HUMAN ECOLOGY OF HEALTH AND SURVIVAL IN ASIA AND THE SOUTH PACIFIC

List of Contributors

Abdoellah, Oekan Soekotjo, Institute of Ecology, Padjadjaran University, Bandung, Indonesia

Edmundson, Wade C., Department of Geography, University of New England, Armidale, N.S.W., Australia

Ellen, R.F., Social Anthropology, Centre for South-East Asian Studies, Eliot College, The University Canterbury, Kent, England

Funabiki, Takeo, Department of Cultural Anthropology, College of Arts and Sciences, University of Tokyo, Tokyo, Japan

Kano, Hiroyoshi, Institute of Oriental Culture, University of Tokyo, Tokyo, Japan

Kobayashi, Kazumasa, Population Research Institute, Nihon University, Tokyo, Japan

Kogi, Kazutaka, ILO Regional Office for Asia and the Pacific, Bangkok, Thailand

Koizumi, Akira, Department of Public Health, Faculty of Medicine, University of Tokyo, Tokyo, Japan

Manuaba, Adnyana, Department of Physiology, Udayana University, Bali, Indonesia

Moji, Kazuhiko, Department of Human Ecology, School of Health Sciences, Faculty of Medicine, University of Tokyo, Tokyo, Japan

Ohtsuka, Ryutaro, Department of Human Ecology, School of Health Sciences, Faculty of Medicine, University of Tokyo, Tokyo, Japan

Strathern, Andrew*, Institute of PNG Studies, Papua New Guinea

Suzuki, Shosuke, Department of Public Health, Gunma University School of Medicine, Maebashi, Japan

Suzuki, Tsuguyoshi, Department of Human Ecology, School of Health Sciences, Faculty of Medicine, University of Tokyo, Tokyo, Japan

* Present Address: Department of Anthropology, University of Pittsburg, Pennsylvania, U.S.A.

HUMAN ECOLOGY OF HEALTH AND SURVIVAL IN ASIA AND THE SOUTH PACIFIC

Edited by
Tsuguyoshi Suzuki and Ryutaro Ohtsuka

UNIVERSITY OF TOKYO PRESS

Proceedings of the International Symposium on The Comparative Human Ecology of Health and Survival Strategy in Asia and the South Pacific, held in Tokyo on March 17-20, 1986.

ISBN 4-13-068125-7
ISBN 0-86008-406-X

Printed in Japan

Contents

Preface

The symposium that forms the basis for this volume can be said to have started during an informal discussion I had with Prof. A. Koizumi in 1984. Professor Koizumi and I had the same feeling: that the scientific activities in Japan aiming at establishing human ecology as a discipline might have reached the level at which many colleagues could discuss the theory and practical applications of human ecology studies in an international symposium. The approval of the University of Tokyo and the Japanese Ministry of Education, Science and Culture for funding of the international symposium was given in autumn 1985.

Since our activities have concentrated in the area of Indonesia and Papua New Guinea for the past several years, we decided to select topics and speakers dealing with actual study experiences in these or related areas, and to invite some speakers who would discuss the general theoretical problems of human ecology. We had the good fortune to get positive answers from most of the invited speakers even though the time for preparing the symposium was limited.

Indonesia and Papua New Guinea (PNG) are both traditional societies being submerged in the high tide of modernization. However, there are many differences between the two. In PNG, many communities are preserving the typical characteristics of the traditional society: they are small, geographically isolated, depend upon horticulture, hunting, fishing and gathering with simple technology, and speak their own unwritten languages. Since the independence of PNG in 1975, the national effort to establish the state in the modern sense has started to infiltrate the remote areas; in various aspects of daily living, the impact of Western culture is changing the traditional ways.

Indonesia seems to be far more complicated and diversified than PNG. Some islands in the archipelago are fully populated; others are very sparsely populated. Subsistence activities vary by island and ethnic group, including seminomadic shifting cultivation, sago gardening, smallholder rubber tapping, irrigated rice farming, highly capitalized plantation of cash crops, itinerant peddling, large-scale commerce, cottage industries, and modern manufacturing, as described by Geertz (1967). Diversification is certainly the character of Indonesia, but most Indonesians live as peasants, forming an agrarian community with fairly advanced cultivation technology. Activities of the national government do not have a strong influence on the rural peasants' lives, even though they are more systematic than in the case of PNG.

It was our intention to reveal the common and unique features of health and survival of human beings living in PNG and Indonesia from the viewpoint of comparative human ecology. The invited speakers included not only human ecologists but also social anthropologists, economists, demographers, and health scientists. All of them approached the subject from their particular standpoints, and the resultant collection has revealed the changing pattern of health and survival in these areas. I cannot say that we have perfectly documented the situation, but I can say that we have demonstrated the expansion and complexity of the problem by this collective effort. One invited guest, Mrs. Zena Daysh from the Commonwealth Human Ecology Council (CHEC), described the conference as an admirable introduction to a new type of scholarly cooperation after her return to Britain, in a CHEC information circular (CHEC POINTS, No. 11, July 1986).

I want to thank the speakers and other participants in the symposium whose active participation made the conference stimulating. Also I want to thank Prof. Wataru Mori, President of the University of Tokyo, for approving the financial support from Ministry of Education, Science and Culture and giving the opening message at the symposium.

Tsuguyoshi SUZUKI
Department of Human Ecology
School of Health Sciences
Faculty of Medicine
University of Tokyo

I. INTRODUCTION

Population and Ecosystem in the Study of Health and Survival Strategy

Tsuguyoshi SUZUKI

Department of Human Ecology, School of Health Sciences, Faculty of Medicine, University of Tokyo, Tokyo, Japan

I. INTRODUCTION

Human ecology has developed in Japan as a discipline in the field of health sciences. The department designated Human Ecology, in which we are now working, was first founded in 1965, as one of nine departments composing the School of Health Sciences, Faculty of Medicine, University of Tokyo. The essential role of human ecology studies in this school was to provide a basic understanding of the man-environment relationship, and it has been emphasized that the environment should be understood in its broadest sense, i.e., as an integration of biological and cultural aspects.

The school was created by reshaping the School of Health Care and Nursing to meet the social request for coping with the new health problems that emerged from the rapid changes after World War II. Professor K. Uraguchi, an eminent toxicologist who studied the health problems which accompany consumption of rice contaminated with fungus toxins, was nominated as the professor of human ecology to smooth the transition. He retired from the University of Tokyo the following year, and Prof. H. Katsunuma, professor of public health, succeeded him in holding the chair as a concurrent post. As one of the leading scholars in the field of public health in Japan, he oriented the discipline of public health toward the art of systematic health activities for people forming a population and defined human ecology in relation to public health as a part of human biology dealing with populations. During the period of about five years under his supervision, a staff was recruited and the education of both undergraduate and graduate students made gradual progress. On these foundations, Prof. A. Koizumi, who also came from the field of public health and returned there several years ago, and is participating this symposium, was committed to the cause of establishing the discipline. Under his guidance, two major facets of studies, population studies and environmental studies, came to the fore. Demographic studies from the viewpoint of human ecology were connected to environmental studies. This was a natural sequence since the population biology of human beings would, if formulated on the basis of the man-environment system, be a discipline that synthesized demographic phenomena into the structure and change of such systems. Human beings are an integration of biological and cultural consequences, and these interactions are always evident at the levels of individuals and of populations.

II. PROBLEMS OF IDENTIFICATION OF A POPULATION OR ECOSYSTEM

A problem we first met in conducting studies of population growth and environmental conditions was defining the area where people were living. In the usual method of public health, an area is administratively defined, which perhaps does not coincide with the area of people's activities. For instance, a person residing in an administrative area often goes to work daily or temporarily outside his or her area. This becomes a hindrance in studying the flow of energy and materials in a human ecosystem. Our first efforts included (1) taking up island ecosystems, not defining them by the islanders' activities but by the usage of the ecosystem as set out in textbooks of ecology for lake ecosystems, estuarine ecosystems, or marine ecosystems. Our actual site was the Tokara Islands, part of an arc composed of numerous small islands in the southwestern part of Japan; (2) enumerating historically and contemporarily the number of islanders using historical documents, family registers (*koseki*), residential registers (*jumin toroku*), and data obtained by household interviews; (3) estimating fertility, mortality, and migration rates based on the above-mentioned data; and (4) studying subsistence activities and estimating the yield of production.

Tokara islanders had been traditionally dependent upon cultivation of sweet potatoes and rice, fishing, and small-scale animal husbandry. With the transition from the feudal system of the Tokugawa era to the centralized governmental system of the Meiji era, the population began to increase in the late 1880s. By analyzing both the family registers, which were institutionalized by the Meiji government, and the historical records on the residential population for older times and the residential registers for recent times, we estimated that the residential population of the islands had reached the carrying capacity by the 1930s and a constant flow of out-migration had continued until the end of World War II. Return migration after the war was beyond the carrying capacity of the islands, and a sudden residential population problem occurred (Fig. 1). This sequence indicated that this island ecosystem had been open in terms of human movement, and the major regulatory factor for population size was migration. During the process of population growth in the post-war period, the relation of population size to cultivated land area on an island basis remained almost unchanged (Fig. 2), and the amount of energy in food produced on each island was roughly equivalent to the energy requirements of the resident islanders (Fig. 3). As long as they lived on the islands, they were self-sufficient in food, although at risk of marginal deficiency. Earnings from work outside the islands might have filled the gap between requirement and supply, and working outside might also have afforded a chance to live away from the islands. Thus, to the inhabitants of an island ecosystem must be added ex-island migrants or islanders temporarily working off the island (Suzuki, 1971, 1972a, 1972b, 1972c, 1973, 1979a, 1979b; Igarashi, 1976, 1978; Kashiwazaki, 1972).

Our second study attempted the identifiable aggregation of a single ethnic group: Japanese immigrants in the lowlands of Bolivia (Suzuki, 1977; Kashiwazaki, 1976, 1983; Ohtsuka, 1980). Recurrent waves of emigration of Japanese occurred from a post-war semistarved country overflowing with returnees from a dismantled empire, and many went to

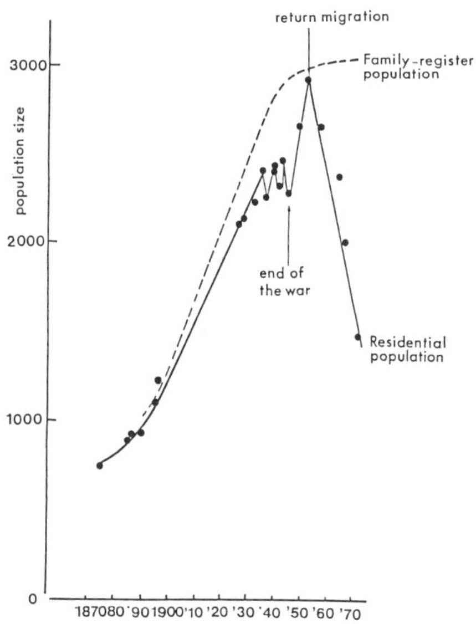

FIG. 1

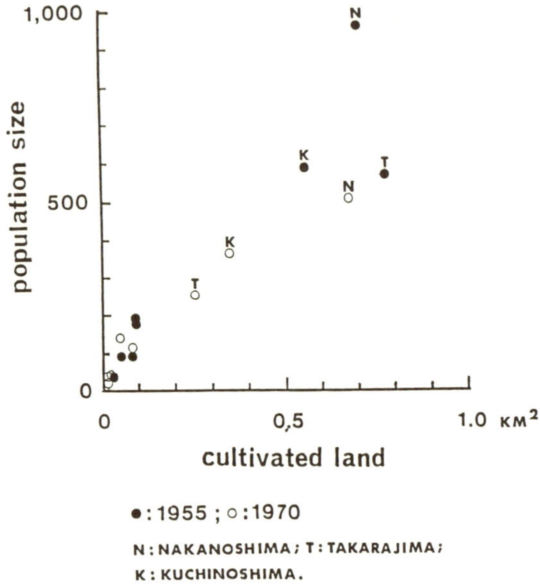

FIG. 2

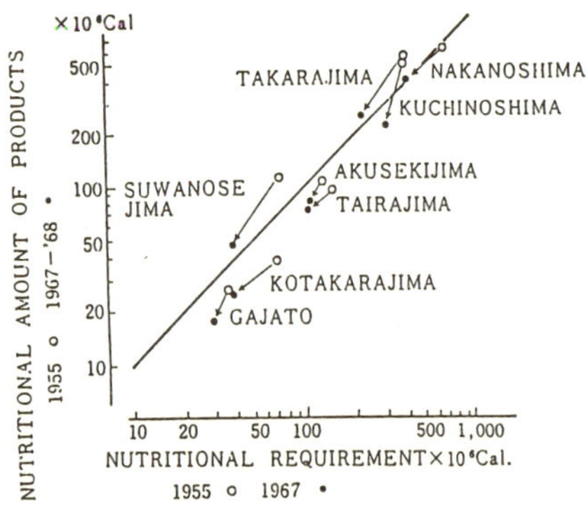

FIG. 3

Latin American countries. One such wave was directed to Bolivia, and immigrants formed several settlements in the tropical rain forest lowlands. Our central interest was in the processes of settlement in tropical forests whereby each component of carried-over biosocial/cultural Japanese traits was expected to be confronted with New World alternatives. The expansion of the settlers' activity range over the passage of time was another interest. Our research was concentrated on a settlement called San Juan, which had accepted 1,648 Japanese immigrants between 1957 and 1973; at the end of 1973, the immigrants numbered 1,034. Simultaneous with the expansion of the settlement itself, the Japanese immigrants rapidly spread to a nearby cities, then to more remote cities in Bolivia, and to cities in Brazil and Argentina. They did not form strong ties with other nearby Japanese settlements composed of immigrants from Okinawa prefecture. The rural-to-urban axis seemed to strongly regulate the direction of activity expansion. This case again educated us in the difficulty of demarcating the activity range of a population.

In both population ecological studies and ecosystem studies, the problem of boundary setting is inherent. In an actual situation of human ecology study, a population may be defined as a unit, or an aggregate of a single ethnic group, in a definable area, and a human ecosystem may be defined as an integrated system of biotic and non-biotic components in a definable area, in which human beings occupy the dominant position. Thus, the common problem is setting the boundary of the area to be defined. For this, Moran (1984) introduced the definition by Rappaport (1967), which was pragmatic and implicitly relied on the concept of territoriality: "The domain of the regulatory operations of a local group defines an ecosystem." Moran accepted this as a basically satisfying solution. This definition is of practical use when a local group is clearly recognized as a unit. However, it is often difficult to identify a local group. In the case of the Tokara islanders, there were three levels of local population: (1) a permanent residential population, (2) a population including permanent residents and people who work off the islands temporarily, and (3) a population whose origin is on a specific island, no matter where their residence is, which mostly corresponds to the family register population. After World War II, the keeping of the family register was entrusted to the family itself. Therefore, it is a reflection of a family's consciousness of origin. Ellen (1982) stated that islands were relatively well definable ecosystems for the study of human ecology, after carefully commenting that boundary setting was arbitrary in any case. I have no disagreement with his thinking, but the fact remains that an apparently closed island ecosystem has free movements of islanders. In our second study, Japanese immigrants in Bolivia, who were certainly identifiable, expanded from a lowland settlement to cities. Insofar as we have been concerned with population biology, boundaries may be a matter of speculation, even though the extent of ambiguity may differ from study to study.

In one of our recent studies, the Gidra inhabiting the Oriomo area in the lowlands of Papua New Guinea were intensively examined. The details of the results will be presented by Dr. Ohtsuka in this symposium. This population is linguistically defined and mostly lives in a tribal land area. Studies from the viewpoint of population biology can be conducted using methodology like that for ecosystem ecology, even though the information to be collected is not identical. Micro-level demography, recent advances in which will be presented by Dr. Kobayashi in this symposium, is a necessity, and the reconstruction of historical change can be achieved only with information obtained by interviews about genealogy. This is disadvantageous to an understanding of the man-environment relation over longer time periods. No observations of contemporary Gidra can reveal historical trends in their full reality, although vestiges may be found in the people's way of thinking, memories, and behaviour.

III. HEALTH OF A POPULATION WITH REGARD TO THE ECOSYSTEM

Greater longevity for each individual in a community has been the target of health activities for a long time. This is still the case in countries with relatively shorter life expectancies. In countries that have achieved longer life expectancy, the increasing proportion of the population who are chronically ill threatens to lead to the bankruptcy of health care systems. Efforts devoted to reduction of mortality simultaneously elicit an increase in morbidity if those who avoid death do not recover full health. This is very likely to occur in societies with advanced aging; i.e., the higher the proportion of elderly is, the greater the cost of taking care of them. This may be relevant to Dr. Koizumi's presentation, and regarding this, I would like to point out that a revision is needed of the hitherto utilized conceptual framework for the definition of health which has relied so heavily on the mortality phenomenon in a population.

In discussing new dimensions for defining health, a unifying viewpoint to cover all human societies from the tribal to the modern state is required. Previously, health has been dealt with as the yield obtained after the battle against epidemics of communicable diseases and malnutrition in pre-industrialized societies and against the numerous artificial menaces associated with industrialization. For foraging tribal societies, health was defined based on the analogy of agricultural pre-industrialized society. However, accumulated information on hunter-gatherer populations does not necessarily support this thinking: at one extreme pole, there seem to be affuluent foragers in good health, although this may or may not be an illusion. At the "advanced" level, the post-industrialized society that has emerged in several industrialized societies show a reduction in mortality and an aging population structure. Societies of this type must be assessed using indicators different from those for industrialized societies.

The continued functioning of a population is realized by ensuring the successive reproduction of new generations within it. Thus, indicators showing the extent of reproductive stability are necessary to evaluate the health of populations. The net reproduction rate (NRR) is one such indicator, which integrates fertility and mortality up to the reproductive age and thereafter during reproduction. For populations with incomplete natality and mortality data, the ratio of daughters to mothers, of sons to fathers, or of children to women is also applicable. When the land, or the economy of a society, is or could be, adequate to carry the increasing population, a high level of reproduction is desirable. On the contrary, high levels of population increase are disastrous in societies with limited land or economy. For instance, societies that have reached the stage of state formation and that function as a mostly closed ecosystem suffer from this problem, and it is still regarded as serious in contemporary countries forming semi-closed human ecosystems. Optimal rates of population growth, or zero growth, must be selected in such a situation based on the answers to the following two questions: (1) How can the optimal rate for each population be found? and (2) How can this level be maintained along with reproductive stability? If it is possible to set the optimal reproduction rate level with allowance for occasional fluctuations in fertility and mortality, the deviation from this set level can be used as an indicator of stability.

The next aspect, which has also been neglected in formulating health indicators (Suzuki, 1980), is concerned with the productivity of a population. A population can be divided into two subgroups, one productive and another dependent. If we can characterize every member of a population at a given date or in a given time period as working or not working for biological/medical or social/cultural reasons, the proportion of the working to the total population will indicate the health level of a population regarding productivity. More precisely, the working population can be thought of as those with no health problems and those with some health problems, and the non-working population as those with or without work ability in combination with the existence or absence of health problems. Thus, six categories classified by work ability and by health problems are presented in Table 1. This categorization is applicable to any population. For example, the non-working population with work ability and without health problems includes the unemployed in industrialized countries. Maximizing the proportion of the working population without health problems should be the ultimate target in all health service activities and related fields.

Table 1

		Health problems	
		+	−
Work ability	+	Working	Working
		Non-working	Non-working
	−	Non-working	Non-working

In a closed human ecosystem, production and consumption form one body; i.e., all that is produced is consumed within the system. Balance between production and consumption in the entire population is the first item to be checked. Moreover, whether or not a good system of product distribution exists is important for the survival of members who cannot produce the basics of life by themselves. An interesting example that shows the importance of a good system for the survival of a population was provided by Weinstein *et al.* (1983), who conducted a simulation analysis of population growth in a hypothetical farming and herding community of Quechuan Indians in the high Andes. Three types of energy resource-sharing networks (no resource sharing between families, sharing within extended families up to a total of ten families, and families in deficit receiving surplus energy from some other family in the population) were hypothesized. In a 250-year simulation, the population with no sharing networks quickly died out, and the populations with moderate or large sharing network reached the same approximate population equilibrium. These results indicate the importance of a good distribution system.

Even in an egalitarian society, a bad distribution system may exist, but in a hierarchical society, the flow of energy, materials, and information becomes stagnant due to social stratification. The extent of unevenness of distribution is thus an indicator of the health of a population.

A population with reproductive stability, work efficiency, and a balanced distribution of consumption is likely to be highly capable in adapting to its environment, or these qualities may be a result of its having adapted to a specific environment. These three factors, production, consumption, and reproduction, are not independent of each other, and the interrelatedness of these three is the first area to study in a population. Next, the character of a population as defined by these three indicators must be examined based on its relation to the human ecological complex consisting of natural conditions, technology, social organization, and cognitive structure of the environment. The health levels of communities on the population level, not on the individual level, can thus be evaluated by the procedures mentioned above.

IV. SURVIVAL STRATEGY OF A POPULATION

Survival strategies of a population are based on the people's cognizance of the man-environment relationship. If they consider that their environment is and will in future be full of resources to utilize for themselves, nothing unusual will be undertaken. In this case, survival strategy means maintaining a traditional way of life. On the contrary, if they consider the environment as being deficient at present or in the near future, actions to recover the deficit or to provide against forthcoming deficit will be taken. The issue lies not in what kinds of deficit they actually have, or will have, but in what they consider to be deficient. Not only material goods but also information may be involved in these considerations. Thus, preparation for the future depends on predictive cognizance regarding change in the relationship of man and environment. When people live under cyclically changing environmental conditions, they easily recognize the cycle and prepare for it. When there is no hope of taking countermeasures against the increasing harshness of the environment, they may prefer to leave it. The fact that a population has survived in a limited range, forming a human ecosystem, suggests that the members of this population continue to consider their living environment as satisfactory, manageable, or at least tolerable.

Individuals, families (or a unit of living), populations, and states each have a survival strategy. Therefore, how they think about it and how they take actions regarding it must first be studied within each level and then the interrelation among the different levels can be investigated; e.g., the confinement or the encouragement of a certain behaviour of individuals that may be imposed by the family's or the population's strategy. Formation of a strategy in a society with a complicated structure may be a matter better dealt with by specialists in the field of social sciences, but human ecologists may also be interested in it. We have hitherto confined ourselves to the study of populations on a relatively small scale with rather simple structures.

Migratory movement is a strategy to find a better place to live. In our studies on the post-war emigration of Japanese, it seemed almost like an epidemic. Many people felt that staying in Japan did not afford a chance for better living (a population susceptible to migration), and the government encouraged emigration to lessen the burden of national poverty at that time (input of motives). There were specific persons who played the role of vector in the "migration fever" in each community. Similar problems in transmigration from one island to another in Indonesia will be discussed by Mr. Oekan Soekotjo Abdoellah in this symposium. Migration is one of the most important elements in the study of survival strategy.

The three aspects of reproduction, production, and consumption, each of which is crucial in evaluating the health status of a population as discussed above, must again be separately and integratively examined in the study of survival strategy. In other words, survival strategy is composed of reproductive strategy, production strategy, and consumption strategy. Because of the dynamic inter-connected relations between the three, any one singled out for study will be void of meaning. For instance, female participation in production, the extent of which is variable according to the society, reduces the reproduction capacity of the entire population. In order to maintain constant reproduction with female participation in production, support by other members in the society is needed, which may result in a reduction of the number of people available for direct production. The length of time women devoted to agriculture became longer or shorter in a Sundanese village depending on whether or not a babysitter was available (Moji, 1980).

Studies on survival strategy primarily need two kinds of information: (1) on actual behaviour or activities of people; and (2) on people's intentions of people in conducting a specific activity. If the strategy is a traditional one, behaviour based on it is often unintentional. People do not necessarily recognize the real reasons for their actions, and the strategy itself may be hidden. In addition to these two, we need to know how people think about future changes, i.e., their predictive cognizance, as the future consciousness of people is related to the perceived relationship of man and environment. In rapidly changing situations, prediction is difficult but inevitable. In contrast, it is both easy and useless in stable situations.

When the cognizance is uniform among the members of a population and the number of actions available is limited, the survival strategy is not diversified. When there is split cognizance, different actions emerge when there is a possibility for multiple actions. Strategies, actual behaviour, and resultant features of reproduction, production, and consumption is a necessary set of information in the study of the health of a population.

V. CONCLUDING REMARKS

In this paper the evaluation of health from the viewpoint of survival of a population has been discussed. The health of an individual has long been evaluated on the basis of longevity; more recently the duration of productive activity has been incorporated into the assessment of health. It was proposed here to evaluate health using three indicators: (1) reproductive stability in relation to a pre-set optimum level; (2) the proportion of the working population without health problems to the total population; and (3) the distribution system for materials and information. I have dealt with reproductive stability only in terms of biology, although human reproductive stability should be considered both biologically and culturally. However, cultural reproduction is not a commonly understood term at present, and must await future study.

REFERENCES

Ellen, R. (1982). *Environment, Subsistence and System.* Cambridge: Cambridge Univ. Press, pp. 78–79.

Igarashi, T. (1976). Ecology of islanders on a remote island—Tokara Islands, Akusekijima. *Karada-no-kagaku*, **71**: 26–32 (in Japanese).

Igarashi, T. (1978). Demography of Tokara islanders. *Kagoshima Chirigakkai Kiyo*, **23**: 33–50 (in Japanese).

Kashiwazaki, H. (1972). The population change after World War II on the Tokara Islands. *Minzoku-eisei*, **38**: 151–168.

Kashiwazaki, H. (1976). Daily living of Japanese immigrants in Bolivia. *Karada-no-kagaku*, **70**: 122–127 (in Japanese).

Kashiwazaki, H. (1983). Agricultural practices and household organization in a Japanese pioneer community of lowland Bolivia. *Human Ecol.*, **11**: 283–319.

Moji, K. (1980). Labor allocation of Sundanese peasants, West Java. *J. Human Ergol.*, **9**: 159–173.

Moran, E.F. (1984). Limitations and advances in ecosystems research. In Moran (ed.) *The Ecosystem Concept in Anthropology.* Boulder, Colorado: Westview Press Inc. (AAAS Selected Symposiu 92),m pp. 19–20.

Ohtsuka, R. (1980). Diversified agricultural strategies among Okinawan settlers in eastern Bolivia. *J. Human Ergol.*, **9**: 133–145.

Rappaport, R. (1967). *Pigs for the Ancestors.* New Haven: Yale Univ. Press.

Suzuki, T. (1971). Interaction of man and environment on island ecosystems. *Proc. 18th General Assembly of Japan Medical Association*, pp. 964–972 (in Japanese).

Suzuki, T. (1972a). A preliminary essay on the analysis of population growth. *Tohoku-Igaku-Zasshi*, **85**: 179–187 (in Japanese).

Suzuki, T. (1972b). On the fertility of women living on Kuchinoshima in the Tokara Islands. *Minzoku-eisei*, **38**: 78–86 (in Japanese).

Suzuki, T. (1972c). On the fertility of women living on Takarajima in the Tokara Islands. *Minzoku-eisei*, **38**: 146–150 (in Japanese).

Suzuki, T. (1973). Human populations and their habitats. *Tokyo Igaku*, **81**: 107–119 (in Japanese).

Suzuki, T. (1977). Ecology of migrants. *Shizen*, **2**: 54–63 (in Japanese).

Suzuki, T. (1979a). Natality and mortality reconstructed from the family register (*koseki*) and the list of residents register. *Minzoku-eisei*, **45**: 79–84 (in Japanese).

Suzuki, T. (1979b). Reconstruction of demography in history using the family register (*koseki*). *Minzoku-eisei*, **45**: 85–91 (in Japanese).

Suzuki, T. (1980). An essay on health indicators from the ecological standpoint. *Tokyo Igaku*, **87**: 61–68 (in Japanese).

Weinstein, D.A., H.H. Shugart, and C.C. Brandt (1983). Energy flow and the persistence of a human population: A simulation analysis. *Human Ecol.*, **11**: 201–225.

II. SURVIVAL OF HUMAN POPULATIONS

Man Surviving as a Population: A Study of the Gidra in Lowland Papua

Ryutaro OHTSUKA

Department of Human Ecology, School of Health Sciences, Faculty of Medicine, University of Tokyo, Tokyo, Japan

I. INTRODUCTION

To gain an understanding of human adaptation and survival in the field of human ecology, primary efforts have thus far been directed to fieldwork in regional ecosystems. Researchers have been concerned with various theoretical and/or methodological issues to ensure the validity of their findings. Based on our research among the Gidra-speaking Papuans, the present paper aims to treat the following three problems in particular: (1) human aggregation as a unit of adaptation or survival; (2) the duration over which human adaptation or survival is assessed; and (3) the inter-connectedness of variables in adaptive mechanisms, paying major attention to those variables concerning production and reproduction, that is, subsistence patterns and food and nutrient intake and inter-generational population replacement, respectively.

The fieldwork among the Gidra was conducted at three periods: an eight-month survey in the inland village of Wonie in 1971–72 by myself, a three-month survey of all 13 Gidra villages in 1980 by T. Kawabe and myself, and a six-month survey of all villages in 1981–82 by five researchers (T. Kawabe, T. Akimichi, T. Inaoka, T. Suzuki, and myself). The 1971–72 survey attempted a functional-ecological analysis of the man-environment relationship, with the human activity system as the key component (Ohtsuka, 1977a, 1977b, 1983). The major purpose of the 1980 and 1981–82 surveys was to elucidate the adaptive mechanisms of the whole population and village-to-village differences in them in light of environmental and cultural conditions (Ohtsuka *et al.*, 1985a, 1985b, 1985c; Suzuki *et al.*, 1984; Kawabe, 1986). One of my own efforts was devoted to long-term demographic analysis treating both the living and deceased (Ohtsuka, 1986).

II. THE GIDRA AS A POPULATION

As a unit of animal survival, biologists prefer to treat a population (or deme) since it is organized independently in the genetic sense. This idea is basically the case for humans as well: it is natural for a human population to form a unit based on marriages and cultural identity. There have never existed strict boundaries of marriages within a single local group with a small population, which makes comprehensive analysis of adaptive mechanisms suitably appropriate. Nonetheless, considering Melanesians, Bayliss-Smith (1977) suggested that any small human population that operates within well-defined boundaries and in relative isolation constitutes an "island ecosystem" for human ecology; this agreed with Fosberg's (1963) point in the well-known symposium on "Man's Place in the Island Ecosystem." In fact, Melanesians, especially speakers of Papuan (Non-Austronesian) languages, are characterized by linguistic diversity: Wurm (1982) estimates the total number of Papuan languages at about 750. Owing to the fact that there are approximately 2.9 million speakers, the number of speakers of each language is only 3,900.

The Gidra-speaking Papuans are one such group since they consist of 1,850 people (in 1980) in 13 villages and occupy 4,000 square kilometres (km^2) in the Western Province lowlands, Papua New Guinea (Fig. 1). Besides the language itself, they possess in common a creation myth, a totemic clan organization and its moiety system, and an age-grade system, all of which form a common cultural identity. On the other hand, our analysis of contemporary Gidra villagers' birthplaces revealed that 97% (1,791 out of 1,850), or 95% of married villagers (755 out of 798) were born within their territory (Ohtsuka *et al.*, 1985b). These characteristics demonstrate that the Gidra can be treated as a population or an entity of adaptation and survival over generations (cf. Wright, 1969; Birdsell, 1973; Bodmer and Cavalli-Sforza, 1974).

III. DEMOGRAPHIC INFRASTRUCTURE

The population of each village ranged from 104 to 241 in our 1980 census, the mean and SD being 142.3 $\pm$ 34.8. Since the 13 villages are scattered with distances between them varying from several to 20 km, each village tends to manage daily sustenance independently from neighbouring villages. Judging from village size, however, it seems impossible that marriages could have been organized within each separate village.

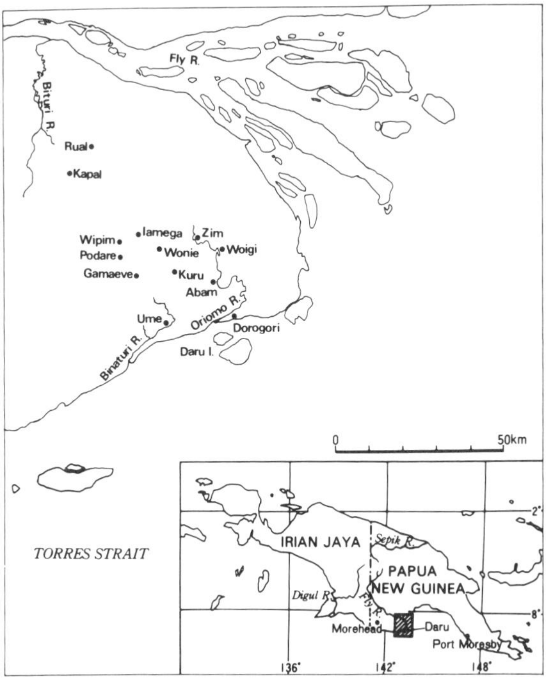

FIG. 1. The location of 13 Gidra-speaking villages in the eastern end of the Oriomo Plateau. The dotted lines show network of paths (Including canoe routes).

According to Wobst's (1974) simulation analysis, the minimum equilibrium size for hunter-gatherers in order to provide all members with mates upon reaching maturity ranges between 175 and 475. The rate of village endogamy among the contemporary Gidra members is about 70% (Ohtsuka *et al.*, 1985b). In my view, this high rate of village endogamy reflects the independent condition of daily living on the one hand, and on the other satisfies the theoretically minimum endogamous size.

For analyzing marriages outside village endogamy, we used the rate of inter-village migration of the married, which is defined between villages A and B as follows:

$$\frac{1}{2} \times \left(\frac{\text{Number of married of A who were born in B}}{\text{Total number of married of A}} + \frac{\text{Number of married of B who were born in A}}{\text{Total number of married of B}} \right)$$

Our previous analysis using the above formula disclosed that the inter-village migration rate was not correlated with the distance between the villages but with the scored contiguity of the foot or canoe path network for each two-village pair (Ohtsuka *et al.*, 1985b). The contiguity score is defined as follows: a contiguity score of 1 implies that the two villages are linked by a path with no village in between; a score of 2 or more is the number of villages inbetween plus 1 (Fig. 1). The means and SDs of the inter-village migration rate of the village-pairs by the contiguity score are shown in Table 1, where the mean and SD of the rate of village endogamy are also given in the category of contiguity score 0. Table 1 illustrates that the larger the score between 0 and 3, the lower the migration rate by ten times per point. Among the village-pairs with contiguity scores of 4 and 5, no migration occurs.

The organization of marriages, as the basis of reproduction, is thus characterized by a high rate of village endogamy, with the bulk of the remainder being maintained by inter-village migration within the village pairs with a contiguity score of 1. Another characteristic of inter-village migration is the lack of subdivision of villages. This is typically evidenced by the fact that there is no village-pair with a contiguity score of 1 in which no inter-village migration occurs. It is thus concluded that the Gidra population consists of villages as sub-populations, concurrently maintained by an overlapping inter-marriage network of adjacent villages throughout the territory. This suggests that the adaptive mechanisms of the Gidra should be simultaneously analyzed at two levels, i.e., the village level and the whole population level.

IV. ENVIRONMENTAL DIVERSITY AND SUBSISTENCE

Microenvironmentally, the habitat of the Gidra is fairly heterogeneous. Of the 13 villages, one (Dorogori) is located on the coast facing Daru, the capital of Western Province, with about 7,000 dwellers; four villages (Abam, Woigi, Zim, and Ume) are situated along the permanently run-

TABLE 1. Inter-Village Migration Rate of the Married by the Contiguity Score of Two-Village Pairs (Mean ± SD)

Contiguity score	N	Mean ± SD
0*	13	0.7068 ± 0.1254
1	23	0.0762 ± 0.0528
2	38	0.0056 ± 0.0115
3	17	0.0004 ± 0.0017
4	7	0
5	3	0

* Intra-village marriage rate.

ning Oriomo or Binaturi Rivers; and the other eight are inland. Of the eight inland villages, Rual and Kapal are located in the northern part and upper tributaries of the Bituri River flow within their village lands and so these two can be distinguished from the other six proper inland villages with no permanently running river: Iamega, Wipim, Podare, Gamaeve, Wonie, and Kuru. Thus, the Gidra villages can be categorized into coastal, riverine, inland, and northern groups. It should be noted that the village of Dorogori was relocated a half-century ago from beside the Oriomo River several km from its mouth.

The natural environment largely conditions each village group's adaptive mechanisms, and the four following items are specifically relevant to subsistence and daily activity patterns. First, the land of the inland villages consists of not only monsoon forest but also savanna due to its relatively higher terrain, whereas the land of the other village groups is predominantly monsoon forest and swamp. Second, hunting activity is favourable in the inland villages, while fishing tends to take the place of hunting in the riverine, northern, and, especially, coastal villages. Third, The savanna abounds in wallaby (*Walabia agilis*), which is more easily hunted than the other major game animals like pig and cassowary, and supplies the inland villagers with a large amount of meat. Sago palms luxuriate in swampy land with less saline water (cf. Nishikawa *et al.*, 1979). The people of the coastal (Dorogori) village have no favourable place for sago around the village, and consequently they must travel several hours northward up the Oriomo River by canoe to harvest sago. Fourth, the means of travel and/or transport of goods differ between the village groups. The northern and especially inland villagers travel on foot and carry such heavy burdens as sago bundles, garden crops. and firewood by themselves, while the riverine and coastal villagers utilize canoes for these purposes.

The four village groups also vary in their degree of modernization, which is typically indicated by the frequency of visits to Daru, the sole center of modernization in the area. In fact, local products (e.g., garden crops, sago, coconuts, and game meat) are sold at the local market in Daru and, in turn, imported foods (e.g., rice, wheat flour, tinned fish, and corned beef) are purchased from the supermarkets there. The 3-km trip requires one to two hours' travel by sailing canoe, so the coastal villagers frequently visit Daru; each adult visits an average of once or twice a month. The riverine villagers have had engine-powered canoes for a dozen years, and at present two or three canoes from each village, with about several to ten villagers on each voyage, go to Daru every two weeks or so. In contrast, the people of the inland and especially northern villages have to walk over long distances to riverine villages to take passage in the canoes.

Consequently, their visits to Daru are still infrequent and transportation of market goods is fairly difficult. This different degree of access to Daru conditions the degree of dependence on imported foods. It is also related to many other conditions, for instance, the prevalence of out-migration to urban areas, and the degree of receptivity to medical services.

The inter-village difference in ecological (environmental and cultural) conditions is typically reflected in their food consumption and nutrient intake. We studied food consumption on six different occasions: once in the dry season and once in the wet season in the inland village of Wonie in 1971–72, and once each in four selected villages (Rual in the north, Wonie inland, Ume riverine, and Dorogori coastal) in the dry season of 1981. Each study was conducted for 12 or 14 successive days in six to eight selected households. This paper will deal with the five dry season records partly because, despite the considerable difference in the kinds of foods consumed, the nutrient intake varied to a small extent between the dry and wet season records in Wonie in 1971–72, and partly because it is meaningful to compare records from the same season.

The design and methods of the food consumption study and the calculation of the nutrient intake (together with our own analysis of food composition) have been discussed in detail elsewhere (Ohtsuka *et al.*, 1984, 1985a). In this paper, I will use the major results, i.e., the amount of energy and protein intake in each record, which was adjusted to the amount consumed per day per adult male, and the breakdown of the source foods into eight categories: (1) wild plants collected, (2) *Metroxylon* sago, (3) coconut (mainly the dry meat), (4) garden crops (mainly bananas, taros, and yams), (5) purchased plant foods (mainly rice and wheat flour), (6) land animals hunted (mainly wallabies, pig, and cassowary), (7) aquatic animals fished and collected (mainly fish, prawns, and shellfish), and (8) purchased animal foods (mainly tinned fish and corned beef).

The results are illustrated in Table 2, from which the following observations are evident. Energy intake varies from 2,980 to 3,650 kcal in the five records. Compared with FAO/WHO nutritional recommendations (1973), the riverine villagers' energy intake is below the requirement for the "very active" energy expenditure level, while those of the other records exceed it; the coastal villagers' intake was lower than that of the inlanders. A conceivable reason for this comes from different energy expenditures, which seems to be related to the means of travel and transportation. Intake of protein varies among the five records more than that of energy. The protein intake in all records exceeds the FAO/WHO's safety level (about 32 g for a Gidra adult male weighing 55.7 kg). To adjust for the quality of protein in the diet relative to that of milk or eggs

TABLE 2. Energy and Protein Intake Per Day Per Adult Male in the Five Food Consumption Records, and Their Breakdown by Eight Categories of Food Sources

		Total	Wild plants	Sago	Coconut	Garden crops	Purchased plants	Land animals	Aquatic animals	Purchased animals
Energy (kcal)										
Northern	(1981)	3,553	227	1,912	101	975	205	82	45	6
Inland	(1971)	3,323	117	1,827	317	918	0	140	4	0
	(1981)	3,550	2	1,551	10	1,591	216	179	0	0
Riverine	(1981)	2,980	27	588	417	1,237	537	76	95	2
Coastal	(1981)	3,221	2	209	194	1,216	1,326	27	118	130
Protein (g)										
Northern	(1981)	54.3	9.3	3.4	0.9	11.6	4.6	16.8	7.5	0.2
Inland	(1971)	48.3	1.1	3.3	3.1	9.8	0	30.1	0.8	0
	(1981)	68.0	a	2.8	0.1	22.6	6.2	36.2	0	0
Riverine	(1981)	67.6	1.4	1.0	4.1	16.6	12.9	16.4	15.1	0.1
Coastal	(1981)	73.3	a	0.4	2.9	16.5	22.2	4.0	21.3	6.4

a: negligible amount.

while considering the amino acid score of the foods (net protein utilization, NPU), 80–85% NPU should be applied to the Gidra diet (cf. Norgan *et al.*, 1974). Though any converted values still exceed the safety level, it seems more appropriate to use the values of about 40 g and 45 g, respectively, for the inland (Wonie) villagers in 1971 and the northern (Rual) villagers in 1981 for the marginal level.

The inter-village difference is more prominent when the energy and protein source foods are taken into account. Among the plant foods, the consumption of sago markedly declined from northern to coastal villages, and, at the same time, the energy from purchased plant foods showed the opposite trend. The most important reason for this is attributable to modernization. Modernization is also related to the consumption of garden crops, as typically indicated by the difference between the 1971 and 1981 records in Wonie. These differences in plant food consumption patterns contributed to a lesser extent to the inter-village differences in energy intake but to a greater extent to that in protein intake, since the protein content per unit of energy differs: wheat flour and rice contain, respectively, 3.0 g and 1.6 g protein per 1 kcal energy, while the corresponding values of tubers, bananas, and sago flour are 1.46 g, 0.88 g, and 0.15 g, respectively (Ohtsuka *et al.*, 1984). The amount of animal protein intake was similar in all five records, with the proportion of aquatic animals to land animals differing with the locality of each village, and the proportion of purchased animal foods being high in the coastal village. Thus, the total protein intake reflects the level of intake of plant protein, especially that from purchased foods such as wheat flour and rice.

Regarding recent technological development in subsistence activities, the most important was the introduction of the shotgun and fishing net, which have enabled the villagers to catch land and aquatic animals easily and reliably. These new implements are specifically effective in killing big land animals like pig and cassowary which inhabit the forest, and in catching fish; these land animals and fish are the major sources of animal protein in the northern, riverine, and coastal villages. The inland villagers, whose major game is agile wallaby inhabiting savanna, have not frequently used shotguns. In fact, the bulk of game animals were killed by bow and arrow in Wonie even in 1981. It is thus assumed that the amount of animal foods consumed by the inland villagers has not greatly differed over long periods. In contrast, the amount of animal foods consumed by the northern, riverine, and coastal villagers a couple of decades ago should have been much smaller than that in the 1981 records. In addition, it is assumed that purchased plant foods such as wheat flour and rice have substituted mainly for sago flour during the last couple of decades, and this has raised the amount of protein intake. When we assume that all purchased plant foods consumed in 1981 are substitutes for the sago flour consumed 20 years ago, and the amount of land and aquatic animals consumed 20 years ago was one-half or two-thirds that recorded in 1981, the total protein intake in the northern, riverine, and coastal villages two decades ago is estimated at about 40 g; when NPU is taken into account this value corresponds to 32–34 g, the same as the safety level of FAO/WHO (1973). It can thus be concluded that the environmental availability of animal foods seems to have been favourable in the area exploited by the inland villagers, although modernization has favoured coastal and riverine villagers through their involvement in a cash economy and technological improvements.

V. LONG-TERM DEMOGRAPHIC CHANGE

The man–environment relationship is the result of a historical process of adaptation, for instance, termed "ecological end-states" by Ellen (1982). It is desirable to explore the long-term man-environment relationship to understand present conditions, despite the difficulty of such an attempt in non-literate populations. Attention in our studies was directed toward change in population size as one of the basic components in the man-environment system.

Because of the lack of written records before the 1950s and a lack of data on people's ages except for some of the young people, the Gidra's population increase rate in the past was estimated from their genealogies involving 889 married women who had completed reproduction. The basic principle of this method is that of the net reproduction rate, which measures the inter-generational replacement of females and provides the rate of natural increase (Pressat, 1972; Hassan, 1981).

To ensure the validity of this method, several sociocultural conditions of the Gidra must be considered. First, it is the rule that a female marries a few years after menarche. Second, when a woman becomes a widow or divorces, she will usually remarry if she has not passed the reproductive age. Third, the Gidra have seldom practised birth control or infanticide, as judged from our observations and their oral history. It can thus be assumed that the Gidra have always intended to have as many children as possible (Suzuki, 1985; Ohtsuka, 1986). Regarding marriage customs, exogamy between two moieties is still observed to a considerable degree, and it has been ideal for two marriages to be organized simultaneously by means of an exchange of women; in most independently organized marriages there were extenuating reasons, such as death of the wife soon after the marriage or delayed compensation for unbalanced relations between the clans. These customs make it important for the villagers to memorize the marital relations of their ancestors.

The indicator applied to measuring inter-generational replacement was the average number of daughters who were born to a group of women (classified according to the estimated generations) during their lifetimes and who married. As discussed elsewhere (Ohtsuka, 1986), this rate can be treated as a variant indicator of the net reproduction rate, even though some methodological reservations remain; for convenience, this rate is called the daughter-mother ratio or DMR.

The yearly rate of natural increase, or Lotka rate (P), is calculated from the net reproduction rate (R_0), as follows:

$$P = \sqrt[y]{R_0} - 1$$

where y is the mean age at childbearing. In this study, y was taken to be 22.5, the mean of 20 and 25, within which the mean age for Gidra childbearing was estimated to occur.

The "mothers" in this study were females who had married and died or, if still living, had passed the reproductive age. They were categorized into the following four groups, according to age: Group D = not all female offspring have married; Group C = all female offspring have married; Group B = all female offspring have completed reproduction; and Group A = all female offspring of all female offspring (or all granddaughters of the subject women through the female line) have married. Naturally, the age interval between each group is approximately 20 years. In other words, the estimated central ranges of birth years for the women in Groups A, B, C, and D were, respectively, 1860–1880, 1880–1900, 1900–1920, and 1920–1940.

Table 3 shows the number of children who were born to women of each group and married, and the corresponding DMR and Lotka rate, or annual increase rate. The DMR of three groups, A, B, and C, ranges from 1.0284 to 1.0602. Taking into account the inconsistent trend on the one hand and the small number of subjects on the other, it is reasonable to judge that the DMR was rather constant, fluctuating within a small range. In other words, the annual population increase rate had been about

TABLE 3. Daughter-Mother Ratio (DMR) and Lotka Rate (P) by Mother Group

	Number of married children			P at mean childbearing age	
Group (N)	Male	Female	DMR	20	25
A (176)	186	184	1.0455	0.0022	0.0018
B (211)	228	217	1.0284	0.0014	0.0011
C (266)	283	282	1.0602	0.0029	0.0023

0.2% between 1880 and 1940 (or 1945), the time period of the central reproductive years of these subject women. Since the Gidra had little contact with outsiders prior to World War II (cf. Williams, 1936; Hashimoto, 1983), the 0.2% annual increase rate is supposed to have been the norm during their traditional way of life. In comparison with the palaeodemographic literature, the 0.2% increase rate is close, in a global sense, to Hassan's (1973) estimate during the Neolithic, i.e., 0.1% on the average with great fluctuation.

Interestingly, DMR varies when the women are broken down by birthplace or place of residence or death, as shown in Table 4, in which, owing to the small sample size, women of Groups A, B, and C are combined. The DMR as broken down by birthplace varies more markedly, and this is judged to be largely attributable to the inter-village migration of females upon marriage. The higher DMR of women of the coastal village (Dorogori) may have been related to the greater influence of modernization. More interesting is the fact that the DMR of women of the inland villages was higher than that of those of the northern and riverine villages. In particular, the DMRs of the latter two were less than 1.0, implying depopulation.

This micro-geographical difference can be discussed from the viewpoint of health and disease. No evidence has been found of prevalent venereal diseases, which have been related to depopulation especially by means of increased sterility in the literature (e.g., Schneider, 1955; Polunin and Saunders, 1958), among the Gidra. If they had been a decisive factor in decreasing fertility of the Gidra, the coastal villagers should have been the most affected.

According to Riley (1983), the most important disease relevant to vital events in Papua New Guinea is malaria, which not only kills es-

TABLE 4. Daughter-Mother Ratio (DMR) by Mother's Birthplace and Place of Death or Residence

Birthplace[1] (N)	Northern (82)	0.732
	Inland (332)	1.160
	Riverine (183)	0.891
	Coastal (22)	1.409
Death or Living Place[2] (N)	Northern (85)	0.976
	Inland (319)	1.110
	Riverine (198)	0.899
	Coastal (35)	1.514

[1] Excluded are 34 mothers who were born outside the Gidra land, whose married daughters numbered 44.

[2] Excluded are 16 mothers who died or live outside the Gidra land, whose married daughters numbered 15.

pecially infants and young children, but also reduces fertility. There is a strong possibility that malaria is related to the micro-geographical difference in DMR, since the northern and riverine villages abound in mosquitoes. Also emphasized by Riley is malnutrition, which increases susceptibility to infectent diseases. In this connection, it should be noted that our study of food and nutrient intake suggested a marginal level of protein intake in the northern and riverine villages a few decades ago.

This palaeodemographic analysis has revealed that the reproduction rate of the Gidra markedly differed between the villages. In other words, the Gidra's territory of only 4,000 km, the bulk of which is generally recognized as lowland plain, is heterogeneous in the sense of human reproduction.

VI. CHANGING POPULATION STRUCTURE IN MODERNIZATION

Since the post-World War II development of Daru, the Gidra have been introduced to Christianity, primary school education, and a cash economy. In this course, the Gidra's fertility, mortality, and intra- and inter-population migration patterns have changed. It should be noted that, as indicated by the inter-village differences in food and nutrient intake, the degree of modernization has varied among the villages at any given moment.

As shown in Table 5, the total fertility rates of women belonging to Groups C and D were obtained in two different ways: from the genealogical records, and from an interview survey on reproduction histories for all married women in the four intensively studied villages (Rual, Wonie, Ume, and Dorogori). There was a possibility that the genealogical records excluded offspring who had died in infancy or early childhood, and this possibility was higher for the older-generation mothers who had

TABLE 5. Total Fertility Rate of Groups C and D Based on Genealogical Records and Interview Results

Group (N)	Total fertility rate
Genealogical	
C: Died (197)	3.010
C: Living (69)	3.362
D: Died (53)	2.887
D: Living (183)	4.546
Interviewed	
C (21)	3.714
D (50)	4.640

already died before our 1980 survey. Such exclusions of offspring would result in underestimation of the total fertility rate. However, the difference in this rate between the "Died" and "Living" sub-groups is largely attributable to the different longevity of the mothers in the two sub-groups.

With some reservations about the accuracy of the figures in Table 5, the overall comparison has proved that the total fertility rate markedly increased from Group C to Group D. The increase in the fertility rate is estimated at about one-fourth or one-third, based on comparison between the two groups in either the genealogical records or interview data.

Reliable information on premarital death was obtained for offspring born to 71 mothers, the subjects of our interview survey. The proportion of premarital death among all children born is shown in Table 6. According to the traditional age-grade system of the Gidra, age at death can be placed into two categories, one corresponding to the first age-grade (about 8 years old or younger) and the other to the higher ages. From various kinds of information, the mean age at marriage is estimated at 18 years for females and 28 for males. Table 6 demonstrates that the premarital death rate has declined from Group C to Group D. This becomes more prominent when the proportion of survivors at age 9 (l_9) for both sexes and either that at age 19 (l_{19}) for females or that at age 29

TABLE 6. Premarital Death of Children Born to Interviewed Married Women

Number of Live Births and Number of Premarital Deaths

Group of mothers (N)	No. of live births		No. of premarital deaths	
			≤8 yrs.	8+ yrs.
C (21)	Male	37	11	4
	Female	41	12	3
D (50)	Male	109	17	—
	Female	121	28	—

l_x and e_0 in the Corresponding Model Life Table

Group of mothers	Sex of children	l_x	e_0
C	Male	l_9 = 70818/100000	e_0 = 39
		l_{29} = 59956/100000	e_0 = 38
C	Female	l_9 = 70426/100000	e_0 = 38
		l_{19} = 64440/100000	e_0 = 37
D	Male	l_9 = 84340/100000	e_0 = 53
D	Female	l_9 = 76955/100000	e_0 = 45

(l_{29}) for males are applied to the Model Life Tables. Using the General Pattern of the United Nations Model Life Tables (1982), l_9 and l_{19} of females born to mothers of Group C correspond to the patterns of e_0 (life expectancy at birth) = 38 and 37, respectively, while l_9 and l_{29} of males correspond to the patterns of e_0 = 39 and 38, respectively. In contrast, l_9 of female and male children of Group D mothers accords, respectively, with the pattern of e_0 = 45 and 53. It can thus be concluded that the mortality of children has declined, with life expectancy at birth increasing by approximately 10 years. This implies that the proportion of daughters who marry will increase by about 12–14% from Group C to Group D. In summary, it is estimated that the changes in fertility and mortality between Groups C and D, owing largely to betterment of nutritional status and increased medical services, will increase DMR by about 50% or an annual increase rate of from 0.2% to 2.0%.

Another recent demographic feature is the increased rate of out-migration to urban areas, mainly Daru (about 24% of total out-migrants in 1980) and Port Moresby (about 39%). As demonstrated in Table 7, 17.3% of living people who were born in the Gidra land had migrated out before our census in 1980, with the out-migration rate markedly varying among sex and age groups. If we look at their age-grades, the

TABLE 7. Out-Migration Rate (M_O) and Rate of Inter-Village Migration Balance (M_B) by Village

	No. of births	No. of out-migrants to urban areas	M_O	No. of births who remain in the Gidra land	Balance of inter-village migrants	M_B
Northern						
Rual	111	9	0.081	98	2	0.020
Kapal	155	22	0.142	124	−7	−0.056
Inland						
Iamega	306	40	0.131	265	−25	−0.094
Wipim	159	21	0.132	137	17	0.124
Podare	182	30	0.165	135	−5	−0.037
Gamaeve	205	43	0.210	156	−5	−0.032
Wonie	117	13	0.111	104	4	0.038
Kuru	187	11	0.059	176	−46	−0.261
Riverine						
Ume	193	32	0.166	150	20	0.133
Zim	139	41	0.295	98	6	0.061
Woigi	156	31	0.200	124	8	0.065
Abam	156	31	0.200	124	14	0.113
Coastal						
Dorogori	164	62	0.378	100	17	0.170

proportion of out-migrants is the highest among adolescent males, second highest among married males, and third highest among married females. The very few cases of out-migration of elders agree with the information obtained in our fieldwork, that most out-migration to urban areas has occurred since the 1950s or 1960s in the coastal and riverine villages and since the 1970s in the inland and northern villages.

On the other hand, the proportion of out-migrants to urban areas varied among villages. To measure this, the proportion of the number of each village's out-migrants to the total births, called the out-migration rate (M_O), was calculated. In this connection, migrations between the Gidra villages should also be considered. For this, the balance was calculated for each village's in-migrants and out-migrants who were born and have remained in the Gidra villages; this ratio is called the rate of inter-village migration balance (M_B). As shown in Table 7, M_O is higher in the coastal and riverine villages than the inland and northern villages, and M_B is positive for the coastal and riverine villages and is negative for most inland and northern villages. The correlation coefficient (r) was calculated at 0.589 ($p < 0.05$). Thus, it can be concluded that the large number of out-migrants from the coastal and riverine villages has tended to be offset by inter-village migrants from the inland and northern villages.

Compared with the proportion of absentees in 49 villages in various parts of Papua New Guinea as reported by Ross (1984), the out-migration (absentee) rate of the Gidra is not very high. If the Gidra follow the "Beach-River"-type villages in Ross's report, the out-migration rate of adult males could reach 50%. From the viewpoint of population ecology, the most significant effect of the increase in out-migrants is to change the core structure of their adaptive mechanisms, from a "closed" system to an "open" system, or from a population level to a global or national level, although the villages (sub-populations) of the Gidra as a whole appear to be coping with the changing situation, as seen in the relationship between the out-migration rate (M_O) and the rate of inter-village migration balance (M_B).

VII. SUMMARY AND CONCLUSIONS

The present paper first demonstrated that the Gidra are a biologically and culturally distinct population which has formed a unit of adpatation and survival through generations. Next, it attempted to analyze village infrastructure and functions in the temporal and spatial dimensions, focusing on production and reproduction.

Emphasis has been laid on the heterogeneity of the environmental conditions within the Gidra territory. In the past when daily living was mostly managed in a village ecosystem, the inland villages were favorable for human adaptation because of the availability of animal protein sources and a low risk of malaria. In fact, the reproduction rate of women born in the inland villages was higher than that of those born in the northern and riverine villages.

Since World War II, the living conditions of the Gidra have changed markedly, with a time lag between the villages. The population increase rate has increased due to increased fertility and decreased mortality. During the same period, out-migration to urban areas has drastically increased. The out-migration rate is higher in the coastal and riverine villages than in the inland and northern villages, and the inter-village difference in the out-migration rate is largely offset by the difference in the rate of inter-village migration balance. These suggest that the Gidra's adaptive mechanisms tend to change from a "closed" to an "open" system, while maintaining mechanisms for stabilizing the population size of all villages (sub-populations).

Finally, the present study attempted to illustrate the spatial and temporal variability of adaptive mechanisms within a single population, and implies that in the narrowest sense the research findings from each field study should be carefully examined as to their spatio-temporal dimension in the man-environment relationship of the target population.

Acknowledgments

I am very grateful to the people in the study villages for their kind cooperation, and to the project members of the 1980 and 1981–82 surveys: Professor T. Suzuki, Dr. T. Kawabe, Dr. T. Inaoka, and Dr. T. Akimichi. The fieldwork on which this paper is based was financially supported by a Wenner-Gren Foundation for Anthropological Research grant awarded to Professor H. Watanabe (for the 1971–72 survey), and a Grant-in-Aid for Overseas Scientific Surveys from the Ministry of Education, Science and Culture, of Japan (for the 1980 and 1981–82 surveys; project representative, Professor T. Suzuki). This paper was elaborated through discussion for the Joint Study of the National Museum of Ethnology, titled "Change of Culture and Society in New Guinea," organized by Dr. S. Hatanaka and Dr. S. Yoshida.

REFERENCES

Bayliss-Smith, T.P. (1977). Human ecology and island populations: The problems of change. In T.P. Bayliss-Smith and R. Feachem (eds.), *Subsistence and Survival: Rural Ecology in the Pacific*. London: Academic Press, pp. 11–20.

Birdsell, J.B. (1973). A basic demographic unit. *Current Anthrop.*, **14**: 337–356.

Bodmer, W.F. and L.L. Cavalli-Sforza (1974). The analysis of genetic variation using migration matrices. In J.F. Crow and C. Denniston (eds.), *Genetic Distance*. New York: Plenum, pp. 45–61.

Ellen, R. (1982). *Environment, Subsistence and System: The Ecology of Small-Scale Social Formations*. Cambridge: Cambridge Univ. Press.

FAO/WHO (1973). *Energy and Protein Requirements*. Rome: Food and Agriculture Organization of the United Nations.

Fosberg, F.R. (1963). The island ecosystem. In F.R. Fosberg (ed.), *Man's Place in the Island Ecosystem*. Honolulu: Bishop Museum Press, pp. 1–6.

Hashimoto, S. (1983). On Daru, the provincial capital. In G. Ohshima (ed.), *Peoples of the Torres Strait: Geographical and Ethnological Studies*. Tokyo: Kokin-shoin, pp. 231–248.

Hassan, F.A. (1973). On mechanisms of population growth during the Neolithic. *Current Anthrop.*, **14**: 535–542.

Hassan, F.A. (1981). *Demographic Archaeology*. New York: Academic Press.

Kawabe, T. (1986). Intrapopulation variation of body physique in the Gidra, Papua New Guinea. *Man Cul. Oceania*, **2**: 27–55.

Nishikawa, G., K. Oda and H. Suganuma (1979). Botanical description of the sago palm. *Jpn. J. Tropical Agriculture*, **23**: 123–130.

Norgan, N.G., A. Ferro-Luzzi and J.V.G.A. Durnin (1974). The energy and nutrient intake and the energy expenditure of 204 New Guinea adults. *Phil. Trans. R. Soc. Lond. B.*, **268**: 309–348.

Ohtsuka, R. (1977a). Time-space use of the Papuans depending on sago and game. In H. Watanabe (ed.), *Human Activity System: Its Spatiotemporal Structure*. Tokyo: Univ. of Tokyo Press, pp. 231–260.

Ohtsuka, R. (1977b). The sago eaters: An ecological discussion with special reference to the Oriomo Papuans. In J. Allen, J. Golson and R. Jones (eds.), *Sunda and Sahul: Prehistoric Studies in Southeast Asia, Melanesia and Australia*. London: Academic Press, pp. 465–492.

Ohtsuka, R. (1983). *Oriomo Papuans: Ecology of Sago-Eaters in Lowland Papua*. Tokyo: Univ. of Tokyo Press.

Ohtsuka, R. (1986). Low population increase rate of the Gidra Papuans in the past. *Am. J. Phys. Anthro.* (in press).

Ohtsuka, R., T. Kawabe, T. Inaoka, T. Suzuki, T. Hongo, T. Akimichi and T. Sugahara (1984). Composition of local and purchased foods consumed by the Gidra in lowland Papua. *Ecol. Food Nutr.*, **15**: 159–169.

Ohtsuka, R., T. Inaoka, T. Kawabe, T. Suzuki, T. Hongo and T. Akimichi (1985a). Diversity and change of food consumption and nutrient intake among the Gidra in lowland Papua. *Ecol. Food Nutr.*, **16**: 339–350.

Ohtsuka, R., T. Kawabe, T. Inaoka, T. Akimichi and T. Suzuki (1985b). Inter- and intra-population migration of the Gidra in lowland Papua: A population-ecological analysis. *Human Biol.*, **57**: 33–45.

Ohtsuka, R., T. Hongo, T. Kawabe, T. Suzuki, T. Inaoka, T. Akimichi and H. Sasano (1985c). Mineral content of drinking water in lowland Papua. *Environment International*, **11**: 505–508.

Polunin, I. and M. Saunders (1958). Infertility and depopulation: A study of the Murut tribes of north Borneo. *The Lancet*, **2**: 1005–1008.

Pressat, R. (1972). *Demographic Analysis*. Chicago: Aldine-Atherton.

Riley, I.D. (1983). Population change and distribution in Papua New Guinea: An epidemiological approach. *J. Human Evol.*, **12**: 125–132.

Ross, A.C. (1984). *Migrants from Fifty Villages*. IASER Monograph 21. Boroko (Papua New Guinea): Institute of Applied Social and Economic Research.

Schneider, D.M. (1955). Abortion and depopulation on a Pacific island. In B.D. Paul (ed.), *Health, Culture and Community*. New York: Russell Sage Foundation, pp. 211–235.

Suzuki, T. (1985). The traditional art of curing among the Gidra of the Oriomo Plateau, Papua New Guinea. *Man Cul. Oceania*, **1**: 67–79.

Suzuki, T., T. Akimichi, T. Kawabe, T. Inaoka and R. Ohtsuka (1984). Growth of the Gidra in lowland Papua. In N. Kobayashi and T.B. Brazelton (eds.), *The Growing Child in Family and Society*. Tokyo: Univ. of Tokyo Press, pp. 77–93.

United Nations (1982). *Model Life Tables for Developing Countries*. New York: United Nations.

Williams, F.E. (1936). *Papuans of the Trans-Fly*. Oxford: Clarendon.

Wobst, H.M. (1974). Boundary conditions for Paleolithic social system: A simulation approach. *Am. Antiquity*, **39**: 147–178.

Wright, S. (1969). *Evolution and the Genetics of Population* (*Vols.* 1–4). Chicago: Univ. of Chicago Press.

Wurm, S.A. (1982). *Papuan Languages of Oceania*. Tubingen: Gunter Narr Verlag.

Environmental Perturbation, Inter-Island Trade, and the Relocation of Production along the Banda Arc; or, Why Central Places Remain Central

R.F. ELLEN

Social Anthropology, Centre for South-East Asian Studies, Eliot College, The University, Canterbury, Kent, England

Those centres of production in the eastern Malay archipelago which for so long occupied a crucial place in global trade were connected to the outside world through a series of local networks.[1] Despite some major changes in patterns of articulation with the world economy, human-

---

[1] This paper explores themes discussed in two earlier articles (Ellen, 1978a; 1984), being part of a long-term programme of research on "Change and the social organisation of trade in the central Moluccas, eastern Indonesia". The literary sources on which it is largely based were examined during three months tenure at the Netherlands Institute for Advanced Study at Wassenaar. The argument is also supported by data assembled in 1981 while undertaking a pilot field study for the project on Seram, Amboina, Haruku, Geser, Seram Laut, Gorom, Banda, and the Kei islands. This work was sponsored by Lembaga Ilmu Pengetahuan Indonesia, The Indonesian Institute of Sciences, and funded by the British Academy (through the British Institute in Southeast Asia) and the University of Kent at Canterbury, England. A Nuffield Foundation Fellowship during 1985 and 1986 has enabled me to revise this paper for presentation and publication. I am indebted to all these bodies for their generous support.

Among individuals, I would like to thank R. McGonigle of the Institute of Geological Sciences in Edinburgh and K. Giebel of the Map Department of the Koninklijk Instituut voor de Tropen in Amsterdam, respectively, for seismological and cartographic advice; and Drs. Gerrit Knaap for several useful conversations, numerous written comments, for guiding me through the Landbeschrijving of Rumphius, and for permitting me to consult his then unpublished doctoral thesis (Knaap, 1985). Manuscript sources are from the Algemeen Rijksarchief in the Hague (hereafter ARA), and references to them here appear as footnotes.

induced shifts in productive focus, and level of extraction (both spatially and temporally), the essential shape of these networks has proved remarkably resilient over the course of 400 years (Ellen, 1979). Much of their basic structure has been reproduced while experiencing fundamental fluctuations in content. As far as the Moluccas are concerned, I have indicated in a previous publication (Ellen, 1984: 186) how we might conceptualize these as nesting geographical spheres of exchange, as networks portraying some classic systemic properties, focussed on centres of varying degrees of connectedness and related to extent of spatial inclusiveness. At the highest level of generalization we may recognize three *regional* spheres with strong systemic properties, each articulating with *long-distance* trade routes to the west. These are Banda–east Seram–New-Guinea, Ambon–west Seram, and Ternate–Tidore–Halmahera–New Guinea. Each of these may be subdivided into several *intermediate*, and thereafter *local*, networks (see Fig. 1). Such a schematization does not, of course, rule out locally significant trading relations across the boundaries of these spheres, but is concerned rather with structural and statistical tendencies.

The problem I address here is the impact of environmental change and perturbation on these networks, and the extent to which specific patterns of trade have themselves brought about change in environmental relations, in some cases effected through overt political control. In particular, I ask how such networks cope with physical disturbances, and why their central places are so locationally constant despite histories of severe environmental and political disruption, and the transient fortunes and shape of the periphery. I attempt to link these various themes together with particular reference to the Banda Arc, that chain of islands constituting the circumference of the Banda Sea from Wetar in the south through the Kei archipelago in the east round to Buru in the northwest. In this area the historic central places have been in the vicinity of Banda, Tual, Dobo, Geser, and Amboina.

I. ENVIRONMENTAL CHANGE IN THE MOLUCCAS

Short-term environmental change in the Moluccan islands, that is change on an historical rather than geologic timescale, arises in a number of interconnected ways:

(1) Seismic perturbations (earthquakes, tidal waves, and volcanic eruptions);

(2) Seasonal patterns and occasional climatic perturbations, such as hurricanes. Thus, a high level of annual (particularly wet season) precipitation leads to flash floods on exposed slopes causing erosion, while

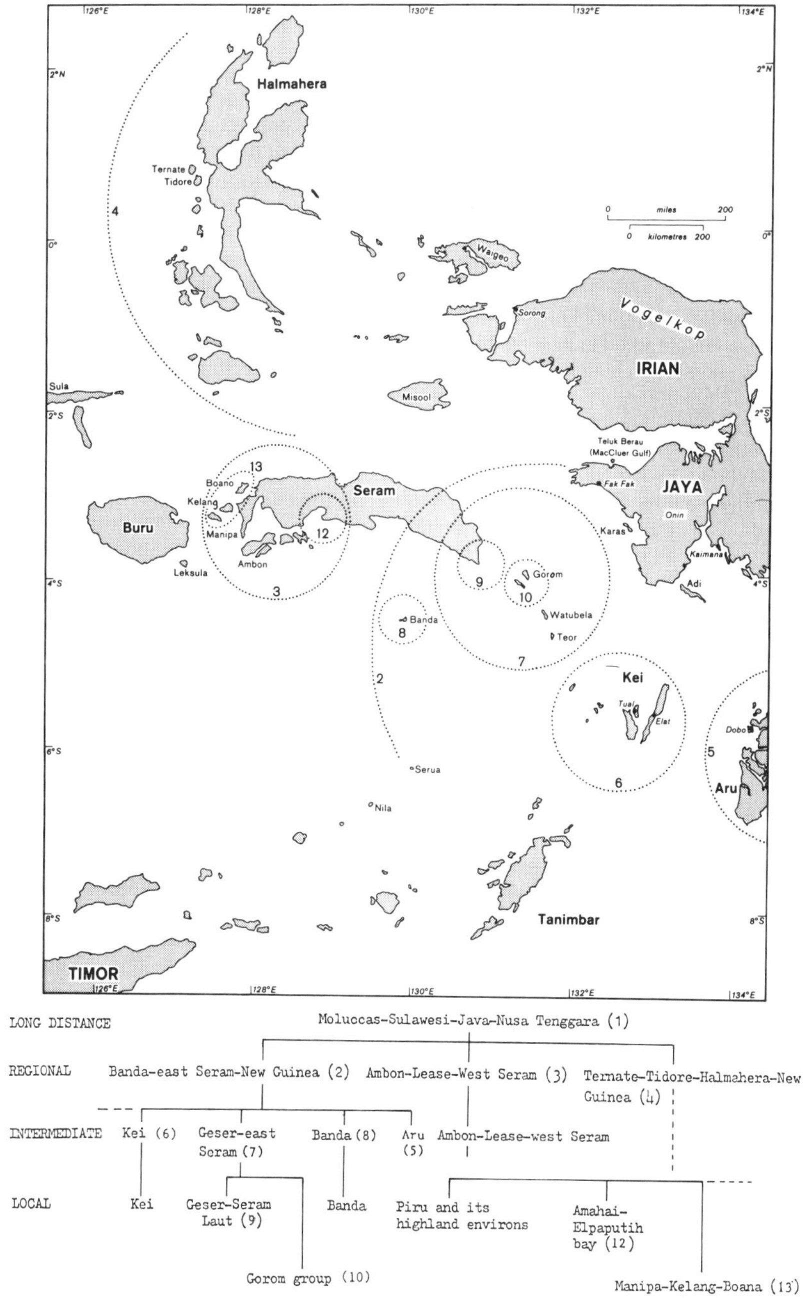

FIG. 1. Schematic outline of nesting Moluccan trading spheres. The legend takes the form of the accompanying hypothetical taxonomy.

wind damage may be a considerable hazard with crops such as coconut palms.

(3) Introduction of new species by human agency, purposeful and accidental. For example, cassava (*Manihot utilissima* Pohl.), tania (*Xanthosoma sagittifolium* Schott), and sweet potato (*Ipomoea batatas* Lam.) were increasingly adopted by Moluccans from the seventeenth century onwards, in part because they required less intensive input for equal or greater yield than taro (*Colocasia*) and the various species of native yam (*Dioscorea*). Cassava is now the main starch staple in many areas, in places having achieved a concomitant cultural status, as with the *embal* cultivar of Kei. Virtually everywhere else it is a crucial secondary food reserve. Maize (*Zea mays* L.) is found everywhere in varying quantities, but in the islands of the southwest (e.g., Wetar, Roma, Kisar, Damer, Leti, Moa, Lakor, Sermata, and Babar) it has become the local staple. With the new staples came many pan-tropical weeds of cultivation, now common on Moluccan forest fringes as well as in plantations, fields, secondary forests, settlements, and along waysides. Many of the trees nowadays found in Moluccan swiddens, groves, and even completely undomesticated settings represent species introduced historically, and even prehistorically, for their useful timber, fruits, and other properties (Ellen, 1985). Among certain animal introductions, only goats and deer have had a major impact on the environment. Both have provided an important protein supplement to the human diet. As a grazer, the deer unchecked may have some effect on low forest bush and secondary associations.

(4) Contraction, decline, and extinction of native species due to over-extraction or pollution. Among maritime species, the dugong is now found only in restricted localities, due partly to direct human predation for meat and tusks, but also, possibly and indirectly, due to depletion through extraction of part of its natural food supply, the economically important alga *agar-agar*. *Trepang,* or sea cucumber, periodically culled by humans, has been extensively extracted in certain places in the past. At the height of Chinese demand and collecting activity during the late 19th and early 20th centuries, it is possible that certain desirable varieties were collected to virtual extinction in some areas. In part, this would account for the seeking of *trepang* in even more distant waters. As Chinese demand rose, commercial *trepang* collectors moving farther away from their home bases, travelling as far as New Guinea and the northern coast of Australia (MacKnight, 1976). In recent times, commercial Japanese fishing has been making inroads into populations of desirable seafood, including prawns and *cakalang* (tuna). In places it is in direct competition with local village fisheries. Among terrestrial animals, wild pig has disappeared on

most of the smaller islands, such as Banda, Gorom, Ambon, Nusalaut, Haruku, and Saparua. Elsewhere, small populations of introduced animals (such as deer) have been either hunted or badly husbanded to extinction.

(5) Sanding (including shifting and the deposition of bars), silting, and erosion along coastlines and in small island groups, often consisting in part of atolls and submerged reefs. This has happened extensively, for example, where coastal mangrove has been progressively depleted. However, the absence of large rivers has meant that patterns of channel erosion and deposition, and other related riverine geomorphological modifications, are unimportant in the Moluccas.

(6) Changes arising from deafforestation.

(7) Expansion and fluctuation in the monocropping of clove (*Eugenia aromatica*) and nutmeg (*Myristica fragrans*) from the 15th century onwards; destruction and control of production from the 17th cetnury; and re-expansion (together with other cash crops, particularly coconut) to the present time.

To these modifications should be added non-agricultural human transformation of the environment: drainage and reclamation in urban areas (Ambon harbour area), landslides and erosion following road building, and also (as in a few areas) complete landscape transformation through the creation of irrigated rice fields (e.g., the transmigration areas of Makariki) and fish farming (Passo, Ambon Island). These, however, are relatively insignificant. The most important (in terms of their implications for undermining economic infrastructures and long-term change) have been seismic and other physical disturbances, deafforestation, and extensive spice monocropping, both in objective ecological terms as well as in the perceptions of the local inhabitants. It is necessary to look at these in a little more detail.

II. DEAFFORESTATION

Changes which begin with deafforestation eventually lead to a wide range of interconnected biotic and geomorphologic modifications. Until quite recently most Moluccan deafforestation could be attributed to the practice of swidden cultivation on the rain forest fringes of the larger islands (particularly Seram, Halmahera, and Buru). Although a small percentage of swiddened land may eventually be recycled into primary forest (particularly following human depopulation of an area), most is drawn into a cycle of relatively short-term fallow or reverts to a secondary growth kept thin through selective human depletion. Alternatively, it is transformed into an entirely new biotope, such as bamboo brush or grassland. Jones (1976:59) has estimated that swiddening has been responsible for the destruction of 0.75 million cubic metres of timber on 7,000 hectares of Seramese primary forest, although in my view this figure is at the very least misleading and probably inaccurate.

In areas of relatively high population density and dependence on swiddens, the fallow periods may be only a few years. Continuous cultivation, or reliance on short fallows, has in places resulted in the creation of grasslands dominated by *Imperata* with very little prospect of use, except as coarse pasture for small herds of cattle. Elsewhere it has led to the establishment of other biotopes, such as bamboo scrub, whose semi-permanent character is maintained at least in part by regular cutting. On steep slopes, deafforestation and swiddening has been accompanied by slope failure (landslide, soil flow, accelerated creep) and denudation of steep hillsides, exacerbated by wet season flash floods. These leach soil and in places remove topsoil completely. Where forest has been removed along ridges and watersheds the process of erosion has been materially hastened. However, in the Moluccas such problems are local and relatively unimportant constraints on human dispersion and resource use, mainly due to low levels of population. By contrast, in eastern Timor, destruction of woodland and erosion has for long been a major problem, with topography characteristically scarred by deep gullies, surface soil wash, over-swiddening, and over-grazing of cattle on anthropogenic grasslands (Metzner, 1977: 202, 251).

Widespread use of iron tools undoubtedly led to an increase in the volume of timber cut from Moluccan forests during the protohistoric and historic periods, and the systematic use of larger pieces in the construction of boats and dwellings accelerated the process still further. Extraction for fuel is a fairly insignificant cause of rain forest destruction, although it has been the responsible agent in the destruction of mangrove swamp and woodland patches near densely inhabited areas. For example, there is some evidence to suggest that the mangrove forest on the extreme southeast tip of Seram has retreated over a 300-year period to leave wide brackish channels, and islands completely surrounded by sand banks and salt water which were once effectively part of the mainland. More recent depletion of mangrove can be seen along parts of the peri-urban rim of Ambon Bay, with the expansion of coastal settlement and pollution, and on the north side of Kuako Bay near Amahei.

By contrast, firewood has been a more significant cause of forest removal in contemporary Timor, where 135,000 m^3 are destroyed a year for this purpose. The Timor model of deafforestation can be applied cautiously to some of the smaller islands of the Moluccas. The development of these places as political and trading centres throughout the historic—and no doubt also during the protohistoric—period led to population growth beyond a level which the timber resources of the islands themselves could sustain. Swiddening and firewood and timber extraction no doubt all contributed towards this situation. Wood, therefore, had to be imported for major construction purposes, including boat building. In a few notable cases virtually all wood had to be imported. Thus, the important island centres of Geser, Kiltai, and Keffing off the southeast corner of Seram import all their firewood from settlements in the adjacent mainland mangrove swamps.

Prior to the emergence of modern commercial logging, and next to swiddening, boat building has had the most significant human impact on Moluccan forests, especially with the growth of long-distance commerce with Java and places further afield. Historically, the greater demands of boat builders coincided with the increased planting of spices, which between them led to the virtual early clearance of certain small islands, through either blanket or selective felling. This was especially the case in such places as the Banda islands, Seram Laut, Gorom, Ternate, Tidore, and Ambon. With the decline of the rain forest on the smaller islands, boats were increasingly built with timber from Seram and Halmahera, and sometimes even from New Guinea. Dutch influence brought new uses for planked timber, led to the introduction of sawing on a large scale and, in the present century, commercial logging as we would understand it. Lumbering began in a small way during the colonial period, but only had a very localized impact in terms of rain forest damage (e.g., around the Amahai timber mill in south Seram). Since 1947 the impact of lumbering has steadily increased, and present evidence is not at all encouraging in terms of rain forest conservation (Ellen, 1985).

The importance of long-distance trade in forest products is well established and is clearly ancient in the Moluccas, but only where timber was cut on an excessive and systematic scale did it do long-term ecological damage. A striking example is the destruction of Timorese forests during the pre-colonial period through the trade in sandalwood (*Santalum album*). And once forest has been heavily depleted, either through sustained extraction at a low level for many decades or through dramatic short-term clearances, it becomes vulnerable to predatory activity which would otherwise not be expected to have much effect, e.g., firewood collection, rattan extraction, or gathering of wood for fencing.

III. PLANTATIONS AND EXTIRPATIONS

At the opening of the European era wide-scale clove production was restricted to the islands off the west coast of Halmahera, mainly Ternate,

Tidore, and Bacan. Since the 16th century, increasing amounts of land in the central Moluccas have been transformed first into groves of clove and, from the late 19th century onwards, coconut. The Hoamoal Peninsula, the islands of Manipa, Kelang, and Boano, Ambelau, the southwest coast of Seram, Ambon, Haruku, Saparua, and Nusalaut were planted with clove groves during the 16th and early 17th centuries, and remained that way until the Dutch extirpations. The Dutch, in an attempt to maintain their monopoly, thereafter confined production to Ambon-Lease. Nutmeg production had always been geographically more confined, primarily to Banda and Gorom, although wild nuts had long been collected from the forests of New Guinea. The Dutch destruction of Banda in 1621 and the imposition of a nutmeg monopoly stimulated planting on Gorom and elsewhere, and also the collection of wild New Guinea nuts, in an attempt to evade the monopoly. The Dutch response to this was also extirpation. Thus, in the space of 100 years parts of the Moluccas witnessed two major ecological traumas: the widespread planting of groves (a pre-colonial silvicultural replacement of rain forest on an almost unprecedented scale), and their subsequent uprooting and burning, a man-induced environmental calamity of similarly gigantic proportions.

The scale and geographic spread of the extirpations were enormous. For example, in 1648 Arnoldus de Vlaming destroyed more than 4000 clove trees in the neighbourhood of Hatumeten, south Seram (van Doren, 1957: 317), and eight years later virtually all clove trees on the westerly Hoamoal Peninsula were destroyed. Between 1692 and 1695 about 1,050,000 trees were removed in the Ambon-Lease area alone (Knaap, 1985: 304). The devastation of the nutmeg groves was comparable. There were extirpations of nutmeg trees in various parts of east Seram in 1637, 1652, 1668, 1672, and 1674. In one year alone more than 11,000 trees were cut in Haya in south Seram. In 1648 4000 trees were cut "on Keffing"[2] and 1449 on Gorom. Gorom was subjected to a further extirpation of 1000 trees in 1670 and 137 trees, plus 200 smaller stands, in 1748 (Reiner de Klerk, 1894 [1756]: 37). In the early years of the extirpations (as is reflected in these figures) the aim was to destroy pre-existing plantations; the smaller extirpations of the later years appear to have been to enforce unequal treaties with unwilling villages that had the temerity to violate the monopoly. There were smaller extirpations of nutmeg groves on the far peripheries of the Banda system as well: on Teor, the Kei islands, Serua, Nila, Dammar, Roma, and Kisser (Warburg, 1897: 125–127). Not content

[2] By this is presumably meant parts of Seram Laut or the mainland of Seram under the control or influence of Keffing. The immediately adjacent mainland, however, is mangrove swamp, and would not have supported clove groves.

with destroying the exchange economy, the Dutch also made attempts to undermine their subsistence base, the groves of sago palm (De Klerk, 1938: 256–7).

IV. LOCAL TRADING NETWORKS AND THE RELOCATION OF PRODUCTION

We can generalize about the effects of the developments outlined in the preceding two sections as follows. Environmental depletion in the form of deafforestation (with all its accompanying side effects), together with spice monocropping, on small island centres led to greater dependence on the periphery of trading networks. It was, consequently, a formative process in the creation of such centres. Once centres had established themselves, their own internal dynamics became additionally important in maintaining their centrality, a tendency accelerated once such places became centres of colonial production and administration. But maintaining a sufficient supply to support a centre (let alone permit any expansion) may easily lead to over-extraction, or over-extension, at certain points of the periphery. This, in turn, may lead to the relocation of production, and to consequent change in the shape of the system. Let us examine some examples.

The increasing demand for timber in Amboina first led to the development of Amahai-Soaku, on the south coast of Seram, as a saw milling location. Exhaustion of nearby forest had, by World War II, resulted in its demise. Now, this kind of relocation is visible at the local level, but not on a wider scale in Moluccan trading systems. The reason lies in the structural properties of the system, and has little to do with the number of intermediaries and the geographic scale of the periphery. Thus, in the Banda system, the periphery is divided up in the classification of Bandanese producers and merchants alike in terms of the dominant secondary centres: Tual, Geser, Dobo. . . . In their model of the world, such specific places stand for entire sectors of the periphery, although they are in fact only secondary trading centres. Relocation of production on the periphery is not directly visible since it takes place within regions with their own centres which are themselves constant. Therefore, "going to Tual" may mean virtually anywhere in the Kei islands for a merchant in Amboina. Timber is still reckoned to come from Geser, even though Geser itself is an atoll with no timber of its own, and regardless of whether it has been imported to Geser from Warus-warus on the east coast of Seram, or from Sorong in New Guinea. A similar widespread usage in Ambonese Malay which expresses a similar spatial compression of distance, although I do not know the extent to which this finds homologues in local languages, is *belakang*, as in *belakang Geser*, *belakang Dobo* . . . (lit. behind Geser, behind Dobo). This refers to, in the case of Geser, the whole of mainland southeast Seram, and in the case of Dobo, to the hinterland of the Aru islands. It sometimes occurs in the nominal form as *dibelakang*, lit. "out the back", a usage which is in some respects similar to the Australian English "outback" or "the back end". I was often amused by informants who told me that someone or other was "out the back" (*ada dibelakang*), when it transpired that they were in fact 30 kilometres (km) away in the mountains and would not be back until the following day.

The convenient property of a highly connected periphery is that such systems have great flexibility:

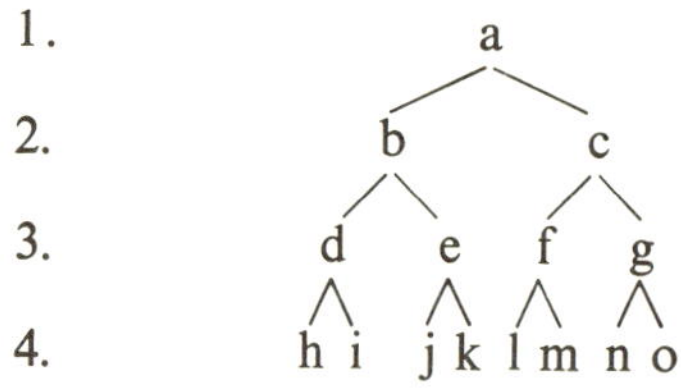

Thus, if there is a shift in production from *h* to *i*, *h* may disappear from the system, but the rest of the structure remains intact. Indeed, the repercussions at levels 1 and 2 may, other things being equal, barely be noticed or comprehended. This is so in the world of traders in Bandaneira or Amboina. The dynamics of the system operate independently of the perceptions of the actors. The more vectors centre *a* has to go through in order to obtain its primary products, the better protected it is from local perturbations in production, including environmental changes. This, of course, has to be weighed against the economic disadvantage of plural middlemen in forcing up the price of the goods.

But trading systems are, in reality, not like taxonomies. There are cross-cutting ties between points at the same level of the periphery and between points of production and different secondary centres. Thus, a more realistic model would be something like:

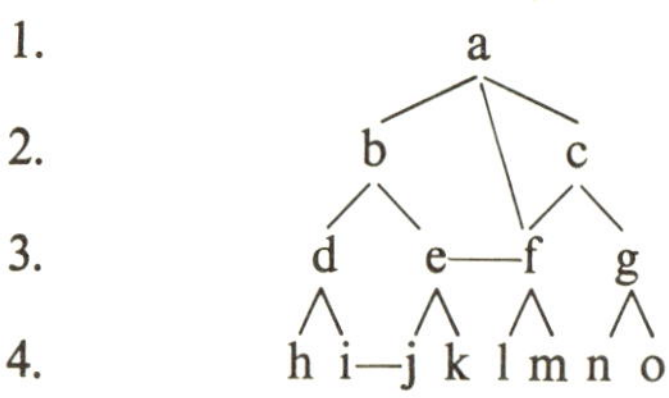

This only serves to increase the interconnections of the system, and gives it even more flexibility. However, there are some cross-cutting trading ties which may at the same time feed back to the centre more directly in a way that makes it more vulnerable, certainly more aware, of what is going on at the periphery. Moreover, the ties which a centre has with various secondary centres, and the ties which those centres have with points of production, are not equally significant. This introduces vulnerability, and must be set against the other vulnerability-reducing features of the network.

Changes in demand in international trade may require local modification. These may be met up to a point by home production, but on any scale will require expansion at the periphery. If the changes in demand are qualitative, this may lead to a gradual shift in the sites of production and the kind of production on the periphery. However, in the history of central Moluccan trade since the 15th century, the primary centres have remained remarkably constant. This reflects patterns of trade and, latterly, the Dutch monopoly. There have been population movements and changes in the ethnic composition of those groups controlling and facilitating trade, but much of this has simply been ethnic replacement within the same niche. The trade in certain high-value commodities, such as bird-of-paradise feathers and *massoi* bark, remained surprisingly stable over many centuries. Centres such as Banda could, therefore, fall back on the entrepôt trade if spice harvests failed or if demand slackened. Moreover, from the 17th century onwards, the Dutch themselves required supplies (such as slaves and food) from the periphery to support their own settlements and to subsidize trading activities. The dominant oscillations have been the expansion, control, decline, and then re-expansion of clove production, and the growth and then steady decline of nutmeg production. Within this period we have also seen the 18th–century growth in trade in *agar-agar*, pearls, *trepang*, and other maritime products, largely in response to demand of the Chinese market. In all this the major systemic innovation was the creation of the Amboina network. Prior to the 16th century, Ambon and the Lease islands were relatively unimportant as trading or political centres, or in production for exchange, although they had been in contact with Japanese, Malay, and more distant Asiatic traders (Abdurachman, 1981: 2). The area now incorporated in this system was probably previously integrated through more local coastal networks with linkages to Ternate and Tidore, while the interiors of the large islands of Seram and Buru must have been relatively unintegrated through trade. Hitu and Luhu, used as watering and victualling points for passing traders, and with connections with Java, provided incipient centres.[3] With the increase in trade, Hitu became important. During

[3] Some slight concrete evidence to support the assertion that, prehistorically,

the 16th century clove cultivation expanded, first in the Hoamoal Peninsula and later on Hitu, where by 1570 it grew in abundance (Abdurachman, 1981: 12). The Portugese and then the Dutch tried to centralise their activities on Amboina, and this led increasingly to its development. The Portugese fort and its associated township fed on each other symbiotically, and gave rise to a new kind of human settlement hitherto unknown in the Moluccas, and resembling much more towns like Malacca (Abdurachman, 1981: 15). It was then almost entirely a creature of European interests. As Amboina developed it began to dominate and bring within its sphere of influence other (older) traditional systems in the Moluccas, in particular the Banda and Ternate-Tidore systems. As Ambon eclipsed Banda as an administrative and economic centre, and as the Dutch became less preoccupied with illegal smuggling and breaking of the monopoly, so Seramese, Goromese and Aruese sold their *massoi*, pearls, *trepang*, gum, paradise feathers, *agar-agar*, and so on directly in Ambon, thus subsuming Banda in the wider Ambonese system (Bleeker, 1856: 129). In this the Amboina and Banda systems contrasted with other trading centres in the region, which despite the monopoly managed to sustain a remarkably free trade in commodities other than nutmeg and clove. Such a "Conradian" model of indigenous east Indonesian commerce, to use Resink's (1959) illuminating allusion, is applicable almost up to the end of the 19th century.

East Seram was an extremely important trading area between the 17th and 19th centuries, and during this period rivalled the Dutch in its volume of trade (Leirissa, 1981: 56). The Bandanese who fled to east Seram after 1621 (settling particularly at Keffing and Guli-guli) were particularly prominent in these activities (Knaap, personal communication), and set themselves up in competition with the new traders occupying their old homeland. Some villages may well have been entirely or predominantly Bandanese in origin, and on some early maps "Banda-Keffing" is marked, suggesting parallels with the old Bandanese settlements of "Banda-Elat" and "Banda-Eli" on Kei. Other villages may have assimilated lesser numbers of Bandanese.

However, the east Seramese trading area itself cannot have been a

---

Ambon-Lease was relatively unimportant in east-west archipelagic or extra-archipelagic trade is to be found in the distribution of artifacts of Javanese or western Indonesian origin. Bronzes and Hindu-Buddhist monuments are found in Banda, Gorom, Kei, and even New Guinea, but not in Ambon-Lease (van Heekeren, 1958: figure 1; Ellen, 1981: fieldnotes). On the fragmentary literary evidence pointing in the same direction, see Van Fraassen, 1976.

Bandanese creation, as is sometimes suggested (e.g., van der Crab, 1862: 62). From the early Portuguese sources we may infer that already in the early 16th century the peoples of Gorom and Seram Laut played an important part in the trade of *trepang*, *massoi*, and bird-of-paradise feathers (Boxer and Manguin 1979: 180, n. 14), while toponymic evidence from the Negarakertagama suggests even earlier antecedents (van Fraassen, 1976).

All this invigorated trade in the east Seram area, and in the entrepôt stakes led to the virtual eclipse of Banda itself in the 19th century. Banda had already suffered a decline with the growth of nutmeg plantations elsewhere in Indonesia and abroad. The situation was only saved by permanent settlement of new Chinese and Arab merchants to occupy the trading role previously, but increasingly ineffectively, performed by the *perkeniers* (Hanna, 1978: 104). Banda was declared a free port for general purposes in 1853.

The east Seramese polities were, therefore, more or less autonomous up to the end of the 19th century, apart from periodic extirpations in the early period in revenge for breaking the monopoly and anti-piracy raids later. Dutch apathy stemmed partly from isolation and ignorance, and partly from lack of commercial and political interest. In response to recommendations made by Bik after 1824, southeast Seram and its various insular extensions were assigned to the residency of Banda, and small posts were established on Keffing, Gorom, Kei Kecil, and Aru. Maintenance and reunification of the Banda system through the drawing of boundaries gave administrative recognition to an indigenous zone of trading and political influence.[4] But with the crumbling of the monopoly and the emergence of new patterns of trade, things finally began to change, painfully slowly. In the early 1860s Van der Crab (1862: 57) noted the independence of the rulers of the various autarkic polities of east Seram, but optimistically declared that they were becoming increasingly subject to Dutch authority. This view was starkly contradicted as late as 1874 by the Italian explorer G. Emilio Cerutti, who could report (writing in French) to the Dutch authorities that although Aru and Kei were claimed in the name of the Dutch crown, and were from time to time visited by the Resident in Amboina, they were in fact commercially and politically quite autonomous.[5]

[4] ARA Min. van Kolonien (2.10.01) 2766, 2767: Report of March-April 1824 to G.G. van de Capellen.

[5] ARA 2.10.10 mailrapporten 1874 6363–354: Soevereiniteitsrechten op de Aroe- en Key-eilanden door het gouvernement.

V. ENVIRONMENTAL CHANGE AT THE CENTRE

Both deafforestation and the vicissitudes of large-scale spice plantings and extirpations were more acute in their environmental consequences at the centres of trading networks, though by no means confined to them. We must now add to these those environmental changes which threatened their integrity in (arguably) a much more fundamental way. Ternate, Tidore, and the Banda group are all tiny volcanic islands, routinely subject to frequent and destructive eruption. The entire Moluccas is an area of great seismic activity, but the islands off the west coast of Halmahera, the Banda group, and the southwestern reaches of the arc of islands ending with Wetar (Nila, Seroa) are particularly vulnerable.[6] The last eruption of Gamalama on Ternate was as recent as 1983. We know from firsthand accounts that these can be devastating. Hanna, in his brief history of Banda, conveys the situation well, and it is instructive to quote him at some length:

> Gunung Api threatened a major eruption at the time of the very first Dutch visit to Banda in 1599, and for the next three centuries seemed recurrently on the point of blowing itself apart.... Concurrent earthquakes, tidal waves, and hurricanes added to the destruction caused by showers of hot lava and ash, which set fire to the thatch roofs and bamboo frames of the traditional-style houses favored by the Dutch before they learned from costly experience to build of stone, plaster and tile.... Enormous shade trees (*kanaris*) were uprooted by the hurricanes and the spice trees were stripped of branches and fruit.... Gunung Api sometimes emitted sulphorous fumes which settled over Neira town... held largely accountable for the

[6] The significance of seismic activity in the Moluccas is evident from the enormous attention it receives in the colonial and scientific literatures. For an exhaustive list of citations up to 1935 see Ruinen (1928) and Tutein Nolthenius (1935), under index headings "vulkanen en vulkanisme", "uitbarstingen", "aardbevingen" and "zeebevingen". For a list of eruptions, earthquakes, and tidal waves in the Banda group in pre-modern time see Verbeek (1901), Brouwer (1920), and Wichmann (1895). One of the earliest detailed first-hand descriptions of an earthquake is that of Rumphius. For 1900 to the present time I have used the earthquake data file of the Global Seismology Unit of the Institute of Geological Sciences in Edinburgh. This records most events from the Moluccas with a magnitude of 7.75 or over on the Richter scale, and those of lesser magnitude for more recent periods. From 1963 events with a magnitude of 4 or greater are recorded. Between 1900 and 1978 there were 54 events of magnitude 5 or above in the Banda group. For the purposes of this calculation these include all events occurring between –4.90 and –5.10 latitude and longitude 129.50 and 131.

> prevalence of illness and mortality rate. . . . [The] especially bad years of the seventeenth century were 1615, 1629, 1638, 1661, 1691, and 1693. The 1615 eruption was so severe that boulders were sent hurtling down upon Fort Nassau. . . . In 1629, a tidal wave swept Neira anchorage and the new town (p. 84).
>
> The stinking vapors and showers of hot, clinging ashes [of the 1691 eruption] persisted for a full five years. . . . The worst of the epidemics, which generally followed soon after the eruptions, were those of 1638, when 375 persons died in Neira Town, and 1693, when 771 slaves died. . . . In the eighteenth century, natural disasters became less frequent but no less destructive (p. 85).
>
> During one awful hour in midmorning on April 2, 1778, there occurred, simultaneously, an especially destructive volcanic eruption, an earthquake, a tidal wave, and a hurricane. This manifestation of nature's malevolence worked devastation in the towns and in the *perken* [the estates] and even in stoutly built fortifications. The damage in the nutmeg gardens was so extensive that one tree out of every two was uprooted or badly splintered. The harvest during the next twelve months dropped to a mere 30,000 pounds of nutmeg and 10,000 pounds of mace, as compared with 800,000 and 200,000 pounds respectively in 1777 (p. 89).

There was a fresh series of natural disasters in the early years of the nineteenth century:

> A hurricane in 1815, an earthquake in 1816, and then, in 1820, a very few years after the return of Banda to the Dutch, one of the most destructive earthquakes in the islands' history (p. 98).

destroying or badly damaging most of the official and private buildings in Neira Town (p. 99). And then on 22 April 1824, coinciding with a visit to the islands of the Governor General Van de Capellen, there was a sudden eruption of Gunung Api (Olveier, 1834; Hanna, 1978: 99). There was an earthquake and tidal wave in 1852, a prolonged series of earthquakes in 1854, and a great fire which burned out a large part of Neira town in 1856. This led to charitable relief from Holland (Hanna, 1978: 104). At times the natural disasters very nearly led to a shift in policy which would have displaced localities such as Banda as central places. The 1778 hurricane "reduced the available supply of nutmeg to a level well below that regarded as optimal for monopoly purposes, such that the Dutch transplanted Banda nutmeg to Ambon," and they reversed the policy with extirpation (Hanna, 1978: 95). The frequency and devastation of such orogenies occasioned official concern for its effect on spice production (Van Vliet, 1853).

Elsewhere, Ternate and Tidore were subject to periodic eruptions, and more recently the entire population of Serua has been resettled on Banda due to an eruption there.

Volcanic eruption was by no means the only physical change threatening trading centres. Geser, Kiltai, and Keffing (as low-lying, exposed, and minute coral atolls and banks) were vulnerable to high tides, frequent flooding, hurricanes, and tidal waves, with virtually no possibilities for cultivating and with only brackish drinking water. Van der Crab (1864: 541) reports that with a spring tide the entire village of Kilwaru on Kiltai was underwater, during which time people temporarily moved to Seram Laut. Bik (1928 [1824]: 41) had long ago remarked that Dobo, the historic primary centre for the Aru group, was no more than an anchorage and sandy spit of land about 1500 feet east from the small island of Wamar. A VOC report of 1792[7] notes the problems of approaching and finding anchorages in Ondor and Kataloka on Gorom during the east monsoon. An American intelligence document says of Geser: "Tidal streams are strong holding poor, and the south going ebb stream meeting southerly winds raises a heavy sea" (ASS 1942: 17). Moreover, the Seram Laut archipelago had a reputation for endemic smallpox, which in 1859 had more or less decimated the population (van der Crab, 1862: 63–64, 69). Over a period of several hundred years, shifting sandbanks, destruction of mangroves, and storm damage have affected the microgeography of southeast Seram.

VI. POLITICAL INSTABILITY AT THE CENTRE

To the environmental threats we must add the political. Although we have little knowledge of Moluccan political history prior to the arrival of the Portuguese, pre-European Banda was most unlikely to have been the congeries of Arcadian republics or Athenian democracies suggested by Villiers (1981). From oral tradition there is evidence of intervillage conflict. There was warfare with Ternate. Likewise, Ternate and Tidore were never at peace for long, and their political relations with the periphery which they controlled was partly in terms of the provision of warriors and war canoes (*cora-cora*). But whatever the situation before European intervention, the arrival of the Dutch led to a period of immense political turmoil, culminating in 1621 with the massacre of the indigenous inhabitants of Banda. In 1624 Van Speult attacked villages in east Seram

---

[7] ARA VOC 3966: 23 (26 September 1792)

and Gorom to which the Bandanese had fled (Tiele 1886: Bouwstoffen vol. 2 ix [c.f. Valentijn II: 54]). In 1633 the first Ambonese *hongi* took place to Seram Laut (Knaap, personal communication; Daghregister 1631–34: 196; Wurffbain 1931a: 85, 90; Rumphius 1910 (I): 93–95). During the 17th and 18th centuries there were periodic Dutch raids[8] on Gorom and other places, as well as raids from Papuan "pirates".

During the 19th century there was endemic rivalry and feuding in southeast Seram (Kniphorst 1883: 311; Kolff 1840: 287–8) and in Dobo. There were, for example, disputes between Kelu and other rulers arising from the war between Kwaai and Keliberao on Keffing (Bik 1928 [1824]: 16). Bik (1928 [1824]: 48) reports on a war between Wamar and Wadheir, in which the latter replaced the former as the power more influential with the Alifuru (native population) of the east coast of Aru, the source of *trepang* and birds' nests. There was migration within and between island groups as a result of endemic local warfare, and Bik (1928 [1824]: 11) also tells us of a headman from Teor living on Seram Laut on account of intervillage warfare on his own island. There are constant references in the mail reports to the liveliness (*levendig*) of trade, but often these are accompanied by or juxtaposed to accounts of unrest and fighting between intrusive traders (*vreemde*) and natives, often resulting in the death of Chinese and Makassans and the plundering of villages by traders. Many of these reports come from Ternate and Dobo in the last quarter of the 19th century.[9] And with the final arrival of secure Dutch administration the records are full of litigation between intrusive traders and local rulers and between the local inhabitants over rights in extraction and ownership of particular commercially valuable resources (Holleman, 1925: 134–47). However, open conflict between rulers of local polities de-escalated into cases brought befor ecolonial magistrates (*raad*) (Adatrechtbundels, 1925: 177–208).

None of this should be surprising, for at the end of the day, we would expect centres to be politically unstable compared with their peripheries, partly because they *are* centres.

VII. WHY CENTRAL PLACES REMAIN CENTRAL

So, why do people persist in locating the centres of networks in such places? Indeed, why do they not only remain there but also expand areas

[8] Rumphius, Landbeschrijving ARA VOC 1124: 120–126.

[9] ARA Mailrapporten (2.10.10) 1871, 6353–503: Onrust onder be bevolking en aanvallen op handelaren; 1872, 6355–609: Handel op Dobo/Aroe-eilanden is levendig, Toestand op de Aroe-eilanden/res. is rustig; 1892, 6498–1191, 1201: Bestrijding van onlusten op de Aroe-eilanden door SS. Java.

of cultivation into environmentally more precarious zones and intensify population levels? Gunung Api in Banda, which was uninhabited at the time of European discovery, now has a population of almost 2000. This is hardly because of investment in physical infrastructures, as until the colonial period this was limited; or because of the demands of spice cultivation, as was once thought. Both nutmeg and clove are now grown widely in coastal areas of the tropics. Part of the answer must be that the dynamics of the system require it; that given the prior existence of the system, there is a built-in conservative force in peoples perception, scheduling, and habitual decision-making which is geared to preservation of the existing systemic order. This involves weighing-up the costs of periodic orogenies against long-term economic security. For, when all is said and done, although these islands are highly active seismically, in any objective global sense, in the experience of individuals and families, crippling eruptions occur only infrequently, and then also irregularly. Thus, between 1900 and 1978 there were 33 events of magnitude 5 and above in the Banda group,[10] but their temporal distribution is highly asymmetric:

1910	**1**
1920	**1**
1934	**1**
1936	**1**
1940	**1**
1951	**1**
1956	**1**
1974	**4**
1975	**20**
1976	**1**
1977	**1**

Thus, in an average lifetime crippling earthquakes are not automatically expected. Such irregular periodicity does not encourage major capital investment in either relocating sites or developing strategies to alleviate or prevent disasters. At the same time, the effects of disasters (though feared) are measurable and predictable. They destroy only easily renewable resources and result in very little loss of life. All this may explain why at the present time people seem so unprepared for such events and fail to respond to them with specially elaborated cultural mechanisms.

This tolerance of imminent physical disaster is reinforced by the security of well-worn short-term material advantages: the constancy of trade in

[10] But see definitions in footnote 6.

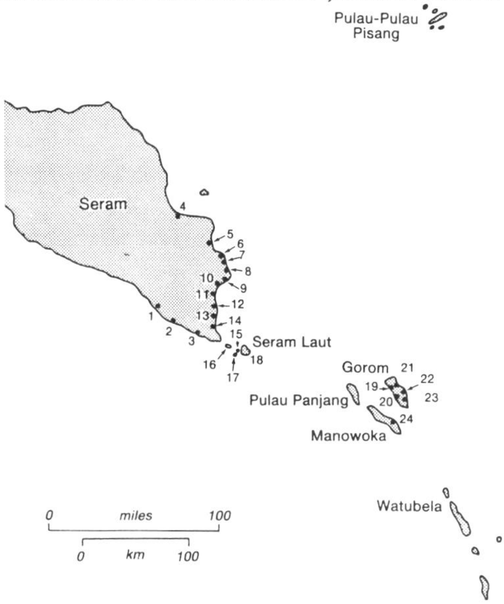

FIG. 2. East Seram and Seram Laut Archipelago, showing some of the places mentioned in the text.
The numbered locations are as follows; 1. Kilmuri 2. Guli-guli 3. Kwamar 4. Waru 5. Gah 6. Warus-warus 7. Air Kasar 8. Sesar 9. Kilbat 10. Kilmoi 11. Danama 12. Kiandarat 13. Kianlaut 14. Kwaos 15. Kilwaru, Kiltai 16. Keffing 17. Geser 18. Kelifura 19. Kataloka 20. Ondor 21. Namalen 22. Mida 23. Rarat 24. Amarsekaru

certain high-value goods, investment in the primary production of nutmeg, clove, and later in the extraction of maritime products; and development of a geographic division of labour involving centres of specialist production. In the early 19th century, Gorom (and other centres in east Seram, including Kilmuri and Kilwaru; see Bik 1928: 16) were centres of a weaving industry exporting to other parts of the archipelago. This export trade had probably been in existence since at least the 17th century, as indicated by a reference in Valentijn (Niggermeyer, 1952: 3883, 3892). Kilwaru, Seram Laut, and Gorom monopolized the trade in *massoi.* In the 1680s there was a division of trading labour in the *massoi* trade and slaving between two villages on Seram Laut. The Seram Laut group provided ironsmiths, goldsmiths, and silversmiths, carpenters, potters, and boatbuilders (Hollander, 1895: 501; Riedel, 1886: 169). Gorom was a centre for the manufacture of trochus shell armbands (Ellen, 1984: 185) and boxes made from sago leafstalk.[11] In western New Guinea Goromese are still renowned as smiths. In the late 19th century carpenters and bricklayers from Geser found work in west New Guinea

[11] Rumphius, Landbeshrijving: ARA VOC 11245: 120–126.

and the Raja Ampat islands (Bruijnis 1933: 96). Before 1621 Banda was an important centre of pottery production.

All this was in turn facilitated by underlying environmental factors. Wind systems and currents restricted those areas in which central places could be effectively located.[12] In those areas which were accessible given the exigencies of navigation and seamanship, further considerations came into effect, such as the availability of harbours which might be used by intrusive traders and refugees as safe havens in otherwise hostile territory.

But more than this, the networks themselves had a cushioning effect and possessed a flexibility which enabled change through internal modification and replacement. This in part stemmed from the conservative system-maintaining behaviour and views of the inhabitants. This was done partly through the replacement of commodities decreasing in demand with those growing in demand. This may point to a hitherto unelaborated characteristic of pre-capitalist mercantile systems, namely that commodities underwrite trading relationships which endure independent of individual commodities themselves. In capitalism, the social relations of trade are entirely subservient to the needs of obtaining not only *particular* commodities, but particular commodities at the cheapest market price.

Moreover, centres can re-arrange their activities to cope with damage to their parts. For "centres" themselves are spaces rather than points. There can be a temporary move to the periphery, or the locus of trade and political power may shift within the centre. The effects of Dutch and native raids were lessened by the ease with which the inhabitants could escape to other islands, or remove settlements further inland. At low tide one can walk across from Seram Laut to Kiltai, and from Kwaos to Keffing (Bik, 1828: 16; Rosenburg, 1867: 132). Keffing to Kilwaru is no more than a half hour away with a good wind, and no more than an hour under most conditions; Kilwaru to Geser is only 15 minutes in a favourable wind. Geser and Kilmuri are less suitably placed for rapid evacuation, and this journey may take 11 hours by sail. In traditional Banda, the polities of Neira were no more important than those of Lonthoir, Rhun, and others, with which they were in alliance. In the north Moluccas, Ternate and Tidore, though often politically hostile, and with distinct social and trading connections, can be seen in wider geographic and economic terms as a single system.

In southeast Seram we know that political and trading power shifted

[12] With the demise of sailing vessels as the most important conveyors of goods such factors became irrelevant, but by this time the social and economic dynamics of the systems themselves had become sufficient to maintain certain locational patterns.

between the islands of Keffing, Geser, Kiltai, and Seram Laut, and more widely still to include places on the mainland of Seram and the polities of Gorom. There have been important trading centres in southeast Seram since before the Portuguese arrived, and we may reasonably infer that they go back much further into the prehistoric period. Serdenha (and variant spellings), mentioned in de Brito's manuscript of 1500, played an important role in regional distribution in the 16th century, although Boxer and Manguin (1979: 180 n. 14) are unable to identify it. But in a sense its precise location is beside the point. It could have been Keffing, Seram Laut, and Gorom individually, but all are historically related by language, culture, and politics, and are part of a 25-km zone in which the centre of the moment shifted about.

In what is perhaps the earliest map of locations in southeast Seram and its adjacent archipelago, that drawn by H. and A. van Langren or Linschoten in 1596 (1955), Guli-Guli only is marked, in approximately its correct location.[13] On a map of 1651, based on information provided by Arnoldus de Vlamingh van Outshoorn, only Seram Laut is marked among a number of small islands and banks off southeast Seram.[14] A 17th-century Dutch map in the Rijksarchief[15] shows Keffing (*Out* [*Ho*]-*ffing*) on the mainland; Geser is shown, but not named. In 1624 Gorom appears to have been the principal power in southeast Seram: it could mobilise 50 *kora-kora* (war canoes) following the Bandanese flight from their homeland.[16] At this time Keffing and Seram Laut appear to have been primarily anchorages for Malay, Makassarese, and Javanese trading vasels.[17] In the 1680s Geser is claimed by Kilwaru, but is no longer itself inhabited.[18] In 1779 Geser and Seram Laut appear to have been the

---

[13] Kaart behorende bij Linchotenvereeriging Deel LX. V. Waarachtigewtwarpinghe ofte afbeeldinge van alle die custen ende Landen van China, Cauchin china, Camboja, Sijao, Malacca, Arracan ende Pegu, enz. 1595. Henricus F. ab Langiren [Sculpfit]; Arnoldus F. a Langren delineauir.

[14] ARA VEL 1345 Caarte van Groote Ceram, midsgaders alle d'Eylanden van Amboina en Banda, 1651. Behoort bij het rapport van Arn. de Vlamingh van Outshoorn.

[15] ARA VEL Kaart van het Eiland Ceram, Bouro, een gedeelte van de Westkustvan Nova Guinea, de Arouw Eilanden, Timor-laut, het Oostelykste gedeelte van Tymor en de daar tusschen gelegen Eilanden; also ARA VEL 475 Kaart van het Eiland Ceram, Bouro, Amboina, en bygelegen Eilanden.

[16] Brief van Herman van Speult aan de GG J. Pz. Coen in d. 15 Juni 1622, Tiele 1886 (vol.1): 315.

[17] Artus Gijsels, gouverneur van Ambon, aan den Gouv.-Gen. Jacq. Specx, 10 September 1632: quoted in Tiele 1886 (vol.1): 203.

[18] Rumphius, Landbeschrijving: ARA VOC 11245.

political centres of gravity as far as the Dutch were concerned, and the heads of these polities signed contracts renewing old agreements with the VOC to supply Banda with victuals, slaves, and manufacturing materials.[19] A proclamation on smuggling issued in 1824[20] by the Dutch authorities and adressed to rulers in the Amboina residency is quite specific in its mentioning of locations, but among the polities of the Seram Laut archipelago only Gorom is mentioned, suggesting that at this time Gorom (Kataloka, Ondor) was in political and commercial ascendency, while Keffing and Seram Laut and other places had been temporarily eclipsed. In a map possibly drawn in 1835[21] Kiltai and Kilwaru are shown in their modern locations, and Kelu and Keffing are on Keffing (Seranrei) Island. On another map dated 1835[22] Geser is marked, but not Kilwaru. By 1875[23] the proportions of islands such as Keffing shown on maps are at last correct. In a map of 1872[24] Keffing is shown as part of the mainland though separated from it by a channel in the mangroves. On this same island are shown Kelu and Kwaai. By the mid-19th century *Klein* Keffing is shown on Seranrei (Keffing Island) and *Groot* Keffing on the mainland (van der Crab 1862: 59). At the present time the Seram Laut archipelago consists of five *desa* units: Kiltai, being half of Kiltai island and part of Seram Laut; Kilwaru, being the other half of Kiltai and part of Seram Laut, Kelu, being half of Keffing island and the remaining part of Seram Laut; Keffing, being the remaining part of Keffing Island; and Geser. Thus, within the "centre" the importance of particular places shifted from time to time, as did the settlements themselves. In the second half of the 17th century Guli-Guli, Kataloka, and Solotkay were sufficiently important for the Dutch to build temporary fortresses. Geser, so important at the end of the 19th century, when its status as a central place was bolstered by its becoming an administrative centre and coaling depot, had been empty not so many years previously. The Dutch had

[19] ARA VOC 3561. pp. 1855 a 1856 Brief van gemelde Bandas gouverneur Pelters aen generael en raden van 14 December 1980 over de Cerammers enz.; see also Hollander 1895:50.

[20] ARA Min. van Kolonien (2.10.01) 2766: Reglement on het Binnenlandsch Bestuur en dat de Financien op Amboina en Onderhoorigheden. Ambon, 15th April 1824.

[21] ARA MIKO 111 973 Geteekende kaart van het eiland CERAM.

[22] ARA MIKO 111 207 1835: Geteekende kaart van het eiland Groot Seram.

[23] E.g. ARA MIKO 111 1875 Schetskaart van het eiland Ceram 1909.

[24] ARA MIKO 111–1082: Figuratieve schets van het eiland CERAM, residentie AMBOINA.

planned to establish a fort on Geser as early as 1785,[25] but it was only in the 1880s that it became the *stapelplaats* of the entire southeasterly archipelago (Kniphorst 1883: 310, based on a report by Sterker). In fact, the Seram Laut and Gorom archipelagos were a network of fluctuating political alliances, reinforced by marriage; integrated social formations covering several islands, with a flexible organization. Northwards on the east coast of Seram there were autonomous *orang kayas* in Danama, Kilmoi and Kilbat, westwards the *orang kaya* of Urung and the *rajas* of Kilmuri, Tobo, and Hatumeten; on the islands the *raja* of Kilwaru and Kelu, the *majoor* of Keffing, and on Gorom the *rajas* of Amar, Kataloka and Ondor. These polities were connected through various alliances which may have shifted over time. For example, the *seri-tahun* alliance covered the area between Kwaos, Urung, and Keffing, and possibly other places; the *tutup-tolu* (three) alliance encompassed Danama, Kilmoi, Kilbat, Gah, Warus-warus and Kiltai and Kilwaru; the *tutu-hitu* (seven) alliance connected Kelu and Amar; while the *raja-empat* alliance connected Kilmuri, Tobo, Sepa, Mengeli, and Werinama (Jansen 1928; Ellen, field notes 1981). There were others as well, but in all this Tidore, which claimed authority over the area, had little influence.

It would appear that the preconditions necessary for permanently abandoning central places are demanding and complex, although (as I have shown) the Dutch appear to have come perilously close to abandoning Banda in the 19th century. What seems to be crucial in the long run is not the finer points of geography, or the crude tabulation of hazards, but the extent to which there is an overarching social system which can cushion a precarious centre (cf. Alkire 1965: 2). Such social systemic properties not only account for the persistence of centres, but explain short-term political shifts as well.

VIII. CONCLUSION

In the real world the conventional wisdom of central place theory has relatively little to offer. Geography (coastline patterns, wind systems, currents, and navigational and sailing factors), given a particular level of technology, tends to funnel networks into corridors and warp ideal Christaller-Lösch landscapes. Here "strategically placed communities may then become nodes through which many strands are drawn, and

[25] ARA VOC 3677. Copie secrete resolutie van 10 Julij 1784 inhoudende 'g gooverneurs voornemen tot sluiting van verdere te samenrottinen door het stabilieren van een fortje op Po. Gisser; Plan van een fortres hetwelk de gouverneur geintentioneerd was om op Po. Grisser [sic!] op te regten.

may be able to establish an oligopolistic control over traffic" (Brookfield with Hart, 1971: 317). Fixed boundaries are inclined to interfere with classical properties, and insular systems anyway are bad exemplars of central place theory. The reasons are topographic: the high proportion of uninhabitable space (in this case sea), approximately 85% in the Moluccas,[26] and the lack of uniformity in the distribution of the land areas. This affects virtually every aspect of the classic Christaller-Lösch predictions: with respect to the spacing of settlements, the shape of market area (that is, degree of "hexagonality"), threshold sizes (the lower limit on number of consumers required before a given type of function, such as commodity specialization, can come into existence), trip frequency (the further the distance, the fewer the trips), and hierarchy and rank size rules. On this latter, Geser, which is highly connected, should have grown substantially in size. Instead it has remained a small town. Riedel (1886: 148) gives a figure of 306 persons for the beginning of the period when it became a Dutch administrative centre; in 1978 the population was only 2200. Of the other alternative "centres within the centre" Riedel gives 527 for Seranrei (Keffing Island), 568 for Kilwaru, and 448 for Seram Laut. In fact, the percentage of the population located at the centre in such systems may be very low indeed. The evidence therefore conforms to the general criticisms of the usefulness of central place theory made by Walter Isard (Smith 1976: 24), on the grounds that it uses untenable assumptions of an isotropic landscape, perfect competition among suppliers, threshold governance of supplier location, single suppliers of each good at each centre, and single-purpose trips by consumers.

REFERENCES

N.B. The following list contains published sources only. Manuscript references are indicated in footnotes.

Abdurachman, Paramita R. (1981). New winds, new faces, new forces. Un-Paper presented at the Conference on Southeast Asian Responses to European Intrusions, British Institute in Southeast Asia, Singapore.

Adatrechtbundels (1925) Uitspraken van gecommitteerde ambtenaren voor Ceram, Ceramlaut, Goram, Aroe- en Kei-eilanden (1853–1857). *Adatrechtbundels*, **24**: 177–208.

Alkire, W.H. (1965). *Lamotrek Atoll and Inter-Island Socioeconomic Ties*. Urbana: University of Illinois Press.

---

[26] To be exact, 85 % of the rectangle bounded by 3°N to 9°S and 125°E to 134.5°E, and this includes the large land masses of the Kepala Burung (Vogelkop) of Irian Jaya, as well as part of East Timor.

ASS (1942). *Area Study of Seran (Ceram)*. Allied Geographical Section, South-west Pacific Area.

Bik, A.J. (1928 [1824]). *Dagverhael eener reis, gedaan in het jaar 1824 tot nadere verkenning der eilanden Kefing, Goram, Groot-Klein Kei en de Aroe-eilanden.* Leiden: A.W. Sijthoff.

Boxer, C.R. and P.-Y. Manguin (1979). Miguel Roxo de Brito's narrative of his voyage to the Raja Empat, May 1581–November 1582. *Archipel.*, **18**: 175–194.

Brookfield, H.C. with D. Hart (1971). *Melanesia: A Geographical Interpretation of an Island World.* London: Methuen.

Brouwer, H.A. (1920). Geologische onderzoekingen op de Sangi-eilanden en op de eilanden Ternate en Pisang. *Jaarb Mijnw Verh.*, **2**: 1–68.

Bruijnis, N.W. van (1933). *Ethnologische economie en de studie van het economisch leven der inheemsche bevolking in het oosten van de Indischen Archipel en Nederlandsch Nieuw-Guinee.* Arnhem: Paap [Thesis, Rijksuniversiteit te Utrecht].

Crab, P. van der (1862). *De Moluksche eilanden: Reis van Z.E. Den Gouverneur Generaal C. P. Pahud.* Batavia: Lange.

Crab, P. van der (1864). Reis naar de Zuidwestkust van Nieuw-Guinea, de Goram- en Ceram-laut eilanden en Oostelijk Ceram. Tijdschrift voor Indische Taal-, Land- en Volkenkunde, **13**: 531–556.

Doren, J.B.J. (1857). *Herinneringen en schetsen van Nederlands Oost Indie: vervalg op de fragmenten uit reizen in die gewesten. Vol.* **1**. Amsterdam: J.D. Sybrandi.

Ellen, R.F. (1975). Non-domesticated resources in Nuaulu ecological relations. *Social Science Information*, **14**: 127–50.

Ellen, R.F. (1977). Resource and commodity: Problems in the analysis of the social relations of Nuaulu land use. *Journal of Anthropological Research*, **33**: (1) 50–72.

Ellen, R.F. (1978). *Nuaulu Settlement and Ecology: An Approach to the Environmental Relations of an Eastern Indonesian Community.* (Verhandelingen van het Koninklijk Instituut van Taal-, Land- en Volkenkunde, No. **18**) Leiden: Martinus Nijhoff.

Ellen, R.F. (1979). Sago subsistence and the trade in spices: A provisional model of ecological succession and imbalance in Moluccan history. In P. Burnham and R. Ellen (eds.), *Social and Ecological Systems* (Assn. Social Anthrop. Monogr. **18**). London: Academic Press.

Ellen, R.F. (1984). Trade, environment and the reproduction of local systems in the Moluccas. In Emilio Moran (ed.), *The Ecosystem Concept in Anthropology.* (AAAS Selected Symposium 92). Boulder, Colo.: Westview Press.

Ellen, R.F. (1985). Patterns of indigenous timber extraction from Moluccan rain forest fringes. *Journal of Biogeography*, **12**: 559–587.

Fraassen, C.F. van (1976). Drie plaatsnamen uit Oost-Indonesie in de Nagara-Kertagama. *Bijdragen tot de taal-, land- en volkenkunde*, **132** (2–3): 293–305.

Haggett, P. and R.J. Chorley (1969) *Network Analysis in Geography.* London: Edward Arnold.

Hanna, W. (1978). *Indonesian Banda: Colonialism and Its Aftermath in the Nutmeg Islands*. Philadelphia: Institute for the Study of Human Issues.

Heekeren, H.R. van (1958). *The Bronze-Iron Age of Indonesia*. Verhandelingen van het Koninklijk Instituut voor taal, land- en volkenkunde **22**. The Hague: Martinus Nijhoff.

Hollander, J.J. de (1895). *Handleiding bij de beofening der land- en volkenkunde van Nederlandsche Oost-Indie*. Vol. **2**. Breda: Broese.

Holleman, F.D. (ed.) (1925). Jurisprudentie van de inheemsche rechtspraak op Boeroe, Ceram, Aroe en Tenimbar (1883–1923). *Adatrechtbundels*, **24**: 131–148.

Jansen, H.J. (1928). Gegevens over Geser, Boela en de Gorong- of Gorom-eilanden. *Adatrechtbundels*, **36**: 490–94.

Klerck, E.S. de (1938). *History of the Netherlands East Indies*. 2 volumes. Rotterdam: Brusse.

Klerk, Reiner de (1894 [1756]). *Belangkrijk verslag over den staat van Banda en omliggende eilanden aan zijne excellentie der Gouverneur-Generaal . . . . met eene korte beschrijving van Banda . . . door C.A.M. van Vliet*. 's-Gravenhage: W.P. van Stockum.

Knaap, Gerrit (1985). *Kruidnagelen en Christenen: de Verenigde Oost-Indische Compagnie en de bevolking van Ambon, 1656–1696*. Doctoral thesis presented at the Rijksuniversiteit te Utrecht.

Kolff, D.H. (1840). *Voyages of the Dutch Brig of War Dourgu Through the Southern and Little-Known Parts of the Moluccan archipelago and along the previously unknown Southern coast of New Guinea . . . . 1825–1826*. London: Madden and Co.

Linschoten, J.H. van (1955). (1596) *Itinerario, Voyage ofte shipvaert van Jan Huygen van Linschoten naer Oost ofte Portuguels Indien, 1579–1592*. Edited by Prof. Dr. H. Kern. Second edition, revised by Dr. H. Terpstra. 's-Gravenhage: Works of the Linschoten-Vereeriging. nos. **57, 58, 60.**

Macknight, C.C. (1976). *The Voyage to Marage: Macassan Trepangers in Northern Australia*. Carlton, Vic.: Melbourne University Press.

Metzner, Joachim K. (1977). *Man and Environment in Eastern Timor: A Geoecological Analysis of the Baucau-Viqueque Area as a Possible Basis for Regional Planning* (Development Studies Centre Monogr. **8**). Canberra: The Australian National University.

Niggemeyer, H. (1952). Ceramesische Baumwoll- und Fasergewebe. *Ciba-Rundschau*, **106**: 3881–3893.

Olivier, J. (1834). *Riezen in den Moluschen archipel: Naar Makassar enz. in het gevolg van den Gouverneur-Generaal van Nederland's Indie*. Amsterdam: G.J.A. Beijerinck.

Resink, G.J. (1959). De archipel voor Joseph Conrad. *Bijdragen tot de Taal-, Land en Volkenkunde CXV* (2), 192–208. Reprinted (1968) as "The eastern archipelago under Joseph Conrad's Western eyes." in *Indonesia's History between the Myths: Essays in Legal History and Historical Theory*. The Hague: W. van Hoeve.

Riedel, J.G.F. (1886). *De sluik- en kroesharige rassen tusschen Selebes en Papua.* 's-Gravenhage: Nijhoff.

Ruinen, W. (1928). *Overzicht van de literatuur betreffende de Molukken. Vol. 1 (1550–1921).* Amsterdam: Molukken-Instituut.

Rumphius, G.E. (1675). *Waerachtign Verhael, van de Schrickelijcke Aerdbevinge, nu onlanghs eenigen tijd herwaerts, ende voornaementlijck op den 17 February des Jaers 1674, voorgevallen, in, en ontrent de Eylanden van Amboina, mitsgaders ongehoorde watervloeden, droevige ongelucken, en wanderlijcke by-sonder-heden, enz. daer op gevolght, gelyck sulex in het Dagh-Register van dien neerstigh en omstanstigh aengeteyckent staet, uytgetrocken is Gedruckt naer de Copye van Batavia, In't Jaer Onses Heeren, 1675* [16 pp.].

Smith, C. (1976). *Regional Analysis. Vol. 1. Economic Systems.* London: Academic Press.

Tutein Nolthenius, A.B. (1935). *Overzicht van de literatuur betreffende en de Molukken (exclusief Nieuw Guinea). Vol.2 (1922–1933).* Amsterdam: Molukken-Instituut.

Verbeek, R.D.M. (1901) *Geologische beschrijving van de Banda-eilanden.* Batavia.

Villiers, J. (1981). Trade and society in the Banda Islands in the sixteenth century. *Modern Asian Studies,* **15** (4): 723–750.

Vliet, L. van (1853). *Proeve van beantwoording der vraag: welken invloed moeten de laatste aard- en zeebevingen in the Molukken, geacht worden te hebben op de productie der specerijen?* Amsterdam.

Warburg, O. (1897). *Die Muskatnuss, ihre Geschichte, Botanik, Kultur, Handel und Verwerthung, sowie ihre Verfölschungen und Surrogate, zugleich en Beitrag zur Kulturgeschichte der Banda-Inseln.* Leipzig: Wilhem Engelmann.

Wheatley, P. (1959). Geographical notes on some commodities involved in Sung maritime trade. *Journal of the Malay Branch of the Royal Asiatic Society,* **32** (2): 5–140.

Wichmann, A. (1895). De statistiek der aardbevingen in den Indischen Archipel. *Ned Nat. Geneesk Congr.,* 493–498.

Wurffbain, J.S. (1931). *Reise nach den Molukken 1632–1646.* 2nd ed. Vol. 1. 's-Gravenhage: Nijhoff.

Big Man Eats Little: Modes of Production and Consumption of the Mbotgote in Malekula, Vanuatu

Takeo FUNABIKI

Department of Cultural Anthropology, College of Arts and Sciences, University of Tokyo, Tokyo, Japan

I. INTRODUCTION

The purpose of this essay is to describe and analyze the pattern and regulation of eating habits among the Mbotgote, inhabitants of Malekula Island in the New Hebrides Archipelago. Although the paper refers to the relationship between a population and its environment and to the allocation of resources and products, which is the purview of Human Ecology, the data and analysis are not quantitative but delineative. In keeping with the theme of this Symposium, the holistic view of human interactions with nature and among themselves, I take up the problem of food production and consumption, focusing on the customary practices of the Mbotgote in preparing and taking meals.

I aim, first, to clarify the socio-religious differentiation and the developmental shift of Mbotgote dietary rules in their normative framework, and then to relate the resultant composite pattern to other social phenomena in different spheres. This essentially structural-functionalist form of analysis complements the holistic approach of Human Ecology in which the parts of separate spheres are assumed to constitute a whole with consistency and determinancy; but it would not accord some rash attempt to leap from reality to quantity and then to theory, without substantiating the difference in levels through ethnographic accounts.

II. THE MBOTGOTE OF MALEKULA

The Mbotgote-speaking people, who in 1975 numbered 81 persons, together with their neighbours, the Nabwol (36 persons), constitute the whole population of the interior forest of the southern part of Malekula.[1]

---

[1] In spite of their separate socio-ritual identity, the Mbotgote and the Nabwol

From general data on the climate of the New Hebrides (Kennedy, 1974: 56–7; British Service, 1973: 96–8) average annual rainfall in South Malekula can be estimated at about 3,500 mm, and average maximum temperatures are around 28°C in May – October and 30°C in November – April. But the interior region of South Malekula which the Mbotgote occupy has more rainfall and lower temperatures than these averages because of its elevation. The Mbotgote's area rises from about 50 metres at the river to 800 metres at the top of the hill. Primary and secondary forests prevail throughout this area with shrubbery and sporadic gardens. Transportation in South Malekula is either by foot or by boat. Vehicles can be used only on the road along the eastern coast of the island. Some hundred metres inland from the coast, there are only faint paths to be found in the thick forest.

The Mbotgote have been well known in Vanuatu for their obstinate seclusion in the forest and a conservative commitment to their way of life. In the mid 1970s [the ethnographic present of this essay], the Mbotgote are the only people adamantly continuing to resist change and remain in the bush-forest as traditionalists; all the other bush-dwellers have migrated to the coast and become Christians. This geographical as well as cultural isolation is due not only to the Mbotgote people's faith and pride in their ritual tradition but also to the economic disadvantage they would have on the coast as latecomers. As Mbotgote land rights are limited to the central area of South Malekula, one or two days' walk from the seashore, moving to the coast would virtually force them to give up their rights and place them in an economically inferior position to those people who settled the area earlier, over the last fifty years or so. On the other hand, because all the other traditional groups and some Mbotgote members deserted their homes in the forest, those who remained now have better access to arable land and to the hunting-gathering forest. Economic advantages and disadvantages thus enable them to cling to their conservative way of life.

This relative affluence is often mentioned by the Mbotgote people in comparison with the past. The forest is now full of wild pigs, and wild yams and taros abound. They say, "You can use anywhere for your gardens." Whether this situation has affected their social formation is a point I will take up later; but before I can discuss this matter, I must end the general description of the Mbotgote by referring to their food production and residential pattern.

The subsistence economy of the Mbotgote is based on horticulture

---

have the same cultural base. In this paper, however, I only refer to the Mbotgote group of 81 persons.

and pig husbandry, though hunting, fishing and gathering also have importance. Their main vegetable staples include taro, yams, bananas, bread-fruits and some greens. Of them, they plant taro and yams in the garden. They sometimes burn a forest for yams, but not for taro. The soil of the interior region is suitable for planting taro, but not for yams. Animal protein derives from pigs, birds, fish, shrimps, etc. Various wild fruits, vegetables, and root crops are gathered from the forest. Mbotgote men also try to artificially create two special items used in rituals: elongated yams and circle-tusked pigs. They do not try to elongate all the yams, but they do try to make all the male pigs into the circle-tusked variety.[2]

The residential pattern of the Mbotgote is very much dispersed. Usually one or two nuclear families, sometimes together with a few friends or relatives, set up a domestic compound at a site halfway up a hill near a stream. I call this residential unit a hamlet, though eitght of the fourteen hamlets at present are "one-family" hamlets. The distance between hamlets varies, but a journey of a few hours is quite normal for Mbotgote people visiting neighbors. The dispersion of Mbotgote dwellings is such that a mere fourteen hamlets are spread out over about 250 square kilometres. But paths are properly maintained, and visiting and receiving neighbors is an everyday affair.

Each domestic compound has two houses. The first is called a *neimo*, domestic house, in which a cooking fire for women and boys is set up in a stone oven. The second is called a *namel*, men's ritual house, which has a fire for the use of adult men. These arrangements are based on the Mbotgote "fire-food regulations," according to which men who have passed through the initiation ritual with penile incision must not share food cooked on the same fire with the uninitiated, i.e., with women and boys. In addition to these domestic compounds, a hamlet usually has another *namel* which is hidden from the uninitiated behind a thick shrubbery of plantains. Initiates use this *namel* for entertaining guests (initiates) from other hamlets in social life and also on ritual occasions. To distinguish this *namel* from the one in the domestic compound, I shall call the latter a "domestic namel".

III. DIETARY RULES AND HABITS

A Mbotgote, through his or her lifetime, changes patterns and manners

[2] I have written elsewhere (Funabiki, 1981) on the inefficiency of Mbotgote pig-raising as a means of producing food protein and its efficiency in serving a social function.

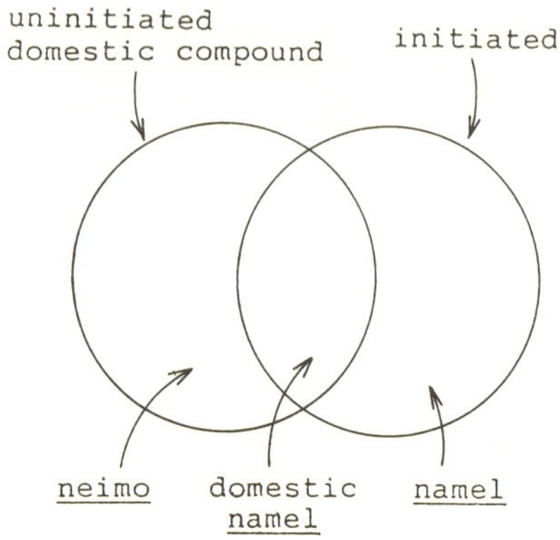

FIG. 1. Mbotgote space categories

of food production and consumption, in conformity with his/her given socio-religious category expressed in the arrangement of space. I shall provide an account of those changes, following the developmental phases of life.

A newly born baby is breastfed by its mother, who also begins to give it half-digested food quite soon after birth, though the period varies between one and four months with the mother's preference and the physical condition of the mother and newborn. But breast-feeding does not cease altogether for up to two years or more, and often ends only when another baby is born to the parents. Birth control in the form of postpartum continence results in a number of Mbotgote families having children at intervals of around two years. After weaning, a mother nourishes her children with food cooked by the fire in the *neimo*. Although food itself is largely produced together by a wife and husband in the garden, it is she who is responsible for feeding the children. Children, therefore, follow their mother's, and female intimates', patterns and manners of consuming food—with neither particular food taboos nor a ritualistic diet.

The male initiation ritual brings about a marked change in a boy's nutritional pattern.

Initiation takes place early in childhood, when a boy is around ten years old. One morning, all of a sudden, he is taken from his natal *neimo* to the *namel* together with other novices. After the rite of penile incision, he is placed in suclusion for one year from all he has been familiar with. This drastic change certainly has a psychological effect on a boy, as is often noted by anthropologists, but it should also be noted that the change has a nutritional aspect. During the ritual seclusion a novice is supposed to live on his own, finding food by himself, though in practice senior initiates can come to his aid. After the period of seclusion, he does not go back to his natal *neimo*. From now on, he must lead a "semi-nomadic" life with his fellows, staying at one hamlet for a few weeks and lodging at its *namel*, then moving to another hamlet. He earns his own living. This phase of bachelorhood lasts from initiation at age ten to age twenty-five or thirty when marriage normally takes place. In this period a boy learns how to obtain subsistence, but also—in particular for immature initiates—how to cope with hunger in nutritional as well as psychological terms.

In terms of nutrition, a young initiate has two ways of getting food: 1) hunting and gathering in the forest and 2) receiving food from the host-family of the hamlet where he is staying, in exchange for game and vegetables or for his assistance in various activities. In due course, he will begin to accumulate economic resources for his future married life by cultivating a portion of land and growing pigs with the aid of married seniors for whom he is a kind of protégé. In the space of fifteen years or so, he gradually turns from a helpless quasi-orphan into a young man ready to have a family.

Transformation is also taking place in another sense. Long before solving the problem of hunger in those practical ways, a boy must solve it psychologically. To show his independence from the *neimo*, where one can always find cooked food, he has to learn to hide his hunger, which is an embodiment of Mbotgote manly behavior. This behavior is slowly transformed into the more formalized attitude of indifference to food. Again, if we translate all these steps into nutritional terms, they constitute the process of a boy's learning how to control his diet.

As girls have no corresponding initiation ritual, their habitual pattern of consuming food does not change throughout adolescence. They follow in their mothers' footsteps, taking care of household affairs, feeding pigs and growing crops. Though the proportion of work done by women differs from one activity to another, e.g., less in gardening root crops and more in raising pigs, there is no normatives sexual division, or taboo on women working in a particular domain. Women therefore can produce food for themselves; and, apart from the game hunted by men, women have easier access to food than men. It should be understood, however, that this advantage is due to the *neimo* as a category of space, rather than to women as a gender.

In the description of children's dietary patterns, I have emphasized that children, like mothers, are given few restraints on eating. What about fathers in domestic compounds? Marriage causes changes in a young man's life. He is required to lead a dual life: domestic activities with his family in the compound and social and ritual ones with the other men who live in his hamlet or visit its *namel.* He travels several times a day between the compound and the *namel.* The geographical distance between the two houses is negligible, but the categorical difference is irreducible. He cannot escape this hectic life until all his children, at least the males, have grown up. But in this period, a father-husband can temporarily escape from the food restraints I have explained, insofar as he takes meals at his domestic *namel* in the compound. In fact, he usually takes a snack in the morning at his domestic *namel*, and after finishing his daily activities he again comes back to the compound to have a full meal cooked by his wife but on his own oven in the domestic *namel.* Then he goes back to the *namel* to chat with visitors and sleep there. He has to produce a lot of food, but he also can consume a lot without constraint at the compound, away from other men. A man makes a big swing between the *neimo* and *namel* categories when he leaves his natal compound and his mother in his early childhood and then, after a long period of bachelorhood, returns to domesticity, this time as father and husband.

A man, however, again leaves his family life when his sons leave home and move out of his care after their initiation, while his daughters help his wife in the household. He may have surplus food and more time to spend outside his compound, away from his family. These are the very conditions necessary for a Mbotgote man to devote himself to ritual, which I have no space to describe in detail but which is the most important activity in a man's life. In this phase he can spend more time in the *namel* and leave home for periods of time to visit other hamlets. Or he may work hard to produce more crops and raise valuable tusked pigs mainly for the purpose of using them in his own rituals. In the end a man quits the compound altogether, although his wife may continue to occupy it along with other women. A man's movement between the *neimo* and *namel* during the developmental phases of his life corresponds to his daily pendulum-like movement between the two categories.

There were eight men at the time of my fieldwork who lived only in the *namel.* Some of their wives were living with other women, either in their own compounds or in those of others. Most of these men were too old to work in gardens; nevertheless, they kept their own tusked pigs, which were indispensable for ritual and social life.

At this stage of life, an old man seems to be drawing near to the state of a "spirit". The reputation for being a great ritual performer gives an old man a religious status corresponding to that of a spirit in ritual. The higher his ritual status, the more frequently he is called and referred to, not by his birth name, but by his ritual title, which is in fact the name of a certain ritual spirit. But it is more appropriate here to consider specifically the old men's manners regarding food. As higher ritual status prescribes for an old man stricter fire–food regulations—i.e., more circumscribed rules for sharing food with other men—he tends to eat separately from others. And, more significantly, he imposes on himself a controlled attitude toward food. An old man is often seen refusing food offered to him and sitting apart from others enjoying a meal, even when there is no risk of his violating rules. Indifference to food is seen as manly and mature. The specific regulations and the related general manners thus make an old man take much less food than his juniors, at least to others' eyes. The reputation for "not eating much" adds to his spirit-like character, as spirits do not consume material food. As a matter of fact, an old man with a distinguished ritual career not only eats separately, but lives an independent and solitary life. There was an old Mbotgote man at the time of my fieldwork who was reputed to be spending much of his time somewhere in the forest unknown to the rest, just as spirits do.

In contrast with men's pendulum movement between the categories, women lead more stable lives in this regard. A woman may move from one hamlet to another at marriage but stays within the same category, *neimo*. The change in women's behaviour is a kind of gradual, one-directional, development through life. In terms of rules and manners concerning food, women follow those belonging to the *neimo*: separation from the initiates but few restraints on eating itself.

As a mother a woman is directly responsible for the prenatal and postnatal nutrition of infants. The observation of Mbotgote adult women incessantly eating taro-pudding during their leisure time could be in part explained by their need as mothers to take in more calories and protein for their infants as well as their own needs. But in fact, all the females, whether mothers or not, have these ways of eating. They are observed to eat at various times and in various places, all day long inside the *neimo* if it rains, or on the way through the forest to visit others' hamlets. The caloric content of starchy food is no sufficient reason either, as the initiated males' ways of eating differ dramatically from the females', as already described. The reasons for the difference in eating patterns between two sexes might be found in the interrelation of the above factors; but here I would summarize for the following discussion: the women have a more static and gregarious life than men and have the opportunity to consume food casually and freely in varying circumstances.

IV. MODE OF PRODUCTION AND CONSUMPTION

In this concluding part, I shall attempt to clarify the basic modes of Mbotgote life in terms of food consumption. For that purpose, I recapitulate the description of Mbotgote dietary habits and patterns by focusing on the relation between production and consumption.

Girls and uninitiated boys do not produce food but consume it without restraints. Initiated bachelors learn to produce food, first to fill their own needs and then to prepare for their future marriages. Hunger is an acute problem for an immature initiate around ten years old, but he is not supposed to beg food, and, in the meantime, he internalizes the manly ethics of abstention (more specifically, in this case, dieting). A man produces most during the period when he looks after his family, and consumes as much. Restraints on consumption are applied to a father-husband, since the same regulations and ethics as for initiates are applied to him; however, he manages them by crossing over the boundary on one side from the *namel* to the *neimo* or the domestic *namel* (see Fig. 1). In the latter, the "quality" of food is still bound by the fire–food regulations, but the quantity is free from inspection by other men. In old age, dieting makes a man's reputation. Its ultimate form is ritualistic ostentatious abstinence from food, which the old man accomplishes by not letting others see him eating. Old women continue the eating habits which they adopted when they became mothers. For a man, ritual diet intensifies from childhood towards old age, though there is a return swing to the *neimo* during married life. Women practice no such dieting, and some of them even intensify their eating, in the direction opposite to men. But this intensification is not measured quantatively: it is not concerned with how much or little an old recluse consumes in the depth of a forest. Intensification refers here to the degree of restraints on Mbotgote men and women at different stages of life.

The summary of Mbotgote food production and consumption has revealed the contrasts and differences between men and women (including children), and among initiated men. These contrasts and differences do not reflect any economic stratification in Mbotgote society. With equally shared usufruct of land and current low population pressure, the Mbotgote people do not differ in economic terms—for example, in access to the means of production. On the contrary, in a seemingly reversed order of normal social status, small children eat freely, and Big Man eats little. In the current Mbotgote society, the allocation of resources in economic production is not a factor regulating the present form of producing and consuming food. It is, rather, the categorical differences in mode of consumption owing to the combination of fire–food regulations, manly ethics and domestic necessity support the whole system of production and consumption. And those contrasts and differences which affect restraints on the mode of food consumption but not on the amount of consumed food, are derived from the two basic modes of Mbotgote living, typified by family life at the *neimo* and men's life at the *namel*. The former life is spent almost entirely in the family's own compound. Food is mostly produced from the family's garden and is consumed primarily for their subsistence. In the latter life, whether bachelors or seniors, men live in a wide network consisting of a number of *namel*, visiting other hamlets and receiving guests from a distance. Seniors who have retired from family life use their agricultural products and pigs in ritual activities. Ideally, this is also the case with young men, though they still lack the experience and ability to fulfill various ritual requirements.

As for the mode of consumption, the one at the *namel* is more regularized, or ritualized, than that at the *neimo*. The ritualization is concerned not solely with "not-eating" but also with "eating". On ritual occasions, seniors are obliged to eat the food cooked and offered to them within five days after the end of the performance. "Big Man's" dieting does not mean merely eating little but eating in a performative way according to the occasion.

The other point I would like to make concerns the relations between the mode of production and consumption and the residential pattern. The small size of the Mbotgote population is due to depopulation around the turn of the century and to the recent emigration to the coast. But aside from the present reduced size, informants' stories and ethnographic accounts of this area tell that forest people in South Malekula have been in a similar social formation from the beginning of this century: relatively small-sized dispersed hamlets forming a wider social network on the basis of systematized graded rituals.

The formation of the small-sized hamlets and the wider network they compose is consistent with the two basic modes of Mbotgote living I have explained. The settled, intensive and secluded mode of production and consumption that characterizes the Mbotgote family at the *neimo* could be safely guarded and conducted in the independent and dispersed small hamlets. On the other hand, the mobile, extended and societal mode of production and consumption practiced by initiates at the *namel* and in the forest is firmly built in the strongly connected network of ritual houses. These factors can help to clarify the present Mbotgote social situation, in which a population of less than one hundred persons is scattered in the larger forest and in which small hamlets are divided into even smaller units. The size of each part is reduced because of the depopulation, but the framework linking the parts remains as before with the two basic modes of Mbotgote living, including the mode of production and consumption of food.

Acknowledgments

The materials on which this essay is based were collected during my initiatory research in 1974 and the following fieldwork in 1975–76. The latter was financially supported by the Harvard-Yenching Institute and the Wenner-Gren Foundation for Anthropological Research.

I would like to thank the Symposium participants for their valuable comments on my original paper.

REFERENCES

British Service of the New Hebrides (1973). *New Hebrides Biennial Report 1971 and 1972*. Vila: British Service of the New Hebrides.

Funabiki, Takeo (1981). "On Pigs of the Mbotgote in Malekula", in Allen, M. (ed.), *Vanuatu*: 175–88. Sydney: Academic Press.

Kennedy, T.F. (1974). *A Descriptive Atlas of the Pacific Islands* (3rd ed.), Wellington: Reed Education (1st ed. 1966).

Comparative "Adaptive Strategies" of Transmigrants in Indonesia: A Case Study in Barambai, South Kalimantan

Oekan Soekotjo ABDOELLAH

Institute of Ecology, Padjadjaran University, Bandung, Indonesia

I. INTRODUCTION

Transmigration as a government programme to balance the population distribution in Indonesia has been in existence since the early part of this century, when the country was still under the Dutch colonial administration. It was first known as "colonization" (Pelzer, 1945). After independence, the name was changed to *transmigrasi.* The policy of transmigration was designed to solve a series of complex problems, including:

1. Alleviation of population pressure in Java;
2. Fostering economic development in the outer islands;
3. Dispersion of people from the political centre to marginal regions of the farflung nation for of defence and security purposes; and
4. Promotion of the cultural assimilation, political integration, and economic consolidation necessary to the developing Indonesia nation.

Evaluations of transmigration have focused on a wide variety of topics, ranging from the selection of transmigrants to site selection, site preparation costs, and even to national defence considerations. However, anthropological or other grass-roots studies of the transmigration process are extremely rare. One American anthropologist has exhibited a sustained interest in transmigration schemes (Davis, 1976). However, even she has devoted little attention to the study of human adaptation in transmigration areas.

It is in this last context that I have attempted to explore the various "adaptive strategies" among groups of transmigrants. Specifically, the focus is on how people from different cultural backgrounds adjust to new environmental conditions and to the same set of ecological and economic constraints. The three ethnic groups selected are the Javanese, Sundanese, and Balinese.

This paper represents only a preliminary analysis of data collected in Barambai, South Kalimantan, in July and August of 1985 in preparatory field work undertaken prior to a dissertation research project which will focus on problems in ecological anthropology. Thus, the main purpose of this paper is not to determine who has adapted and who has not, but rather to enquire into the general modes of adaptation which individuals/groups have chosen to cope with a new situation.

The analysis of adaptive strategies among migrants in this paper must begin with a brief description of the different social and cultural characteristics of each ethnic group, i.e., the Javanese, Sundanese, and the Balinese, as these constitute some of the most fundamental factors which should be taken into consideration by social scientists who are concerned with the study of adaptations of transmigrants.

II. THE SOCIAL CULTURAL CHARACTERISTICS OF JAVANESE, SUNDANESE, AND BALINESE

1. The Javanese

The Javanese refer to themselves as *wong Jawa*, meaning "barley" (Koentjaraningrat, 1975). The area of the Javanese basically includes all of the eastern and central part of Java Island.

The Javanese settlement pattern tends to form nucleated settlements comprising rows of houses along a road or waterway. The Javanese house is built directly on the ground, and different styles of house layout are determined by the shape of the roof (Koentjaraningrat, 1975).

The Javanese subsistence economy depends mainly on irrigated wet rice agriculture. The staple food is rice, although in poor areas cultivators have shifted to maize or cassava.

Javanese are expected to maintain good relations, especially with neighbours, through various systems of mutual aid such as *gotong-royong*. *Gotong-royong*, according to Koentjaraningrat (1961), can be applied to a wide variety of work arrangements which may include aid in the form of goods, money, or services. *Gotong-royong* is one of the most deeply felt values of the Javanese. The invocation of this ideal creates pressure for concern for other human beings (Geertz, 1963; Koentjaraningrat, 1961).

Most Javanese consider themselves to be Muslim. However, Javanese Muslim, can be divided into two categories, *abangan* and *santri*, based on their degree of adherence to the tenets of Islam (Geertz, 1960). These categories can also be regarded as two subcultures with constrastive world views, values, and orientations within the Javanese culture (Koentjaraningrat, 1967). The *santri* rigorously observe Islamic principles. The *abangan*, however, do not follow Islamic law, and many of them do not respect the taboo against eating pork, or perform daily *shalat* or fast during *Ramadan* (Geertz, 1963; Koentjaraningrat, 1967, 1975). In the traditional social context of the village, the *abangan* show themselves to be highly adaptive (Geertz, 1963). The *abangan* believe not only in Allah (God) but also in the rice goddess. This belief is demonstrated in fertility rites and ceremonies connected with agricultural production (Koentjaraningrat, 1975). *Abangan* also believe in impersonal magic power (*kesaktian*), which exists in amulets (*jimat*) and in heirlooms such as Javanese daggers (*keris*). Impersonal magic power is also very intensively used in magic, curing, and surgery, centering on the role of the *dukun* (Koentjaraningrat, 1967).

2. The Sundanese

The Sundanese inhabit all of the western part of Java. Their settlement pattern consists of clusters of separated and dispersed settlements. Sundanese houses can be distinguished from Javanese and Balinese houses by the fact that Sundanese houses are built on stilts or piles with stone bases (Koentjaraningrat, 1975).

The staple food of Sundanese peasants is steamed or cooked rice with salted fish. However, Sundanese cuisine is incomplete without a salad of raw vegetables with a wide variety of chili sauces.

Like the Javanese, the majority of Sundanese are Muslims. The distinction between *abangan* and *santri*, however, is unknown in Sundanese society, although they still believe in the important role of the rice goddess (Hidding, 1929).

Traditional mutual aid, known as *gotong-royong*, also exists in Sundanese society. In addition to *gotong-royong*, they also practise *liliuran* (exchange of labour). A man may go to plow another's *sawah* in exchange for later work in his own fields. Such exchange is not usually considered an instance of *gotong-royong*.

3. The Balinese

The Balinese live on the island of Bali. The settlement pattern of Balinese is a tightly clustered village, usually set on higher ridges between streams with rice fields and coconut groves around them (Geertz, 1963). At the central crossing in each settlement are set the main local public buildings, usually an important temple with a cockfighting arena (Geertz, 1963). The typical architecture is distinguished from others by the numerous tall thatched pagodas of their temples, and by the high brick walls with elaborately decorated narrow gates which conceal the house compounds (Koentjaraningrat, 1975; Covarrubias, 1956).

Like the Javanese and the Sundanese, the cultivation of wet rice dominates the Balinese economy. The main crop is rice, but in poorer and drier areas maize and cassava are important (Geertz, 1963). The rice fields are scattered among several nearby irrigation societies (*subak*), mixed in with those of people from dozens of other communities (Geertz, H., 1963; Geertz, C., 1959). The term *subak* is commonly translated as "irrigation society" due to the central role this institution plays in the regulation of water supply. But the *subak* in fact is very much more an agricultural planning unit, an autonomous legal cooperative, and a religius community organized in order to intensify solidarity among its members (Geertz, H., 1963; Geertz, C., 1959; Koentjaraningrat, 1967).

The Balinese religion and traditional political conceptions derive from Hinduism. Their society is marked by highly structured, unambiguous social arrangements for maintaining family relationships, labour and community cooperation, and social control which are sanctioned by group religious ritual (Geertz, C., 1959). Balinese religion is intricately social and is practiced by virtually all members of the society. Worship is never personal or familial, but always takes place in organized groups (Geertz, H., 1963).

Most Balinese eat pork and raise pigs which are marketable not only in Bali but also in Java in general.

III. TRANSMIGRATION PROGRAM IN INDONESIA AND ITS PROBLEMS: AN OVERVIEW

As mentioned above, the transmigration programme has been in existence since the early part of this century. The policy of transmigration, through trials in various forms, has repeatedly failed in its goal to increase the standard of living of transmigrants. Only a limited number of transmigrants has been able to develop a living above the basic subsistence level. Thus, according to some observers, the transmigration programme seems mainly to have succeeded in transplanting poverty from Java to the outer islands (cf. Swasono, 1969). While benefits for transmigrants have not improved significantly, the costs of transmigration have been increasing rapidly. In 1982, for example, the Indonesian government spent US$500 million to conduct this programme (Kronholz, 1983). Now, for REPELITA IV (1984/1985–1988/1989), covering a target of 800,000 families, will reach at least US$2 billion a year (Arndt, 1984). It is evident that the total expenditure for this programme is extraordinarily high. Given such costs, it is obvious that transmigration can not keep up with the population increase, and also moving people from Java/Bali is far beyond the power of the present government budget (Harjono, 1980; Kronholz, 1983).

Probably the most serious problem of all in the transmigration effort has been the increasing difficulty of finding suitable land for settlements on the outer islands. This problem results from the great difference in soil characteristics between Java/Bali and the outer islands (Arndt, 1983; Karyono *et al.*, 1980; Collier 1979; Jones, G.W. 1979; Harjono, J. 1977; 1980; Guinness, P. 1977). Java has extremely fertile volcanic soil with the potential for maintaining a high carrying capacity. Favourable water conditions permit well-organized irrigation in many areas. By contrast, the outer island transmigration areas are often sited on fragile soils (many being tidal swamp forests with peat soil) and further are often unsuitable for irrigation. These problems have never been fully solved and occasionally are not even admitted. In addition, wild pigs, rats, birds, monkeys, and insect pests regularly take a severe toll of the already indifferent harvests (Arndt, 1983; Christanty *et al.*, 1982; Harjono, 1980; Suratnam and Guinness, 1977). Therefore, food shortfalls are quite common due to the unpredictability of "frontier" harvests. In addition, loss of life due to malaria and other endemic diseases is not uncommon (Arndt, 1980; Guinness, 1977; Harjono, 1977, 1980; Suratman and Guinness, 1977).

From the foregoing, we can see that transmigrants are confronted with economic, ecological, health, psychological, and various social problems. The persistent uncertainty of life makes the migrants anxious. They soon realize that the new frontier conditions raise difficulties far beyond their imagination and beyond their ability to manage alone. They become resentful that the government does not fulfill its responsibilities as it has promised (Abdoellah, 1986). As one of the migrants noted:

> "... I went to the transmigration area in way Jepara, South Sumatra. I had joined the programme because the government promised us land, a house, and food rations for six months. But at the first moment, after arriving at the area, I was shocked. I saw logs lying around the house. There were leaks everywhere in the roof. I had to use an umbrella inside the house to keep dry. I had never experienced anything like this before in Java. I received food rations only for the first three months. I felt deceived by the government.
>
> ... I was very sick for three months because I worked too hard to convert the forest into arable land. When I recovered, I worked as an off-farm wage laborer in the city nearby to meet my family's needs. After a few months, I realized that it would be impossible for me to improve my life.

Finally, I felt that I could not stay any longer, so I left for Java. . . ."

(Translated from Singarimbun, 1980)

Like this migrant, many others have also returned to Java or moved to nearby cities. These responses create other new problems for the government, quite apart from those which concern the transmigration agency. In their desperation migrants exhibit social pathologies, although no adequate data exist to demonstrate their extent.

IV. GENERAL ENVIRONMENTAL CONDITION IN BARAMBAI, SOUTH KALIMANTAN, A NEW FRONTIER AREA

The expanse of mangrove and coastal peat swamp forests in Kalimantan represents quite a different ecotype from the extensive fertile soils in Java. The soil fertility is low and soils are unsuitable for rice cultivation without very expensive reclamation and water work construction (Guinness, 1977). In short, these swamps are inaccessible areas with a fragile ecosystem, which leads to questions about the rationale behind their choice for land development by transmigrants.

The Barambai transmigration area in South Kalimantan is sited in a tidal swamp forest with peat soil. The Barambai project is the first tidal area project using a new system of irrigation channels for paddy fields (Guinness, 1977). The idea of opening swamp area for the transmigration programme was derived from the experience of the Banjarese in South Kalimantan (Van Wijk, 1951), who grow rice and coconut on the dome-shaped peat land and on the alluvial levees along the river banks of the swamplands. The government has hoped that the swamplands could be converted to rice fields by Javanese/Sundanese/Balinese transmigrants.

Before the project began, most of the area was in secondary forest, that is, forest that had once been cleared and then allowed to regrow. A small section was held as "native land" that was still partly under cultivation, and compensation was paid to the owners when the government took it over. The project extends over 5,752 hectares (ha) which are now developed as paddy fields and home gardens, with some portion in dry field crops in sections too high to be reached by gravity irrigation (Guinness, 1977; Suratman and Guinness, 1977). The paddy irrigation system was developed by digging a primary canal 35 metres wide and 5 metres deep to the Barito River and then joining that with two secondary canals 15–20 metres wide in a drainage pool. The idea is to provide limited drainage at low tide during the wet season, and to provide irrigation water from the river in flood season (Hanson and Koesoebiono, 1977; Suratman and Guinness, 1977). Unfortunately, the results have not been completely successful. The water in some areas does not reach the fields during the dry season but floods during the rainy season (see Collier, 1979). The fertility of the fragile soils is not easily maintained. After several years of good harvests, it now has become evident that in some areas annual crops scarcely grow and perennial plants such as coconut (despite their shallow rooting) are dying (see also Collier, 1979; Karyono *et al.*, 1980). The failure in agriculture basically is due to soil toxification or fertility decline. The tricky conditions for crop cultivation on tropical peat and acid sulphate soil conditions not only make the transmigrants lose hope but also cause some soil scientists to be skeptical of long-term stability (see Pons and Driesen in Hanson and Koesoebiono, 1977).

1. Transportation and Market System

The Barambai transmigration area is located about 40 kilometres (km)

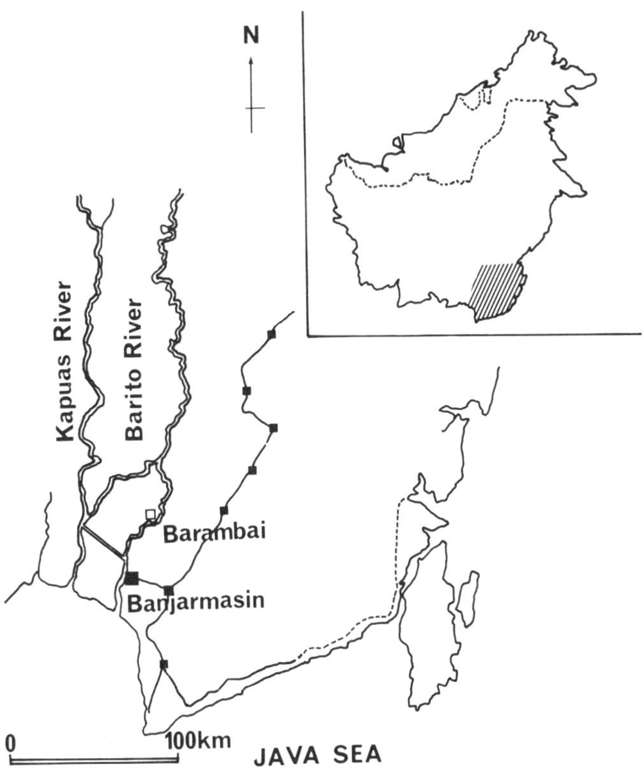

FIG. 1. Sketch Map of South Kalimantan Showing Location of Study Area (Adopted from: LK UGM)

from Banjarmasin, the capital of the province of South Kalimantan, and about 7 km from the capital district of Barito Kuala (Fig. 1). The area which is situated along the reaches of the Barito River can be reached by speed boat in one and a half hours and by *bus-air* (water bus) in four hours from Banjarmasin. Transportation within the area is usually by *kelotok* (ship boat) or *perahu* (proa). Recently, transportation links have been developed both on land and by river.

Marketing products in this area is still very difficult and thus surpluses cannot easily be sold. This sometimes results in waste. In such situations, local traders who control capital are able to buy the agricultural products of transmigrants cheaply in large quantities as they undertake delivery to market. Therefore the transmigrants are dependent on middlemen who are not always fair in their dealings. An *ijon* (harvest pre-purchase) system has also developed in this area which is financed not only by Banjarese as Guinness (1977) mentioned but also by transmigrants, ex-agents of the Banjarese moneylenders who have grown rich by exploiting other transmigrants. For this, they are hated by the other settlers (Guinness, 1977). The government has tried to control marketing activities by establishing agencies such as BIMAS (Agricultural Intensification Program) and BUUD/KUD (Village Rice Purchasing Agency) to serve transmigration settlements. But inadequate planning, mismanagement, and poor coordination have so far rendered these ineffective.

2. Nutrition and Health

During the first eighteen months, transmigrants received monthly rations of rice, salted fish, salt, cooking oil, and kerosene. However, during that time most transmigrants felt that these rations were not sufficient to sustain their families. They complained that their rations were in poor condition when they were received, probably because they had been stored for long periods or had become damaged in transit (Guinness, 1977). In addition, they complained that the rations were sometimes not properly distributed and were received late. The difficulties became more serious when rations were halted. Insufficiency of carbohydrates, protein, vitamins, and minerals led to malnutrition, especially among vulnerable groups in the population. Fortunately, after 14 years the situation has improved somewhat. According to a medical doctor (personal communication) in this area, in general malnutrition is no longer a pressing issue. However, my data show that the average nutritional consumption of the people in terms of calories and protein for each ethnic group except for the Balinese is still below the minimum requirements (Table 1).

Unlike in other transmigration areas, malaria in Barambai is extremely rare. The major diseases are diarrhoea, bronchitis, and skin diseases.

TABLE 1. Nutritional Intake of Barambai Transmigrants (per person per day)

Ethnic group	Calories		Protein	
	Intake (Kcal)	% of standard	Intake (grammes)	% of standard
Javanese	1,860.9	73.4	42.5	83.3
Sundanese	2,098.0	82.9	40.9	80.2
Balinese	2,631.7	104.0	41.3	81.0

V. TRANSMIGRANTS' ADAPTIVE STRATEGIES

The wide range of variables that affect human adaptive strategies derives not only from the natural environment but also from social, cultural, and economic factors. The interactions of these variables make possible a nearly infinite range of adaptive strategies.

In this paper, the term "adaptive strategies" is used with the emphasis on how people of different cultural backgrounds adjust to and cope with a new environment and new economic constraints. In order to evaluate transmigrants' adaptive strategies here, I concentrate only on agricultural, off-farm, food, and allocation of resources strategies which reflect the degree of adaptation and the degree to which an individual/group strives to participate in a new life.

1. Agricultural Strategies

The most important resources as ranked by transmigrants themselves are home gardens and rice fields. In the earlier stage of resettlement, transmigrants were provided with 2.0 ha of land (0.25 ha of home garden and 1.75 ha of rice field). During that time, transmigrants were unable to start farming the rice fields immediately due to a labour shortage and the conditions of the fields themselves, of which part was still secondary forest. Therefore, the transmigrants' immediate strategies were directed at fulfilling their daily needs and initially focussed on developing farming in home gardens.

1.1 Home Garden Production Strategies

The goal of home garden production strategies among the three ethnic groups is different, as reflected in the plant structure of the home garden. Home garden production strategy is influenced not only by physical factors but also by the social-cultural background of the owner (Abdoellah, 1980). Although the transmigrants received similar seedlings, such as cloves, coconut, jackfruit, and rambutan, in the same amounts, from the government, the plant structure of the home gardens is different. Karyono *et al.* (1980) found that the number of ornamental and vegetable plants in Sundanese home gardens is higher than that in Javanese and Balinese gardens. By contrast, in Javanese gardens, they found more starchy food plants than in those of the Sundanese and Balinese. Balinese home gardens tend to lack of plant diversity and is undeveloped. This was borne out in my research on the production of home gardens of each ethnic group (Table 2).

1.2. Rice Field Production Strategy

As in Java and Bali, transmigrants consider rice the most important crop since rice is their main staple food. The goal of rice production, therefore, is for every household to grow enough rice to meet consumption requirements and preferably to produce more for economic security. The government also believes that the "miracle" of new rice technology makes rice growing possible in almost any kind of soil that rice can stand up in. They think, as Geertz suggested (1963), that the only limiting factors are the availability of adequate water and of labour. Based on this thinking, optimism regarding rice production has been high. Unfortunately, the development of rice fields in this area shows that duplicating the high productivity of Java/Bali rice fields is a daydream. Although the productivity of rice fields in this area was higher during the first several years of settlement, it has now become evident that rice production since 1979 has been decreasing annually due to soil fertility decline, soil toxicity, and a lack of fertilizer, labour, capital, and a variety of other innovations adapted to local conditions. Transmigrants can only harvest rice once a year. Table 3 shows the productivity of rice fields/m^2/year by different ethnic groups. It is clear from the table that the productivity of rice fields in this area is very low compared to that in Java/Bali, even to that of upland rice fields.

In order to respond to the deteriorating situation, transmigrants have tried to grow different species of plants such as cassava and sweet potatoes to fulfill their subsistence needs rather than rely solely on rice. They are also aware of the disadvantages of monocropping. The results, however,

TABLE 2. Average Annual Production of Home Gardens (m^2) among Three Ethnic Groups in Barambai

Production in terms of	Ethnic group		
	Javanese	Sundanese	Balinese
Rupiahs (cash valve)	21.7	13.2	9.1
Calories (Kcal)	180.4	152.6	68.1
Protein (gramme)	3.1	4.8	1.6
Vitamin A (IU)	618.7	768.9	154.6
Vitamin B_1 (mg)	0.2	0.1	0.1
Vitamin C (mg)	35.3	29.2	6.0

TABLE 3a. Average Annual Productivity of Rice Fields (m^2) among Three Ethnic Groups in Barambai

Production in terms of	Ethnic group		
	Javanese	Sundanese	Balinese
Rupiahs (cash valve)	14.6	7.7	9.1
Calories (Kcal)	290.0	188.0	176.0
Protein (gramme)	4.7	3.3	2.8
Vitamin A (IU)	412.2	65.2	601.0
Vitamin B_1 (mg)	0.2	0.2	0.1
Vitamin C (mg)	18.1	4.3	21.6

TABLE 3b. Average Annual Productivity of Rice Fields (m^2) in West Java

Production in terms of	West Java	
	Upland fields	Wet rice fields
Rupiahs (cash valve)	24.0	70.5
Calories (Kcal)	945.8	2910.1
Protein (gramme)	18.0	45.0
Vitamin A (IU)	7.5	41.8
Vitamin B_1 (mg)	0.9	1.6
Vitamin C (mg)	0.5	1.6

Source: Oekan Abdoellah *et al*, 1983.

are again very disappointing due to soil fertility decline and soil toxification.

2. Off-Farm Strategies

In order to survive, transmigrants cannot depend on agricultural production alone. They have to diversify their occupations so as to find some other way to support themselves and their families. Thus, Barambai has witnessed an expansion in off-farm sources of employment where transmigrants can earn money.

The major off-farm strategies which are being used by the transmigrants to reduce their dependency on agricultural are working as wage labourers or as traders or small businessmen. My data show that almost 60% of the total income of transmigrants is derived from off-farm sources (Table 4). This indicates that in general the production of agricultural lands is insufficient to fulfill daily needs.

2.1. Wage Employment

Wage employment exists both within and outside Barambai village. However, the opportunities for wage employment within the village are very limited and most are related to agriculture, meaning that they are seasonal, especially at the beginning of the rainy season. Most of the

TABLE 4. Percentage of Income from Off-Farm Activities to Total Income of Transmigrants/Household/Year

Sources of income	Ethnic group		
	Javanese	Sundanese	Balinese
Agricultural products	41.8	31.4	38.0
Off-farm	58.2	69.6	62.0
Total	100.0	100.0	100.0

transmigrants who work for wages within the village are Sundanese and Javanese who belong to the poorest of the poor in this area. By this, I do not mean that only the poorest of the poor transmigrants are involved in these activities because other transmigrants may also be involved, although for different reasons. For example, the poorest of the poor work at wage employment within the village in order to fulfill their direct daily consumption needs, while the other transmigrants are involved primarily for supplementary income which can be used or saved for non-direct daily consumption.

Most of the transmigrants clearly realize that wage employment opportunities within the village are severely limited. Thus, most, including the young generation, try to find jobs in the city, in logging areas, in sugar cane plantations, or in plywood factories where employment opportunities are available. They are hired as skilled and unskilled labour depending on their educational background. Most of the young generation, especially females, work in plywood factories or in the city as servants. Older people usually work as temporary employees on sugar plantations or other government projects as odd-jobbers. Work as a temporary employee or as an odd-jobber is frequently undertaken according to the distinctive occupational characteristics of each ethnic group, influenced by occupations in the sending areas, and thereby represents a group-oriented strategy. To find a job, the transmigrants often use the connections provided by their families, relatives, fellow villagers from the sending area, or other transmigrants from the same ethnic group.

Transmigrants who seek work outside the village in the past initially left only temporarily, mostly after they planted their rice fields when there was little agricultural work to be done. Now the situation has changed since the productivity of rice fields has been decreasing year by year. Most of the transmigrants, especially those of the young generation of both sexes, tend to be ready to leave at any time and outmigrate permanently. They are aware that employment opportunities rarely exist in their village and they cannot depend on agriculture. Therefore the best way to support their families is to look for employment elsewhere, even when doing so may cause a shortage of labour in the household. Families are willing to allow one or more members of either sex to take a job elsewhere in the hopes that they can send them money every month or year. My preliminary data show that income from remittances per year varies from household to household. On average, the remittances form about 14.1%, 24.6%, and 13.5% for the Javanese, Sundanese, and Balinese, respectively, of annual household income.

Wage employment outside the village unfortunately, as Guinness (1977) has also pointed out, often leads to neglect of the farms. The amount of uncultivated land is on the increase, and this land has become an ideal natural breeding ground for pests, creating serious problems for transmigrants who are still struggling in this area. Table 5 shows the size of rice fields owned and the actual amount of undercultivated land. In addition, it is often the case that transmigrants, especially Sundanese and Javanese, leave the transmigration area permanently if they find a good opportunity to survive in other places. The number of transmigrants originally sent by the government and the number who are still trying to survive in this area are presented in Table 6. It can be seen that the number of Sundanese and Javanese transmigrants who have left this area is much higher than that of the Balinese transmigrants, especially since the productivity of the rice fields has been decreasing. This situation makes the pest problem in this area more serious.

2.2. Trade and Other Activities

Trade and other related activities constitute an important income source

TABLE 5. Average Size of Rice Fields Owned and Under Cultivation by Transmigrants (family/m^2, 1985)

Ethnic group	Rice fields			Average family size
	Owned by transmigrants	Under cultivation by transmigrants	%	
Javanese	33,107.7	13,878.6	41.9	5.1
Sundanese	28,544.5	12,509.2	43,8	5.5
Balinese	35,100.7	22,189.8	63.2	6.2

TABLE 6. Numbers of Transmigrants Originally Sent by the Government and Remaining in Barambai

Ethnic group	Number of transmigrant families		% abandoning transmigration
	Originally sent by government	Still in Barambai	
Javanese	630	335	46.8
Sundanese	161	23	85.8
Balinese	100	75	25.0

for only a small number of households. However, it may be appropriate to consider them as an important off-farm strategy since, as shown earlier, the production of agricultural lands cannot support transmigrants' daily needs.

Some of the transmigrants have started to open *warung* (a kind of small shop) to sell foodstuffs and ready-made food. The customers of each *warung* are usually people who belong to the same ethnic group. It is very rare that the Sundanese and Javanese go to Balinese *warung* to buy something unless it is an emergency situation or they cannot find what they need in Sundanese and Javanese *warung*. However, the Sundanese and Javanese do patronize each other and call each other "brother."

The *warung* operations usually bring very little profit. The income from *warung* is also uncertain. On some days they have substantial sales, but on the others they may be able to just cover the cost of the investment. The fluctuations in income are also related to agricultural conditions in this area. When farming is good, *warung* business is also good. Although the owners of *warung* realize that this business brings very little profit, they intend to continue because it still provides supplementary cash income. In addition, the *warung* also permits members of the family who would not otherwise be economically productive—children too young to work or a wife who must stay at home to care small children—to make some contribution to the family income.

Some of the transmigrants, especially the Balinese, are also moving into positions as local middlemen. They buy not only agricultural products such as cassava, sweet potatoes, or rice but also chickens or other animals from the other villagers who need cash, and then they sell them to the market nearby.

Most of the Balinese raise pigs which are marketable to Chinese in South Kalimantan, while their children try to help their parents by selling ice or snacks.

3. Food Strategies

Food strategies are influenced by many interrelated factors which are not only physical but also social-cultural. Human beings eat food not only to satisfy biological needs for survival but also as a cultural activity. Hence, cultural and social values and habit play important roles in eating.

In general, food strategies can be divided into three major types: diversification of food; storage of foodstuffs; and conversion of surplus agricultural products into durable valuables which can then be stored and traded for food in an emergency (Colson, 1977). In this paper, I concentrate only on diversification of food, which, I think, is one of the most important strategies for survival in transmigration areas due to the fact that specialization in one kind of food, say rice, is dangerous. It is too risky to become dependent on rice as the main staple food, especially in areas unsuitable for rice growing. Put simply, the strategy avoids narrow dependence by emphasizing diversification.

Table 7 shows the different food strategies among ethnic groups as reflected in their food habits. The results clearly show that for the Sundanese rice is the only staple food; some of the Javanese try to diversify their staple food; and none of the Balinese eat only rice as the staple.

The different food habits among ethnic groups are influenced by the cultures of their home regions. Rice for the Sundanese (see Abdoellah, 1985) and some of the Javanese has a high social value. For them, taro, cassava, and corn are food only for the people who cannot afford better. They may think that eating mixed staple foods is animal-like. Therefore, it is very difficult to induce the Sundanese and some Javanese to eat less rice and more non-rice staple foods. Consequently, in transmigration areas they often sell their home garden products to buy rice when their rice production is insufficient. If they do not have enough money to buy rice, they borrow money from other transmigrants or local people who act as moneylenders (*pengijon*). This is not the case for the Balinese and those Javanese who do not depend on one staple food, i.e., rice. They can eat taro, corn, or cassava which are produced from either their home gardens or rice fields. The Balinese sometimes eat only rice during the rice planting season when they consider they need more energy.

4. Allocation of Resources Strategies

The allocation of resources among ethnic groups is different due to differences in lifestyle. For example, the Sundanese consider outward appearances more important than do the Balinese and some of Javanese.

Most Sundanese use money mainly for food and consumption purposes, especially for luxury consumption items such as radios, luxury textiles, and jewelry, although very often during the *paceklik* (season of

TABLE 7. Staple Foods of Transmigrants in Barambai, South Kalimantan (by % of sample of households)

Staple food	Ethnic group		
	Javanese	Sundanese	Balinese
Rice only	61.6	100.0	—
Mixed			
rice, cassava, corn, and taro	38.4	—	100.0

Source: Karyono *et al.*, 1980

shortage) they must sell these items again at lower prices to survive. By contrast, the Balinese try to allocate their resources more carefully. For example, they are more likely to use harvested rice sparingly, calculating their needs for the whole year and selling any surplus when rice prices are highest. If they have money, they often speculate by buying rice from other transmigrants, especially from the Sundanese and Javanese who need cash, during the harvest season where rice prices are low. During the *paceklik* season when the rice prices are highest, they sell it again, and benefit by saving the proceeds or using them as capital investment for raising pigs or buying rice fields. As seen in Table 5, the holding of Balinese rice fields per family is much larger than that of the Sundanese and Javanese.

The Sundanese and Javanese also very often sell their rice during the harvest season, as mentioned above, not only to repay debts but also to gain social prestige through *selametan* such as wedding and circumcision ceremonies which usually take place after the harvest season. The cost of *selametan* is very often far beyond the reach of the family budget. To meet the essential *selametan* cost, it is very common for people to borrow money from the moneylenders on the understanding that they will repay it with 10% interest or more per month or with unhulled rice priced at about half the market price. Thus, sometimes Sundanese and Javanese transmigrants have no rice left over after repaying their debts. Again this is usually not the case for Balinese. Although they must perform ritual ceremonies as Sundanese and Javanese do, they usually calculate an appropriate budget based on their ability to pay.

These different resource allocation strategies contribute to the different economic conditions of the three groups of transmigrants. In general, the Balinese are much better off economically than the Sundanese and Javanese.

VI. CONCLUSION

The transmigrants to Barambai clearly cannot depend on a single strategy, but must adopt mixed strategies in order to survive. I have described above four general kinds of adaptive strategies observed among transmigrants, i.e., agricultural, off-farm, food, and resource allocation strategies. Of course, these strategies do not always represent clear-cut and mutually exclusive alternatives.

From this preliminary exploration of my data it is obvious that the transmigrants' strategies are not only influenced by environmental and economic constraints in their new life but also are influenced by the social-cultural background of the transmigrants, which has a significant influence on adaptation by providing different alternatives for each ethnic group. Finally, it should be noted that this paper is based only on preliminary observations. Further study is needed to understand fully the nature of transmigrants' adaptive strategies and to explore the long-range impact of their strategies not only on the physical environment but also on the social environment. Clearly it is a subject of great importance.

Acknowledgments

I owe a great debt to the people of Barambai among whom I worked. They not only cooperated with me but also offered unlimited hospitality. I wish to thank Bapak Hamdani B.A., Bapak Maksum, Bapak Effendy, Bapak Markoni, and Bapak Kawidjaya, who became constant companions with whom I shared hardships and joy. Thanks are also directed to Dr. Moch. Taufiq who was my co-researcher during the preliminary fieldwork. It is impossible to estimate his contribution. Lastly, my special thanks to Dr. James N. Anderson, Dr. Otto Soemarwoto, and Dr. Surna T. Djajadiningrat, who wisely encouraged and guided me.

The preliminary field work was made possible by grants from the Ford Foundation Jakarta, the Ministry of Population and Environment, Republic of Indonesia, the Institute of Ecology, Padjadjaran University, Bandung, Indonesia, and the Lowie Fund, Department of Anthropology, University of California Berkeley.

REFERENCES

Abdoellah, O.S. (1980). Structure of Homegarden of Javanese and Sundanese in Bantarkalong, West Java. Graduate major thesis, Department of Biology, Padjadjaran University, Bandung, Indonesia (unpublished, in Indonesian).

Abdoellah, O.S. (1985). Food Consumption of Sundanese in Kampung Salamungkal, West Java. In S. Suzuki, O. Soemarwoto, and T. Igarashi (eds.), *Human Ecological Survey in Rural West Java in 1978 to 1982*. Tokyo: Nissan Science Foundation, pp. 116–29.

Abdoellah, O.S. (1986). Transmigration policies in Indonesia: Government aims and popular response. In Scott. M. Morgan and Elizabeth Colson eds. *People in Upheaval* Staten Island, N.Y.: Center for Migration Studies (in press)

Arndt, H.W. (1983). Transmigration: Achievements, problems, prospects. *Bulletin of Indonesian Economic Studies*, XIX (3): 50–74.

Arndt, H. (1984). Little land and many people. *Far Eastern Economic Review*, November 1.

Christanty, L. Iskandar, and O. Abdoellah (1982). Homegarden and its possibility for implementation in transmigration areas. *TROPSOIL CRSP*, Lecture series, Univ. of Hawaii.

Collier, W.L. (1979). Social and economic aspects of tidal swamp-land development. *Symposium on Tidal swamp-land Development Aspects.*

Colson, E. (1979). In good years and in bad: Food strategies of self-reliant societies. *Journal of Anthropological Research*, **35**. 1, Spring.

Covarrubias, M. (1956). *Island of Bali*. New York: Alfred A. Knopf.

Davis, G. (1976). Parigi: A Social History of the Balinese Movement to Central Sulawesi, 1907–1974. Dissertation, Dept. of Anthropology and the Committee on Graduate Studies of Stanford University.

Geertz, C. (1959). Form and variation in Balinese village structure. *American Anthropologist*, 61.

Geertz, C. (1960). *The Religion of Java*. Chicago: The University of Chicago Press.

Geertz, C. (1963). *Agricultural Involution: The processes of Ecological Change in Indonesia*. Berkeley & Los Angeles: Univ. of California Press.

Geertz, H. (1963). *Indonesia: Culture and Communities*. New Haven: Hraf Press.

Guinness, P. (ed.) (1977). Transmigrants in South Kalimantan and South Sulawesi. *Report Series No. 15*, Population Institute, Gajahmada University, Jogjakarta, Indonesia.

Hanson, A.J. and Koesoebiono (1977). Settling coastal swamp-lands in Sumatra: A case study for integrated resource management. Bogor Agricultural University, Indonesia.

Harjono, J. (1980). Patterns and policies in migration and resettlement in Indonesia. In *Migration and Resettlement Rural-Urban Policies*, Vol. II. Manila: Social Welfare and Development for Asia and the Pacific.

Harjono, J. (1977). *Transmigration in Indonesia*. Oxford in Asia Current Affairs.

Hidding, K. (1929). Nyi Pohatji Sangyang Sri. PhD. Thesis, University of Leiden, Dubbledeman.

Jones, G.W. (1979). The transmigration programme and development planning. In R.J. Pryor (ed.), *Migration and Development in Southeast Asia: A Demographic Perspective*. Oxford: Oxford University Press, pp. 213–221.

Karyono, L. Christanty and O. Abdoellah (1980). Potential of homegarden in tidal transmigration areas South and Central Kalimantan. *Seminar Ecology of Homegarden III*. Institute of Ecology, Padjadjaran University, Bandung, Indonesia, (in Indonesian).

Koentjaraningrat, R.M. (1975). *Introduction to the Peoples and Cultures of Indonesia and Malaysia*. Sydney: Cummings Publishing Company.

Koentjaraningrat, R.M. (1961). Some social anthropological observations on *gotongroyong* practices in two villages of Central Java. Monograph series, Modern Indonesia Project, Cornell University, Ithaca, NY.

Koentjaraningrat, R.M. (ed.) (1967). *Villages in Indonesia*. Ithaca, New York: Cornell University Press.

Kronholz (1983) Go East Young Man. *The Wall Street Journal*, Sept. 6.

Pelzer, K.J. (1945). Pioneer settlement in the Asiatic tropics. American Geographical Society, Special Publication no. 29.

Singarimbun, M. (1980). Tanah Seberang Tak Menarik: Studi Kasus Daerah Krasak. *Prisma* 5 (May) Th.VIII (in Indonesian).

Suratman and Guinness, P. (1977). Transmigration in South Kalimantan and South Sulawesi. *Working Paper Series No. 1*, University of Gadjahmada, Indonesia.

Swasono (1969). The Land Beyond: Transmigration and Development in Indonesia. Ph.D. dissertation, University of Pittsburgh.

van Wijk, C.L. (1951). Soil survey of the swamps of South Borneo in connection with the agricultural possibilities. *Contributions of the General Agricultural Research Station, Bogor, Indonesia*, 123.

The Long-Term Development of Farm Agriculture in Java: A Rice Economy?

Hiroyoshi KANO

Institute of Oriental Culture, University of Tokyo, Tokyo, Japan

I. INTRODUCTION

Java is famous for being a small island that has been able to feed its large and very dense population through its predominantly agricultural economy. The remarkable capacity of Javanese society for adapting to a huge population increase has usually been explained as a result of the highly elastic and labour-absorbing nature of its rice farming, which Geertz (1963) has categorized as the "*sawah* ecosystem."

This paper attempts to confirm and critize this widely shared premise on the characteristics of rural economy in Java by analyzing some macro-statistical data, which will show the quantitative change in production of main food crops in Java during the period from the 1920s to the 1970s and the regional diversity of its changing pattern. This analysis will also throw light on some features of the survival strategy which has been adopted by the rural population of Java in the decades since the 1910s when the area was still under Dutch colonial rule.

II. THE IMPORTANCE OF DRY LAND AND NON-RICE CROPS IN JAVANESE AGRICULTURE

Table 1 shows that the proportion of dry land (*tegal*) to the total area of arable land in Java has been relatively high for the decades since the 1910s, although it seems that the proportion of dry land has decreased remarkably since the beginning of the 1960s, probably because of the rapid increase in land used for yard space (*pekarangan*). For example, thc dry land area of Java in 1960 (4.91 million hectares (ha)) was much bigger than that of Japan in the same year (2.68 million ha), though both had almost the same paddy field acreage (Japan = 3.01 million ha, Java = 3.48 million ha) (Kayou, 1977). These figures indicate the remarkable

TABLE 1. Area of Arable Land in Java (100 ha)

Year	Arable land			Year	Arable land		
	Paddy field	Dry land	Total		Paddy field	Dry land	Total
1916	2,870	2,740	5,610	1937	3,362	4,487	7,849
1917	2,920	3,024	5,944	1938	3,368	4,503	7,871
1918	3,000	3,476	6,476	1939	3,377	4,523	7,900
1919	3,053	3,565	6,618	1940	3,384	4,544	7,928
1920	3,121	3,730	6,851	1941	3,408	4,553	7,961
1921	3,136	3,793	6,929				
1922	3,137	3,830	6,967	1950	3,415	4,725	8,140
1923	3,144	3,851	6,995	1951	3,424	4,742	8,166
1924	3,194	3,897	7,091	1952	3,429	4,729	8,158
1925	3,200	3,955	7,155				
1926	3,213	4,121	7,334	1953	3,430	4,720	8,150
1927	3,222	4,243	7,465	1954	3,453	4,856	8,309
1928	3,254	4,310	7,564	1955	3,452	4,887	8,339
1929	3,268	4,335	7,603	1956	3,460	4,820	8,280
1930	3,274	4,372	7,646	1957	3,468	4,863	8,331
1931	3,288	4,370	7,658	1958	3,474	4,898	8,372
1932	3,291	4,394	7,685	1959	3,484	4,908	8,392
1933	3,299	4,404	7,703	1960	3,483	4,912	8,395
1934	3,301	4,425	7,726	1961	3,486	4,888	8,374
1935	3,311	4,442	7,753	1962	3,493	4,884	8,377
1936	3,334	4,464	7,798	1980	3,491	2,658	6,149

Sources: 1916–20: *Verslag van bestuur en staat van Nederlandsch-Indië, Suriname en Curaçao* (Bijlage C van het verslag der handelingen van de Tweede Kamer der Staten-Generaal), The Hague, Algemeene Landsdrukkerij, 1917–21.

1921–41: Centraal Kantoor voor de Statistiek, *Indisch verslag*, Batavia, Landsdrukkerij, 1931–40.

1940, 1950–80: Biro Pusat Statistik, *Statistical Pocketbook of Indonesia*, and *Statistical Yearbook of Indonesia*, 1957–82.

importance of dry land farming in Javanese agriculture.

Table 2 shows the average harvested area and production of seven major crops (wet land rice, dry land rice, maize, cassava, sweet potatoes, soybeans, and peanuts) in Java in several periods between 1921 and 1980, as calculated from the contemporary statistics for each period. What is impressive at first sight is the large proportion of the harvested area and volume of production of maize and root crops (sweet potatoes and cassava) in the total harvested area and production of seven crops. This indicates that these non-rice crops, which can be grown on dry land, have played an important role as foodstuffs supporting the huge population growth of Java in this century, although their role has declined slightly in the last decade because of the marked gains in rice production due to the introduction of high-yielding varieties in the 1970s. Yet another

TABLE 2. Average Harvested Area and Production of Seven Major Crops in Java

Crops		1921–30	1932–40	1951–60	1961–70	1971–80
Wet land	1000ha	2850	3292	3760	3524	4283
rice	1000t*	3595	4222	4969	5461	9428
Dry land	1000ha	397	402	251	371	282
rice	1000t*	247	264	149	286	259
Maize	1000ha	1755	2042	1728	2108	1836
	1000t	1696	1974	1516	2103	2309
Cassava	1000ha	733	847	942	1086	1055
	1000t	5690	7011	6922	8570	9012
Sweet	1000ha	167	179	227	265	152
potatoes	1000t	1066	1188	1317	1444	1040
Soybeans	1000ha	180	320	468	510	579
	1000t	106	225	322	353	467
Peanuts	1000ha	202	224	296	297	336
	1000t	155	168	181	204	272
Total	1000ha	6284	7306	7645	8161	8523

* In milled rice.
Sources: Same as Table 1.

noteworthy point is the remarkable growth in pulse cultivation, i.e., soybeans and peanuts, which have traditionally been important sources of protein and fat for the Javanese.[1]

However, non-rice crop production has not always been important in all of Java. For example, Fig. 1 and Fig. 2 indicate, respectively, the proportion of land planted in wet rice/maize and the pulses (soybeans plus peanuts) to the total area planted in the seven major crops for each of 65 regional units, which include the *afdeelings* in 1920 or *kabupatens* at present.[2] These figures show that the eastern part of the island has produced much more maize and pulses than the western part. This different pattern of production is also reflected in the staple food composition in the two regions, as is evident from Fig. 3 which shows regional differences in the annual per capita consumption of rice and maize.

III. REGIONAL DIVERSITY IN CHANGING PATTERNS OF AGRICULTURAL PRODUCTION

Figure 4 shows the distribution of the above-mentioned 65 regional

[1] Soybeans are consumed mainly in the form of processed foods such as *tahu* (bean curd) or *tempé* (bean cake).

[2] Java (including Madura Island) was divided into 80 *afdeelings* in 1920, while at present it is divided into 83 *kabupatens*. As the geographical boundaries of the two sets of divisions are not always identical, some divisions must be integrated into a regional unit for the sake of historical comparison.

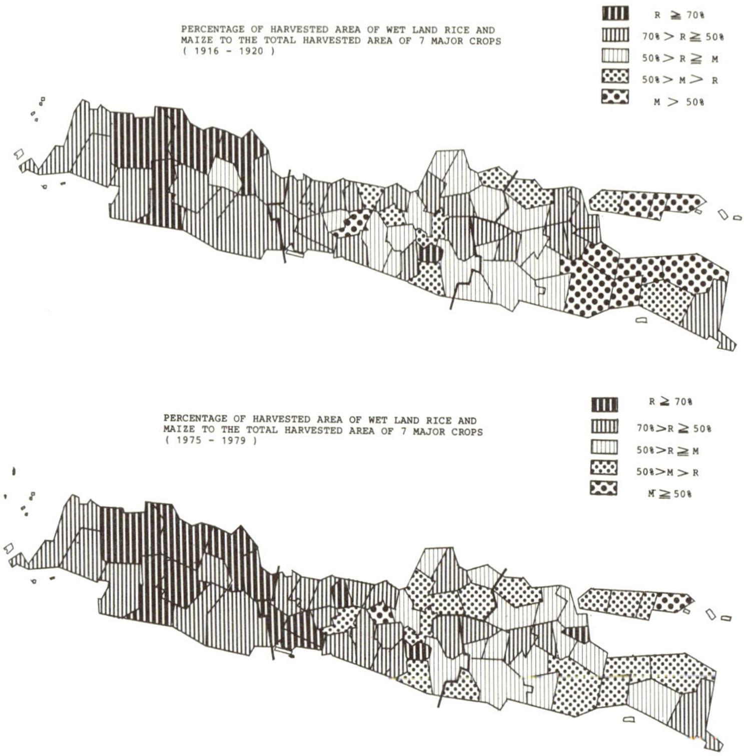

FIG. 1. The proportion of harvested area of wet land rice and maize.

units according to the proportion of land devoted to the seven crops during 1916–20 and 1975–79. These 65 regional units are integrated into nine greater regions (A to I in Fig. 5). Although these divisions and the names of the regions were made by the present author simply for analytical purposes, they do reflect ecological regional characteristics.

A. Pasisir Barat (Western North Coast region)

Most of this region consists of alluvial plains along several rivers which flow into the Java Sea. Historically the agricultural development of this region began rather late due to problems of water control. However, in the course of development during this century, simultaneous with urban development of the Jakarta metropolitan area, this region has become a rich granary supplying rice to the urban population.

B. Priangan (West Java Highlands)

This region includes several basin areas shaped by rivers flowing among

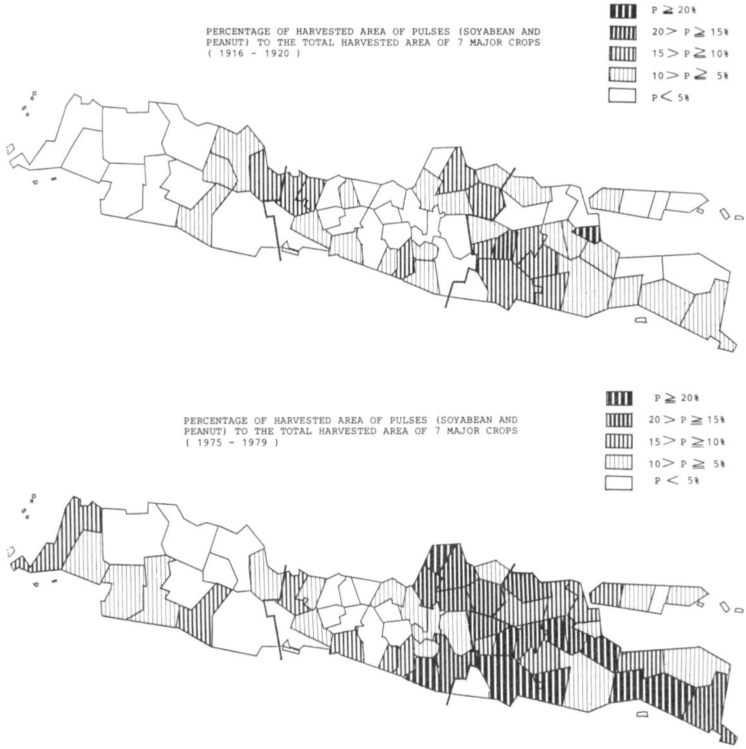

FIG. 2. The proportion of harvested area of pulses (soybeans and peanuts).

the many volcanoes and folded mountains along the southern coast of the island. These basins are the major rice producing areas within this region. However, the development of wet rice cultivation in this region also began rather late, as shifting cultivation was the dominant type of agriculture for a long period.

C. Pasisir Tengah (Central North Coast)

In this coastal area of Central Java, west of Semarang, the coastal plain is rather narrow, and the economy depends on non-agricultural activities such as fishery and trading. The rate of population increase during the last six decades has been relatively low, since many have migrated away from this region, especially to the metropolitan area of West Java.

D. Pasisir Timur (Eastern North Coast)

This region includes the coastal area of Central and East Java lying between Semarang and Surabaya. Most of it is covered by flat plains,

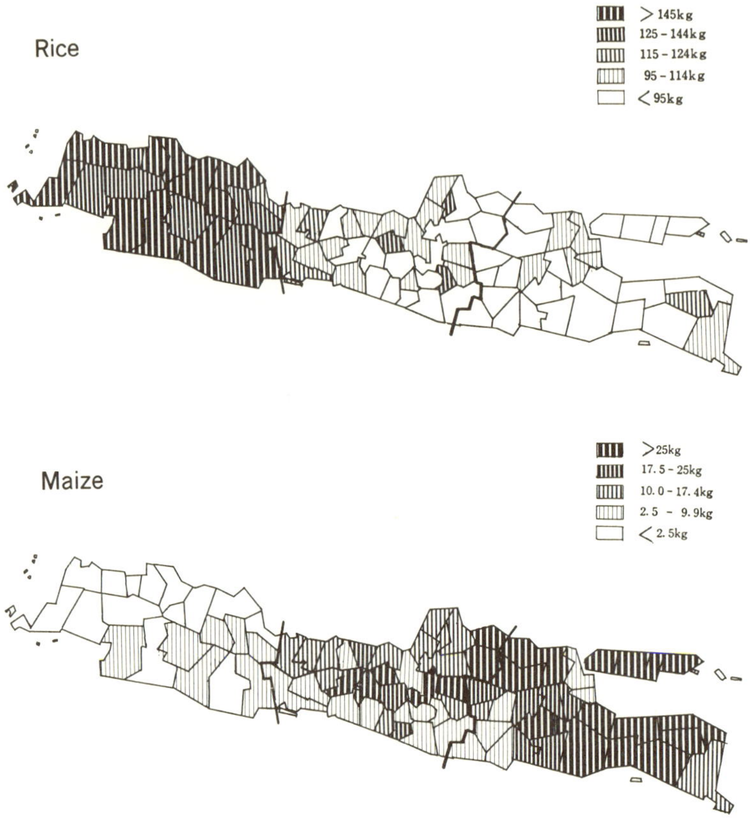

FIG. 3. Annual per capita consumption of rice and maize (1976).

including the basins of rather long rivers such as the Serang, the Juwana, and the lower stream of the Solo River. However, because of problems of irrigation and flood control, the proportion of paddy fields to the total area of land is relatively low.

E. Pegunungan Tengah (Central mountains in Central Java)

At the foot of the volcanoes and within the hill areas in this region the major type of agriculture is dry land farming, though wet rice is cultivated in the small valleys between mountains.

F. Jawa Tengah Selatan (Southern coastal plains of Central Java)

This region consists of two separate areas: the Banyumas plain in the southwest corner of Central Java and the piedmont plain south of Mt.

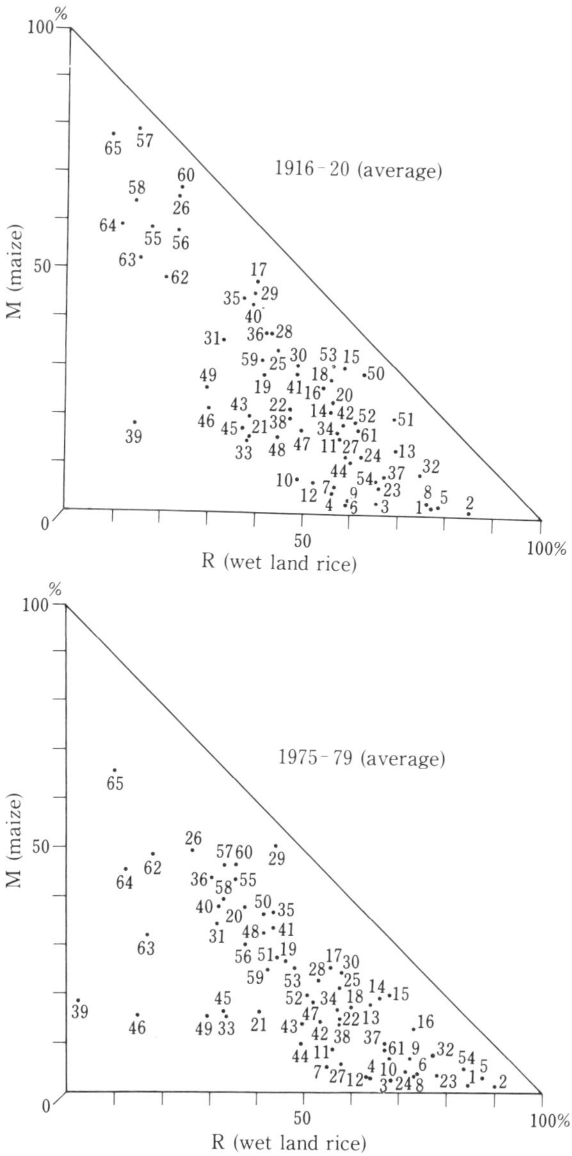

FIG. 4. Distribution of 65 regional units according to the proportion of harvested area of wet land rice and maize.

Merapi, which were parts of the old principalities of Jogjakarta and Surakarta. Most of these plains are gently sloping and thus well suited to

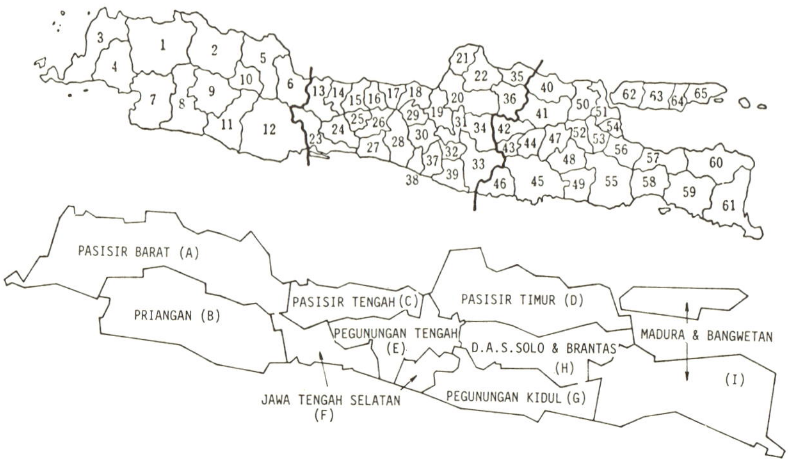

FIG. 5. Sixty-five regional units and nine integrated regions.

gravity irrigation, and rice cultivation in this region has a longer history than in other regions.

G. Pegunungan Kidul (Southern hill areas)

This region includes the hill areas covered by limestone along the south coast of Central and East Java. Because of the scarcity of well-irrigated land, agriculture in this region is mainly devoted to dry land farming.

H. D.A.S. Solo and Brantas (Solo and Brantas Basin Areas)

This region consists of the basin of the upper Solo River and the fertile delta of the Brantas River. Most of the land is located on well-irrigated plains and the population density is as high as in Jawa Tengah Selatan.

I. Madura and Bangwetan (Madura Island and the East Hook of East Java)

"Bangwetan" is an old Javanese term meaning "the east land," which refers to the easternmost region of East Java.[3] Since the proportion of wet rice land to the total area is relatively low and rainfall in the dry season is very scarce, agriculture is highly oriented to dry farming. But the soil is very fertile and the productivity of land is higher than in other regions. The population density has remained relatively low, although great numbers of people have flowed into this area during the last two centuries, mainly from Central Java and Madura Island. Madura Island

[3] See also Hüsken, Frans, *Regionale verschillen in de agrarische ontwikkeling van Java: Variates op het involutie-Patroon*, 1981.

is flat and water for irrigation is scarce, so wet rice cultivation is not practicable. People have left this island for many years, principally for the Bangwetan area of Java proper.

Table 3 shows the aggregate harvested area of seven crops in the above-mentioned nine regions for the periods 1916–20 and 1975–79. The triangle diagramme in Fig. 6 based on these data indicates the regional diversity of crop composition and its changing pattern during the last six decades. These data can be summarized as follows: In West Java (regions A and B) and most of Central Java (regions C, E, and F) the proportion of the wet rice area has increased, while in the easternmost part of Central Java and the western part of East Java (regions D, G, and E), the proportion of wet rice area has clearly decreased and that of maize or other crops has increased. However, in the eastern half of East Java, where the proportion of land planted in maize had been high, the cultivation of wet rice has increased remarkably.

These data indicate the different trends in agricultural development in each region, which deserve keen attention when the relation of agricultural development and population growth in Java is discussed.

IV. DIFFERENT PATTERNS OF AGRICULTURAL DEVELOPMENT AND POPULATION GROWTH

Figure 7 shows the rate of increase in the total harvested area of seven major crops in 65 regional units during the six decades from 1916–20 to 1975–79, while Fig. 8 shows the population growth rate for the same period.[4] A positive correlation is found between the two for each unit ($r = +0.5040$). In the eight areas in Table 4, the population growth rate has been much greater than the rate of increase in the total harvested area of the seven crops. It is noteworthy that five among these areas (marked by asterisks) contain urban cores that have undergone rapid development and they are surrounded by rural areas in which agricultural development has also been phenomenal. This implies that economic differentiation has expanded within these regions between urban areas specializing in non-agricultural activities and the rural areas which supply them with agricultural products.

Table 5 shows the rates of increase in the harvested area of the seven crops (referred to as the total harvested area hereafter) and the rates of population growth in nine integrated regions for the last six decades. Region A, which includes the Jakarta metropolitan area has shown a much greater rate of increase in both total harvested area and population

[4] Statistics for each regional unit are not available.

TABLE 3. Harvested Area of Seven Major Crops in Nine Integrated Regions

Region		Wet land rice		Dry land rice		Maize		Cassava	
		1916–20	1975–79	1916–20	1975–79	1916–20	1975–79	1916–20	1975–79
A. Pasisir Barat	ha	644,181	1,167,436	120,518	56,051	20,990	36,034	42,340	76,584
	(%)	(72)	(80)	(13)	(4)	(2)	(3)	(5)	(5)
B. Priangan	ha	293,963	511,450	67,305	43,686	25,782	38,104	72,243	123,673
	(%)	(59)	(65)	(13)	(6)	(5)	(5)	(14)	(16)
C. Pasisir Tengah	ha	223,049	243,624	7,635	2,800	103,200	71,078	29,856	26.771
	(%)	(57)	(65)	(2)	(1)	(26)	(19)	(8)	(7)
D. Pasisir Timur	ha	540,295	554,669	35,252	20,034	319,501	454,032	100,947	105,545
	(%)	(49)	(40)	(3)	(2)	(29)	(33)	(9)	(8)
E. Pegunungan Tengah	ha	244,666	261,274	11,664	7,857	229,946	184,707	79,099	89,059
	(%)	(40)	(45)	(2)	(1)	(38)	(32)	(13)	(16)
F. Jawa Tengah Selatan	ha	258,421	357,858	22,677	9,733	36,905	33,887	48,143	62,280
	(%)	(62)	(70)	(5)	(2)	(9)	(7)	(12)	(12)
G. Pegunungan Kidul	ha	174,392	221,524	86,582	69,235	93,961	145,985	100,583	248,951
	(%)	(34)	(26)	(17)	(8)	(18)	(17)	(20)	(29)
H. D.A.S. Solo & Brantas	ha	313,584	417,503	13,550	6,532	102,917	150,668	71,212	93,440
	(%)	(53)	(52)	(2)	(1)	(17)	(19)	(12)	(12)
I. Bangwetan & Madura	ha	266,989	555,606	58,041	26,112	734,805	650,855	99,731	191,260
	(%)	(21)	(33)	(5)	(2)	(58)	(39)	(8)	(11)

Region		Sweet potatoes		Soybeans		Penuts	
		1916–20	1975–79	1916–20	1975–79	1916–20	1975–79
A. Pasisir	ha	33,856	24,500	7,267	11,850	30,891	82,725
Barat	(%)	(4)	(2)	(1)	(1)	(3)	(6)
B. Priangan	ha	22,858	24,937	3,651	15,641	16,588	28,747
	(%)	(5)	(3)	(1)	(1)	(3)	(4)
C. Pasisir	ha	5,065	7,468	16,181	16,385	8,162	9,602
Tengah	(%)	(1)	(2)	(4)	(4)	(2)	(3)
D. Pasisir	ha	30,250	16,311	32,272	129,291	37,751	84,264
Timur	(%)	(3)	(1)	(3)	(10)	(3)	(6)
E. Pegunungan	ha	27,538	12,108	3,073	6,296	10,114	14,855
Tengah	(%)	(5)	(2)	(1)	(1)	(2)	(3)
F. Jawa Tengah	ha	20,559	5,635	17,103	24,083	13,250	20,815
Selatan	(%)	(5)	(1)	(4)	(5)	(3)	(4)
G. Pegunungan	ha	17,583	7,346	29,604	101,206	14,427	60,897
Kidul	(%)	(3)	(1)	(6)	(12)	(3)	(7)
H. D.A.S. Solo	ha	23,275	10,666	36,254	94,396	27,868	27,868
& Brantas	(%)	(4)	(1)	(6)	(12)	(5)	(3)
I. Bangwetan	ha	54,523	30,856	15,881	167,957	42,866	61,293
& Madura	(%)	(4)	(2)	(1)	(10)	(3)	(4)

1. *Landbouwatlas van Java en Madoera* (*Agricultural Atlas of Java and Madura*), Mededeelingen van het Kantoor voor de Statistiek No. 33 Deel I, Weltervereden, 1926.
2. *Produksi tanaman bahan pangan di Jawa dan Madura 1975, 1976, 1977, 1978 & 1979*. Biro Pusat Statistik, Jakarta, 1977–1981.

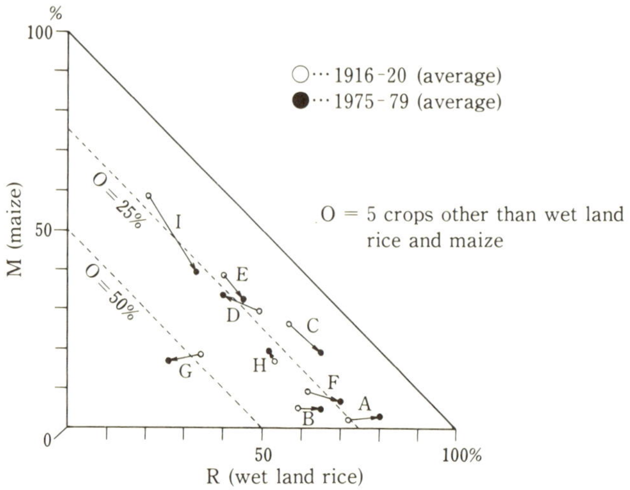

FIG. 6. Crop composition and change in nine integrated regions.

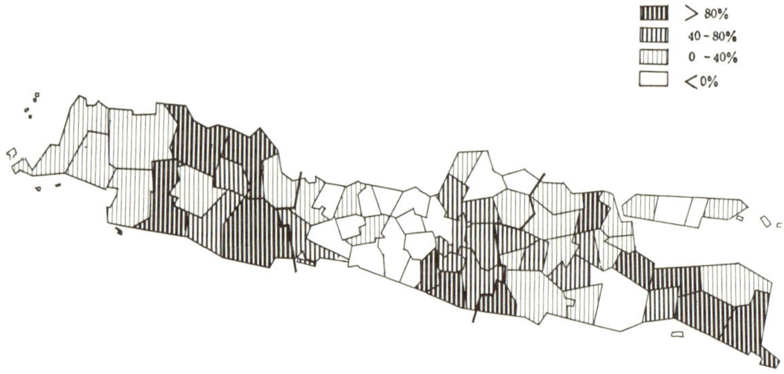

FIG. 7. Increase rate in total harvested area of seven major crops in 65 regional units.

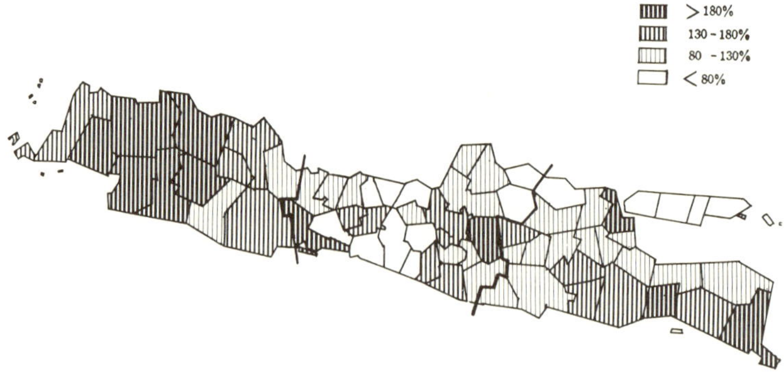

FIG. 8. Rate of population increase in 65 regional units.

TABLE 4. Eight Regional Units in which Population Growth Has Been Greater than the Increase in Total Harvested Area of Seven Major Crops

No.	Regional unit	Population growth (%)	Increase in harvested area (%)
1	Jakarta = Bogor*	370.4	30.5
7	Sukabumi	188.6	1.5
9	Bandung*	270.0	32.1
19	Semarang = Salatiga*	157.6	−24.4
25	Purbalingga	175.0	−9.9
34	Sragen	233.6	59.3
51	Gresik = Surabaya*	250.0	38.3
55	Malang*	159.5	−10.7

growth. These figures reflect the fact that this region has absorbed many migrants from other regions, while the development of agriculture on the outskirts of Jakarta to supply food to the growing urban population has also been remarkable.

Region B has the second highest rates of population growth and increase in total harvested area. This expansion has been due to two factors. The first one is similar to what happened in region A, that is, an influx of population from other regions into urban cores within this region, such as Bandung, and the development of agriculture in the surrounding areas induced by this urban development. The second factor is a greater natural population increase compared to other regions, made possible by the expansion of arable land and continuous intensification of agriculture. The second factor may be the more important one, if it is taken into account that in 1920 the population density as well as the proportion of arable land to the total area and the intensity of cultivation in the Priangan highlands was much lower than that in Central and East Java.

Against expectations, the rate of population growth and increase in total harvested area in region G are quite high. Usually this region is thought to be the economically poorest, and it does not produce sufficient food (*daerah minus*). People have continually left this region for richer areas. However, the figures in Table 5 call this popular view into question, because they indicate that the rate of increase in the total harvested area here has been far higher than that of all of Java and that the rate of population growth has also been higher than the other regions of Central and East Java. In fact, this region has nearly succeeded in absorbing a growing population within its own boundaries, at least during the last sixty years.

On the other hand, in regions C and E the total harvested area has decreased slightly and the rates of population growth have been the lowest, reflecting the migration out of these two regions during the

TABLE 5. Total Harvested Area of Seven Major Crops and Population in Nine Integrated Regions

Integrated region	Harvested area 1916–20 ha	Harvested area 1975–79 ha	Population 1920 ×1000	Population 1977 ×1000
A. Pasisir Barat	900,044	1,455,180	5,680	19,025
	(100)	(162)	(100)	(335)
B. Priangan	502,390	786,238	3,520	10,413
	(100)	(156)	(100)	(296)
C. Pasisir Tengah	393,148	377,728	2,658	5,054
	(100)	(96)	(100)	(190)
D. Pasisir Timur	1,096,268	1,364,176	4,565	10,029
	(100)	(124)	(100)	(220)
E. Pegunungan	605,920	576,156	3,334	6,537
Tengah	(100)	(95)	(100)	(196)
F. Jawa Tengah	417,058	514,291	3,184	6,526
Selatan	(100)	(123)	(100)	(205)
G. Pegunungan	517,132	855,144	2,835	6,867
Kidul	(100)	(165)	(100)	(242)
H. D.A.S. Solo	583,295	801,073	3,557	7,400
& Brantas	(100)	(137)	(100)	(208)
I. Bangwetan	1,272,836	1,683,939	5,484	11,909
& Madura	(100)	(132)	(100)	(217)
Java	6,287,517	8,243,143	34,818	83,753
	(100)	(131)	(100)	(241)

time period under consideration. The increases in the total harvested area in regions D, F, H, and I are at an intermediate level, with population growth rates slightly lower than average.

If productivity differences between areas and between the kinds of crops are considered negligible for the purposes of analysis, the total harvested area of the seven crops gives an approximation of the total food production volume in each area. Thus the increase in the total harvested area reflects a growth in the capacity to absorb population within an area through the development of agriculture. It is interesting to use this assumption to investigate the geographical correlation between the rate of increase in the total harvested area and the rate of population growth in each region. If a strong positive correlation were found between the two variables it would mean that the population growth in that region had been supported by agricultural development. On the contrary, if no such correlation were found, it could be concluded that population growth had depended upon factors other than agricultural development, such as urban development or the expansion of nonfarm activities.

Table 6 shows the rates of increase in the following four items in the 65 regional units during the last six decades: (1) the harvested area of rice (including dry land rice); (2) the aggregate harvested area of five non-rice crops; (3) the total harvested area of seven crops; and (4) population. From this data the following four correlation coefficients can be calculated for each of nine integrated regions, three provincial divisions (West, Central, and East Java), and all of Java: (1) the simple correlation

TABLE 6. Rates of Increase in Harvested Area and of Population Growth in 65 Regional Units

No.	(1)	(2)	(3)	(4)	No.	(1)	(2)	(3)	(4)
1	29.1	41.1	30.5	370.4	34	51.7	71.4	59.3	233.6
2	151.3	266.0	158.4	253.7	35	−2.7	−27.6	−18.2	43.7
3	1.6	202.3	19.4	130.2	36	−11.1	46.0	21.7	70.8
4	36.1	58.3	39.1	193.8	37	102.3	116.0	106.6	160.3
5	97.2	17.8	84.3	155.4	38	13.4	−49.9	−26.2	56.3
6	25.8	−11.5	14.9	123.2	39	64.3	658.2	310.4	164.7
7	− 8.9	36.6	1.5	188.6	40	−15.1	23.9	7.7	60.9
8	72.2	298.0	94.4	199.7	41	−12.1	15.5	1.5	94.0
9	45.8	0.2	32.1	270.0	42	44.6	73.4	56.5	130.5
10	74.0	23.5	58.1	134.2	43	15.7	−11.1	0.7	103.1
11	52.3	94.3	66.5	125.5	44	14.2	90.4	42.1	129.1
12	86.0	81.4	84.5	169.5	45	− 9.8	57.5	24.4	116.3
13	4.5	43.4	15.8	103.2	46	27.5	209.4	116.8	95.3
14	10.2	−19.0	− 1.9	92.1	47	30.7	26.8	28.8	114.5
15	22.7	−19.9	5.3	100.9	48	31.5	63.1	48.0	134.4
16	− 0.2	−54.8	−22.6	78.7	49	20.7	20.2	20.4	135.7
17	17.3	−34.8	−13.5	90.1	50	32.7	202.3	94.4	106.4
18	−10.0	−26.4	−17.2	68.0	51	− 7.4	152.6	38.3	250.0
19	−19.8	−28.1	−24.4	157.6	52	20.5	87.6	46.4	89.3
20	2.5	116.6	52.2	129.7	53	12.4	53.1	30.1	98.8
21	− 8.5	75.9	23.0	129.8	54	37.0	−49.3	7.4	82.9
22	7.4	−15.5	− 3.4	98.0	55	30.2	−24.8	−10.7	159.5
23	66.4	70.9	67.3	182.8	56	163.4	90.5	113.2	82.8
24	2.7	−21.4	− 4.6	70.9	57	324.7	76.4	120.0	92.0
25	7.9	−27.2	− 9.9	175.0	58	88.5	24.5	41.0	180.9
26	45.8	27.8	32.2	142.6	59	68.4	112.1	91.0	168.3
27	−16.4	−16.2	−16.3	43.5	60	41.8	− 8.4	5.5	94.7
28	− 4.3	−34.6	−21.3	42.2	61	264.2	224.2	250.0	404.9
29	− 2.0	−17.5	−11.3	81.9	62	1.0	21.5	16.8	52.2
30	11.8	−21.6	− 5.1	72.5	63	8.0	−17.2	−13.0	44.7
31	52.3	48.9	50.2	167.2	64	53.7	−15.3	− 5.7	57.3
32	52.6	26.4	46.3	123.3	65	16.7	− 0.4	1.2	34.4
33	9.3	110.8	55.8	117.3					

(1) Increase in harvested area of wet land rice (%).
(2) Increase in harvested area of six crops other than wet land rice (%).
(3) Increase in total harvested area of seven major crops (%).
(4) Rate of population increase (%).

between the rate of increase in the harvested area of rice and the rate of increase in the harvested area of non-rice crops (referred to as R12 hereafter); (2) the simple correlation between the rate of increase in the total harvested area and the rate of population growth (R34); (3) the partial correlation between the rate of increase in the harvested area of rice and the rate of population growth (R_{14}); and (4) the partial correlation between the rate of increase in the harvested area of non-rice crops and the rate of population growth (R_{24}). The results of calculation of these correlation coefficients are shown in Table 7, and indicate the following tendencies.

(1) For the whole of Java the R_{12} value is 0.3301, meaning that the cultivation of non-rice crops has not necessarily developed in parallel with the development of rice farming. The R_{34} value is a little higher than others, indicating a weak correlation between population growth and development of farm agriculture as a whole. However, neither R_{14} nor R_{24} is high and the respective values do not differ much from each other. In other words, for Java as a whole population growth has no strong regional correlation with the expansion of rice cultivation or non-rice crop cultivation. It is concluded from this analysis that agricultural development has not been the key factor supporting population growth on Java. In addition, the expansion of rice farming has not played a greater role

TABLE 7. Geographical Correlation between Harvested Area and Population Growth

Region	R_{12} (rice—non-rice)	R_{34} (total—pop.)	R_{14} (rice—pop.)	R_{24} (non-rice—pop.)
A. Pasisir Barat	0.3553	0.2067	0.0915	0.1111
B. Priangan	0.4684	−0.3368	−0.0231	−0.1806
C. Pasisir Tengah	0.0253	0.8679	0.9462	0.9220
D. Pasisir Timur	0.5394	0.4058	−0.4775	0.7290
E. Pegunungan Tengah	0.9274	0.4381	−0.2042	0.3652
F. Jawa Tengah Selatan	0.9175	0.9273	0.4944	0.4008
G. Pegunungan Kidul	0.8905	0.6347	0.2042	0.2185
H. D.A.S. Solo & Brantas	−0.0228	0.6205	0.7017	0.5468
I. Bangwetan & Madura	0.7262	0.7761	−0.1392	0.6954
West Java	0.3720	0.0825	0.0763	0.0072
Central Java	0.4698	0.5260	0.5458	0.1784
East Java	0.3332	0.6511	0.2852	0.4876
JAVA	0.3301	0.5040	0.3186	0.2893

than that of any other food crop. This finding is sufficient to refute the popular view of the modern agricultural history of Java.

(2) If the level of observation is shifted to the three provincial divisions, remarkable differences between them are seen. First, in West Java very little regional correlation between population growth and expansion of agriculture (both rice and non-rice production) is evident. In some regions of West Java rapid population growth in a certain area where urban development has occurred has been supported by agricultural development in other areas, but not in the area itself. In general, population growth in West Java has been made possible by economic development based mainly on the expansion of non-agricultural activities. In contrast, the R_{34} values are quite high in Central and East Java, meaning that the role of agriculture as the support of local population increase has been much more important than in West Java. However, the importance of rice farming has not been equal within these regions. In the case of Central Java, the R_{14} value is far higher than R_{24}, while in East Java the reverse relation is obtained. Therefore the expansion of non-rice crop farming has played a bigger role in East Java in supporting population growth.

(3) Analysis at the level of the nine integrated regions reveals more marked regional diversity. The most meaningful findings can be summarized as follows: In regions C, F, G, H, and I the geographical correlation between agricultural development and the population growth is obviously high as shown by the values of R_{34}. This means that the tendency toward self-sufficiency in food within each local area has been much stronger in Central and East Java than in West Java. However, the remarkably high correlation between the expansion of rice farming and population growth are only found in regions C and H, while in regions D and I the increase in the harvested area of non-rice crops is more closely correlated with population growth than that of rice. These findings make it clear that the role of subsistence farming for rice production as the supporter of rapid population growth in Java has been rather limited during the last six decades.

V. CONCLUSION

There is a great deal of regional diversity in agricultural production in Java, which does not depend solely on wet rice farming. In the eastern part of the island the increase in dry land production of maize has played a significant role in farm agriculture. In fact, the agriculture in the so-called [22] *kejawén* (heartland) area, usually identified as the core of rice culture in Java, has also been greatly dependent on non-rice crops.

During the last six decades the development of rice farming has been remarkable in West Java and the eastern half of East Java. In contrast, the expansion of agriculture in the eastern half of Central Java and the western half of East Java has been strongly oriented toward non-rice crop production. In general, the development of rice production in West Java has been induced by the development of non-agricultural activities in the urban centers and the expansion of trade between these urban centers and their rural hinterlands. In other words, subsistence farming for self-sufficiency in food has been less important than highly commercialized farming. However, the development of agriculture in Central and East Java has been much more strongly oriented toward subsistence, but not toward the rice monoculture for commercial production that is the norm in many West Java regions.

The role of non-rice crop production as a support of population growth in Java has never been less important than that of rice production. Non-farm activities such as handicrafts and small-scale trading have also played a significant role in supporting rapid population growth.

The importance of non-farm activities in the economic life of rural Java has been pointed out by a number of on-the-spot surveys carried out by social scientists and anthropologists,[5] as well as through field work done several years ago by the present author in a village in the Jogjakarta region of Central Java. According to the author's estimation, the proportion of income from rice fields to the total household income in that village was only 35.2%, while the income from garden farming and non-agricultural activities amounted to 10.7% and 46.3%, respectively, of the total household income (Kano, 1981). Some aspects of these features of the rural economy in Java have been confirmed too in this paper through the analysis of regional agricultural statistics, leading to the conclusion that Java's rural economy cannot be fossilized into a rice economy, though rice is undoubtedly important.

REFERENCES

Geerta, C. (1963). Agricultural Involution: The Processes of Ecological Change in Indonesia.

Kano, H. (1981). Sawahan: A Central Javanese Village under the "Development Order," pp.139–160.

Kayou, N. (1977). Basic Statistics on Japanese Agriculture (revised edition, in Japanese), p. 54.

---

[5] See, for example, White, Benjamin, *Production and Reproduction in a Javanese Village*, 1976.

Recent Advances in Micro-Level Demography of Fertility

Kazumasa KOBAYASHI

Population Research Institute, Nihon University, Tokyo, Japan

I. INTRODUCTION

"Human ecology of health and survival strategy" is an attractive field of study not only for human ecologists themselves, but also for demographers. The components of demographic dynamics are important explanatory variables for understanding ecological and socio-economic phenomena. To explain demographic processes, we need appropriate environmental and socio-economic variables. The well-known inter-disciplinary nature of demography stems from this. Demography is related to anthropology, human ecology, public health, geography, history, sociology, economics, political science, and others. Human ecology, which deals with adaptive mechanisms of human populations surviving in local ecosystems, is the most closely related to demography. Demographic studies, in fact, constitute one of the basic research components in human ecology.

Demography has a number of research fields classified by different demographic variables (mortality, fertility, migration, etc.) or different kinds of methodology or different research topics (mathematical demography, biological demography, historical demography, social demography, economic demography, population geography, etc.). In medical and health sciences, mortality (and life tables) research has been the most popular field of study related to demography. Fertility has received much less interest except for clinically-oriented contraception, family planning, and infertility studies. Fertility is the most important element of demographic dynamics due to its central role in generation reproduction. While mortality research tends to remain a relatively isolated field in population studies, fertility research is complexly related to studies of other aspects of demographic dynamics. Because of this, fertility research is a stimulus for demographic studies as a whole.

Demographic fertility research in the field of human ecology has been probably most actively carried out by the human ecologists in Japan who are affiliated with the Department of Human Ecology of the University of Tokyo. Among them, Igarashi and Takasaka have conducted a series of micro-level intensive studies of human fertility in Sundanese villages, West Java, Indonesia.

Igarashi (1985) reported the results of his demographic survey in 1983–1984 at Kampung Salamungkal; his principal interest was the variables that affect the length of reproductive lifespan (age at menarche, age at first marriage, and age at menopause) and those that affect pregnancy intervals (duration of breastfeeding, post-partum abstinence, and post-partum amenorrhea). He discusses post-partum amenorrhea as a key variable to understand the level and pattern of Sundanese fertility and proposes a unique birth interval model for Sundanese women.

Takasaka (1985) accumulated data for individual women currently and previously married in 13 of the 26 *kampungs* of a village called Loa in repeated visits to the village from 1978 to 1984. The data collected by him include detailed pregnancy histories with post-partum amenorrhea following the last delivery, pregnancy status, and outcome of current pregnancy. Whether individual women are presently pregnant or not were examined by use of the immunologic urine test for diagnosing pregnancy, and a follow-up observation on the pregnant women was carried out to confirm the outcome of pregnancy. Igarashi and Takasaka have brought us valuable knowledge on Sundanese fertility, comparisons of which with V. J. Hull's micro-demographic anthropological studies on Javanese fertility (Hull, 1977, 1980) are very interesting and suggestive.

The central theme of fertility research is to explain the mechanisms of determining levels and patterns of fertility. In recent decades frameworks and methodologies of fertility analysis have been developed in demography, especially regarding proximate determinants or intermediate variables of fertility. Detailed data on fertility behaviour and reproductive processes are required for analyzing the impact of the proximate determinants, and micro-demographic field surveys at the village level for obtaining such data. This paper aims at briefly overviewing the recent advances of micro-demography of fertility and discussing some perspectives on developing the micro-study of fertility in the field of human ecology by referring to the above-stated Sundanese fertility research.

II. BONGAARTS'S MODEL OF PROXIMATE DETERMINANTS

The first systematic classification of the proximate determinants of fertility was proposed by Davis and Blake (1956). Following their work, Bongaarts (1976, 1977, 1978, 1982) proposed a model which incorporates four proximate factors—marriage, contraception, abortion, and post-partum infecundability—and has taken evidence from appropriate sources that most of the variation in fertility levels between national populations can be accounted for by just these four. The model developed by Bongaarts is multiplicative and expresses the actual level of fertility (in terms of the total fertility rate, *TFR*) as a function of the relationship between a total fecundity rate (*TF*) and the fertility-reducing effect of the four main proximate determinants:

$$TFR = C_m \times C_c \times C_a \times C_i \times TF$$

where C_m is the index of marriage (nuptiality), C_c the index of contraception, C_a the index of abortion, and C_i the index of post-partum infecundability.

The four indices above can only take values between 0 and 1. When there is no fertility-inhibiting effect of a given proximate variable, the corresponding index equals 1; if the fertility inhibition is complete, the index equals 0. If there is no fertility-inhibiting effect at all in the four proximate determinants, *TFR* equals *TF* in the above equation. In demographic literature fertility means actual reproductive performance as applied to an individual or a group. Foetal deaths (abortions and stillbirths) are not counted in measuring fertility; only live births are included. Fecundity is the capacity (of a man, a woman, or a couple) to participate in reproduction (i.e., the birth of a live child). The total fertility rate is a summary index of fertility for a population, being the sum of all age-specific fertility rates usually taken for a specified period of time. The concept of the total fecundity rate is similar to that of *TFR*.

In Bongaarts's model $C_i \times TF$ is the level of *TF* reduced by the inhibiting effect of post-partum infecundability alone, and this is the total natural marital fertility rate. $C_c \times C_a \times C_i \times TF$ is a level obtained by lowering the total natural marital fertility rate due to the inhibiting effect of contraception and induced abortion. This is the total marital fertility rate. It is further reduced by the fertility-inhibiting effect of celibacy C_m to the level $C_m \times C_c \times C_a \times C_i \times TF$, which is the total fertility rate (*TFR*).

In applying the model to actual populations the principal purposes of analysis are to explain the observed level of fertility (*TFR*) by estimating the extent to which fertility is reduced from maximal levels by each proxximate determinant and to compare the relative impact of different determinants. In actual applications of the model, direct data for any of the indices C_m, C_c, C_a, and C_i are rarely available and the indices must be estimated using indirect methods (for details, see Bongaarts & Potter, 1983).

In the basic list of proximate determinants of fertility Bongaarts includes three additional variables: frequency of intercourse, spontaneous intrauterine mortality, and prevalence of permanent sterility (Bongaarts, 1982). The frequency of intercourse is taken as an index of fecundability (defined as the probability of conceiving per month among cohabiting women who are not pregnant, sterile, or temporarily infecundable) assuming that the fecundability of a population is directly dependent on the frequency of intercourse. In assuming this Bongaarts examined the weight of the frequency of intercourse on the basis of the following theoretical model determining fecundability:

$$\text{Fecundability} = p_1 \times p_2 \times p_3 \times p_4,$$

where

p_1 = probability that a menstrual cycle is ovulatory;
p_2 = probability of having at least one coitus coincide with a fertile period of two days (on the grounds that the duration of the fertile period is about two days);
p_3 = probability of insemination during the fertile period; and
p_4 = probability that fertilization results in a recognizable conception.

For convenience in model calculation Bongaarts takes the product of $p_1 \times p_3 \times p_4$ as 0.45 based on different studies, and p_2 is given by the following equation:

$$p_2 = 1 - (M - n)(M - n - 1) / (M^2 - M)$$

where n is the number of coital acts occurring during an interval of M days that include the fertile period. It is assumed that intercourse takes place at random during the interval M, with at most one coitus per day. Model estimates using the above equation suggested that the biological mechanism linking coital frequency and fecundability is fairly realistic (Bongaarts & Potter, 1983).

The three determinants, frequency of intercourse, spontaneous intrauterine mortality, and permanent sterility, are excluded from the formula for decomposing TFR mentioned previously by Bongaarts on the basis of the results of a sensitivity analysis to determine variations in the total fertility rate induced by variations in different proximate determinants. The three determinants above were shown to be generally much less important causes of variations in fertility (*ibid.*).

The model of Bongaarts is a macro-model. In applying the model to actual populations and estimating the indices C_m, C_c, C_a, and C_i, the necessary base data for parameter estimation must be obtained largely from macro-statistics. The aggregated data include the proportion currently married and the proportion currently using contraception among married women, use-effectiveness of contraception, the proportion currently believed to be fecund, the induced abortion rate, and the duration of post-partum infecundability (*ibid.*).

III. IMPACTS OF PROXIMATE DETERMINANTS AT THE INDIVIDUAL LEVEL

New approaches which permit investigations of the inter-relationships between different proximate determinants at the individual level have recently been developed. In national fertility surveys in several Latin American countries the Sexual Activity Table was used to collect the basic information from each woman. Using this table, information on pregnancy status by outcome, absence of sexual relations by type, and contraceptive use by method was obtained for each woman over the year preceeding interview (Gaslonde and Carrasco, 1982; Hobcraft and Little, 1984). Hobcraft and Little have extended Gaslonde-Carrasco's approach, and this new approach will be outlined here.

The fertility of a woman is measured in this approach by using the proportion of time spent during a certain period of observation in the state of pregnancy leading to a live birth. Let the period of observation be L months and the length of time (in months) spent by the woman concerned during the period of observation in pregnancy leading to a live birth be $d(p)$. Then the observed fertility rate f for that woman is

$$f = (12/9)\,[d(p)/L].$$

In general, a woman may be in various states of reproduction during the period of observation. The principal states of a woman after menarche are classified as follows:

1. Pregnant
2. Not pregnant
    21. Infecund
    22. Not infecund (i.e., fecund)

221. Abstaining from sexual relations
222. Not abstaining from sexual relations
    2221. Practising contraception
    2222. Not practising contraception.

In the above, states 21, 221, and 2221 as well as the state of pregnancy leading to a foetal death (not specified in 1 above) are factors reducing fertility. In the above equation, $L - d(p)$ is the total length of time spent during the period of observation in these four states.

Hobcraft and Little (1984) gave a detailed classification of the states regarding reproduction for their theoretical formulation, which is listed below with their symbols:

[Pregnancy]

p_1 = pregnancy leading to a live birth
p_2 = pregnancy leading to an induced abortion
p_3 = pregnancy leading to a spontaneous abortion
p_4 = pregnancy leading to a stillbirth

[Infecundity]

l = lactational infecundity
i_1 = non-lactational infecundity following a live birth
i_2 = infecundity following an induced abortion
i_3 = infecundity following a spontaneous abortion
i_4 = infecundity following a stillbirth
i_5 = permanent sterility

[Abstention from sexual relations]

m_1 = virginity
m_2 = divorce
m_3 = widowhood
m_4 = separation
m_5 = sexual abstinence following a birth
m_6 = terminal abstinence

[Contraception]

c_k = contraception using method k ($k = 1, 2, \ldots, k$)

[Remainder]

f = fecund (remainder) at risk of conception

In this model different states may occur simultaneously in some cases. In such cases the hierarchy between the states must be noted. For example, if a divorced woman is breast-feeding a child duıing a month (i.e., simultaneous occurrence of l and m_2), priority should be given to the state of divorce and the fecundity-reducing effect of breast-feeding must be discounted since the woman is not exposed to the risk of conception (Hobcraft and Little, 1984).

A particular problem regarding pregnancy is that in order to identify pregnancies leading to different outcomes we must set the reference period for the survey as ending at no more ten months before the interview date (*ibid.*).

Let $D(p_1)$, $D(i_1)$, and $D(f)$ be the length of time spent by a woman during the period of observation (L months) in exposure states p_1, i_1, and f, respectively. Then the proportion

$$NMFR = (12/9) \frac{D(p_1)}{D(p_1) + D(i_1) + D(f)}$$

corresponds to the natural marital fertility rate, which is referred to as "potential fertility rate" by Hobcraft and Little (1984).

The sum of the allocations of time to the other exposure states, $D(s)$, is

$$D(s) = L - [D(p_1) + D(i_1) + D(f)]$$

and, therefore,

$$D(p_1) + D(i_1) + D(f) = L - D(s).$$

The observed fertility rate, FR, is

$$\begin{aligned} FR &= (12/9) \frac{D(p_1)}{L} \\ &= (12/9) \frac{D(p_1)}{D(p_1) + D(i_1) + D(f)} \times \frac{L - D(s)}{L} \\ &= NMFR \times \frac{L - D(s)}{L} \\ &= NMFR \times [1 - D(s)/L]. \end{aligned}$$

The above $D(s)/L$ is the reducing effect of proximate determinants s. Suppose s is composed of $s_1, s_2, \ldots$; then $D(s_1)/L$, $D(s_2)/L$, . . ., respectively, are the reducing effects of the respective determinants $s_1, s_2, \ldots$.

The measurements so far described are all for an individual woman. It is easy to obtain average figures for a group by ages, by social strata, or as a whole, because the model of Hobcraft and Little is not a multiplicative decomposition like Bongaarts's model, but an additive decomposition. Birth-order-specific effects of proximate determinants can also be estimated by generalizing the procedures suggested by Hobcraft and Little (Palloni, 1984).

IV. USE OF THE LIFE TABLE ANALYSIS OF BIRTH INTERVAL

Palloni has proposed another approach to estimate the effects of proximate determinants using the life table analysis of birth interval (Palloni, 1984). Palloni's method is primarily age- and parity-specific.

Let $h_i(X)$ be the unconditional density function of reaching parity $i + 1$ at age X from parity i. Then the age-specific fertility rate at age X, $FR(X)$, is the sum of $h_i(X)$ between $i = 0$ and $i = \infty$, that is,

$$FR(X) = \sum_{i=0}^{\infty} h_i(X)$$

and from this follows the measure of total fertility rate, TFR:

$$TFR = \sum_{X=\alpha}^{\beta} FR(X)$$

where α and β are, respectively, the minimum and maximum age at childbearing (Palloni, 1984).

If we divide $h_i(X)$ into $h_i(X, Z_j)$s, where $j = 1$ 2, . . . and Z_1, Z_2, . . . represent different states of reproduction during the birth interval of order i, we obtain $FR(X, Z_j)$ and $TFR(Z_j)$ for different states regarding reproduction. Suppose we calculate $h_i(X)$ for those women who were married continuously with neither contraception nor induced abortion during the birth interval of order i and let it be $h_i(X, Z_1)$, then $FR(X, Z_1)$ and $TFR(X, Z_1)$ are the age-specific natural marital fertility rate and the total natural marital fertility rate, respectively.

V. DISCUSSION AND CONCLUSION

For the study of fertility-regulating mechanisms in a population, fertility-reducing effects of the proximate determinants are the most important aspect to be investigated. This aspect is sociobiological and requires in general an individual-level analysis of data collected from intensive micro-demographic field surveys. Among the approaches introduced in the present paper, that by Hobcraft and Little seems to be most suitable for micro-level village surveys of human ecology. The Hobcraft-Little method of estimating the fertility-reducing effects of proximate determinants is basically to analyze proportions of time spent by the respective women in different states regarding reproduction. The time analysis of reproductive processes is, theoretically speaking, the most basic method of bio-demographic fertility research. Results of analysis by this approach tend to be sensitive to the quality of information, and the accuracy of the dating of events must be secured in field surveys.

The first step in classifying a group of reproductive women according to their current state of reproduction is to classify them into those pregnant and not pregnant. The attempt at diagnosing pregnancy in individual women using the immunologic urine test carried out by Takasaka in his Sundanese village survey was verified to be efficient and reliable. His follow-up observation on the 55 women who were pregnant revealed 10 pregnancies terminating in foetal death. Takasaka also collected information from 269 women in the same Sundanese village on the duration of post-partum amenorrhea following the last live birth (Takasaka, 1985). Igarashi, whose field is located in another Sundanese village, collected information on the duration of breast-feeding from 162 women using a follow-up approach and from 122 women in a retrospective survey. The follow-up data were found more reliable than the retrospective data. Regarding the duration of post-partum abstinence, data were collected from 120 women by a retrospective method. Data on the duration of post-partum amenorrhea were also collected by Igarashi by both follow-up (74 women) and retrospective (131 women) methods (Igarashi, 1985).

The above example suggests the possibility of collecting micro-demographic data on fertility at the village level, which would seem to be more reliable than data collected through a large-sample retrospective survey. Igarashi calls our attention to a series of problems often encountered in micro-demographic field surveys, and particularly in developing societies. The detailed discussions by Igarashi on age estimation for Sundanese women in reproductive ages in comparison with T.H. Hull's studies confirm that sufficient knowledge of the local culture is needed—the way of thinking of the inhabitants about age, linguistic knowledge of the expressions regarding developmental stages of individuals, historical events in the local society, etc. Collecting as reliable age data as possible is of utmost importance in demographic research. Demographers are, however, in general not well trained in age estimation for individual inhabitants at the village level; for this we need the skills and methods of human ecologists. With regard to collecting and interpreting data on the duration of breast-feeding and post-partum amenorrhea, we again need sufficient knowledge of relevant local norms and local words for the associated behaviours and phenomena (Igarashi, 1985).

In conclusion, micro-demographic research has been increasingly required for fertility analysis; in view of the complex relations between fertility and biological and sociocultural factors, human ecology is expected to become more important in micro-level fertility research.

REFERENCES

Bongaarts, J. (1976). Intermediate fertility variables and marital fertility. *Population Studies* **30** (2): 227–241.

Bongaarts, J. (1977). A dynamic model of the reproductive process. *Population Studies* **31** (1): 59–73.

Bongaarts, J. (1978). A framework for analyzing the proximate determinants of fertility. *Population and Development Review* **4** (1): 105–132.

Bongaarts, J. (1982). The fertility-inhibiting effects of the intermediate fertility variables. *Studies in Family Planning* **13** (6/7): 179–189.

Bongaarts, J. and R.G. Potter (1983). *Fertility, Biology, and Behavior: An Analysis of the Proximate Determinants*. New York: Academic Press.

Gaslonde, S. and E. Carrasco (1982). The impact of some intermediate variables on fertility: Evidence from the Venezuela National Fertility Survey 1977. *WFS Occasional Papers* 23. Voorburg, Netherlands: International Statistical Institute.

Hobcraft, J. and R.J.A. Little (1984). Fertility exposure analysis: A new method for assessing the contribution of proximate determinants to fertility differentials. *Population Studies* **38** (1): 21–45.

Igarashi, T. (1982). Some notes on methods of age estimation: An attempt in a Sundanese village, West Java. *Southeast Asian Studies* **20** (2): 260–284 (In Japanese with English summary).

Igarashi, T. (1985). Some biosocial variables that may account for fertility patterns in the Sundanese society. In S. Suzuki and O. Soemarwoto (eds.), *Health Ecological Survey in Indonesia in 1983/84* pp. 67–97.

Palloni, A. (1984). Assessing the effects of intermediate variables on birth interval-specific measures of fertility. *Population Index* **50** (4): 623–657.

Singh, S.,B. Casterline and J.G. Cleland (1985). The proximate determinants of fertility: Sub-national variations. *Population Studies* **39** (1): 113–135.

Takasaka, K. (1985). Fertility and birth interval of women in a Sundanese agricultural community. In S. Suzuki and O. Soemarwoto (eds.), *Health Ecological Survey in Indonesia in 1983/84* pp. 38–66.

III. HEALTH AND SURVIVAL IN TRANSITION

Health Resource Aspects of Man-Environment Systems

Akira KOIZUMI

University of Tokyo School of Medicine, Tokyo, Japan

I. INTRODUCTION

First of all, I would like to address the ecological concept of *habitat*. Each species has its own *habitat* and lives its life using the limited resources there. Generally speaking, a living being looks for its necessary resources in Nature and chooses a *habitat* where it can easily acquire them. However, human beings build their *habitats* by making use of Nature, processing natural goods or reforming them. Other living beings seek their living materials as widely as possible, but do not demand what lies beyond their limits. Human beings, however, explore all the possibilities they can imagine. It is interesting that human *habitats* are remarkably varied in contrast to that of other living things and also have experienced tremendous changes from a historical point of view. In this variety of life-styles and these changes, however, there has been no fundamental change in the biological characteristics of mankind.

It is common in our contemporary life to drive a car or to travel by jet plane. These substitutional activities on a large scale could be thought of as supplementing the walking function by using an internal combustion engine or an electric motor with artificially released energy. In the same way, a telegraph or a wireless and the wide use of radio or television use mechanical means to extend our physical communicating functions like seeking, hearing, speaking, writing and drawing. In the same way, it is possible to regard an electric computer as a partial expansion of our brain. Our modern life-styles owe much to machines and artificially released energies, supported by complicated social organization.

A mobile machine like a car and high-speed forms of transport like jet planes or superexpress railways have many advantages, but they also carry a certain risk. In ancient times, when human beings built small artificial environments and tried to secure their lives against the forces of Nature, the environment was surely connected directly with human welfare. Although in the contemporary world too we are preoccupied with human survival and welfare, the optimal environment today presumably means living circumstances which enable us to satisfy our cultural desires in addition to being protected from both natural and artificial dangers.

The Japanese philosopher Tetsuro Watsuji in his book *Fudo* [*Climate*] described what he called Europe's pastorality as a "synthesis of wetness and dry." According to his interpretation, people develop the traits of acceptance and endurance in the Asian monsoon climate with its combination of heat and wetness, while in the dry desert climate of the Middle and Near East people become submissive and fond of fighting. Watsuji characterized the fundamental structure of Europe as one of rationality. It was also his view that artificiality tends to be combined with rationality in Japan, while in Europe naturalness tends to be combined with rationality.

The Nobel laureate Yasunari Kawabata referred to the Japanese view of Nature and humanity in a speech titled "Japan, the Beautiful, and Myself. He said: "The snow, the moon, the blossoms, words expressive of the seasons as they move one into another, include in the Japanese tradition the beauty of mountains and rivers and grasses and trees, of all the myriad manifestations of nature, of human feelings as well. The spirit, that feeling for one's comrades in the snow, the moonlight, under the blossoms, is also basic to the tea ceremony. A tea ceremony is a coming together in feeling, a meeting of good comrades in a good season."

The Japanese people have traditionally been possessed by the desire to adapt themselves to Nature, but they seem to have lost their desire to protect Nature since they came to pursue a materialistic civilization as a result of rapid westernization.

II. HABITAT AND WELFARE ENVIRONMENT

Now I would like to examine the functions of a welfare environment from both the macroscopic and microscopic sides. From the macroscopic point of view, let me cite the preservation of the biosphere, which can be regarded as the supporting film of human existence. The biosphere has been ruined by indiscriminate deforestation in past times, and by recent excessive fishing, violent mining of mineral resources and fossil fuels, and the resulting environmental pollution.

A study which aims to examine the influence on health of physical and chemical environmental factors as well as their impact on the entire ecosystem has been carried out under the new name of environmental science. And the results of this study have been applied to setting up specific goals for environmental control. Thus, the macroscopic problems of the welfare environment are closely related to scientific technology and industrial production.

In the microscopic sense, I would like to consider the *habitat* in the sense of living circumstances closely connected with our lives. Any example of food, clothing or shelter shows that the physiological functions of our bodies in nature are supplemented by an artificial environment in our *habitat* today. For instance, body temperature is adjusted with clothing and shelter. In reinforcing the physiological functions, an artificial environment not only enlarges existing functions but also corrects lost or declining ones. Typical examples are eyeglasses and hearing aids, and the same can be said about false teeth, artificial arms and/or legs, and pacemakers. A hemodialysis which must be done periodically is also one of these physiological reinforcements.

An artificial environment differs from eyeglasses in public demand and in cost, and there is also a difference between daily and periodic use. In either case, however, the environment has the same essential role of supplementing our physiological functions.

We often use the words "a child-care environment" in relation to infant problems. This expression points to the importance of the social condition of the environment, as well as its physical and chemical condition. The main role of a child-care environment is a physiologically supplemental function: an infant child needs a helper until he or she grows enough to take care of him or herself. A child-care environment has another positive role, however: to develop a child's mind and body. In this sense it is a mental environment, which has a great influence on human nature including its emotional aspects. A welfare environment has the same influence on adults. Especially where the aged are involved, it is inevitable that cases in which the aid of a family member or another person is required will increase.

The preservation of the biosphere is important in the macroscopic consideration of a welfare environment. Similarly, from the microscopic viewpoint, the human *habitat* must be continuously adjusted to contribute to health maintenance and health improvement. For example, it is necessary that a child-care environment be continually checked to be sure that it is provided with enough security to protect an infant child from accidents, and that nutrition and medical care are sufficient for good health.

A welfare environment which is concerned with individuals and their families will lay a strong foundation for a social welfare environment.

It is necessary for the producers of such an environment to be constantly prepared to satisfy the needs of its consumers. A regional welfare environment program, which is responsible for the whole environment of many human beings, must stay in close contact with a regional comprehensive health care program.

III. LIFE EXPECTANCY AT BIRTH

Now I would like to discuss life expectancy at birth, particularly in Japan. In 1984, life expectancy was reported to be 75.54 years of age for Japanese males and 80.18 for females, the highest rates for any country in the world.

It is, however, only recently that Japanese life expectancy at birth reached such a high level. In 1971, life expectancy passed 70 for males and 75 for females, the achievement of a long-cherished goal for Japanese health authorities. Table 1 gives life expectancy data for each year since 1947 and selected earlier years.

Life expectancy in Japan lagged behind that in other developed countries until quite recently. For a considerable time, the longevity of the

TABLE 1. Life Expectancy at Birth (years)

Year	Male	Female	Year	Male	Female
1921–1925*	42.06	43.20	1964	67.67	72.87
1926–1930*	44.82	46.54	1965*	68.74	72.92
1935–1936	46.92	49.63	1966	68.35	73.61
1947*	50.06	53.96	1967	69.91	74.15
1948	55.6	59.4	1968	69.05	74.30
1949	56.2	59.8	1969	69.18	74.67
1950–1952*	59.57	62.97	1970*	70.31	74.66
1951	60.8	64.9	1971	70.17	75.58
1952	61.9	65.5	1972	70.50	75.94
1953	61.9	65.7	1973	71.70	76.02
1954	63.41	67.69	1974	71.16	76.31
1955*	63.6	67.75	1975*	72.73	76.89
1956	63.59	67.54	1976	72.15	77.35
1957	64.24	67.6	1977	72.69	77.95
1958	65.98	69.61	1978	72.97	78.33
1959	65.21	69.88	1979	73.46	78.89
1960*	66.32	70.19	1980	73.32	78.83
1961	66.03	70.79	1981	73.79	79.13
1962	67.23	71.16	1982	74.22	79.66
1963	67.21	72.34	1983	74.20	79.78
			1984	74.54	80.18

* Complete Life Table. Figures after 1947 include Okinawa Prefecture.

Source: Abridged and Complete Life Tables, Ministry of Health and Welfare, Tokyo.

Scandinavian people, particularly the Swedish, continued to be far beyond Japan's reach, and it took many years to reach the level of England, Wales, the U.S.A. and France (Table 2).

Statistics have proven that life expectancy has increased rapidly in Japan and a high standard of health has been reached. Who could have foretold such a development some decades ago? It is not easy to discover the causes. One is a sharp decrease in the rate of death due to infectious diseases, mainly in the period from 1950–55, but even this great decrease could not bring life expectancy into line with other developed countries at the time as the death rate from epidemics in Japan had previously been so high. There are many factors involved in the extension of life expectancy, and all of them are interrelated; it would be a mistake to single out any one factor.

No one can dispute the effect that antibiotics, in their fight against infectious diseases such as tuberculosis, gastroenteritis, pneumonia and bronchitis, have had on the lowering of the mortality rate. At the same time, easy access to medical care cannot be ignored as an auxiliary factor. Improvement in nutrition may also have been beneficial in enhancing the effects of antibiotics.

Rapid economic growth began in Japan around 1955. In 1961, a new era was entered with the introduction of a nationwide health care insurance system. Economic growth allowed a major portion of people's medical expenses to be publicly financed, and Japan became a nation with a high level of access to medical care services. Improvements in medical technology were also made possible by economic progress.

The nutritional levels of the Japanese diet have been enhanced, with

TABLE 2. International Comparison of Life Expectancy at Birth

Country	Year	Male	Female
Japan	1980	73.32	78.83
Iceland	1979–1980	73.70	79.70
Sweden	1980	72.76	78.81
Norway	1979–1980	72.75	79.00
Denmark	1979–1980	71.20	77.30
Netherlands	1979	72.40	78.90
Switzerland	1968–1973	70.29	76.22
France	1978–1980	70.05	78.20
England & Wales	1977–1979	70.20	76.40
Canada	1975–1977	70.19	77.48
U.S.A.	1979	69.90	77.80
Puerto Rico	1979	69.60	76.07

Note: Years show the period on which the statistics are based.
Source: Demographic Yearbook, UN, 1981.

the average intake of calories, protein and fat still below that level of Western countries. This helps to sustain a comparatively low death rate by aiding in the prevention of degenerative diseases. It is now widely accepted that the eating habits of the Japanese are better for health than those of Western countries, particularly in preventing heart disease.

In spite of the reported rapid increase in life expectancy in Japan, a mathematical model based on analysis of recent trends indicates that the rate of increase has been declining and will level off in the future. At the same time, national medical expenditure has been growing continuously in Japan; therefore, we examined the relationship between changes in life expectancy at birth and per capita national medical expenditure. To remove the influence of long-term price fluctuations on these figures, a correction was made using the consumer price index published by the Bureau of Statistics of the Prime Minister's Office.

If we express life expectancy at birth (average of males and females) as "x" for a year, and per capita national medical expenditure for the same year as "Y," the relation between "x" and "Y" is shown by the following equation:

$$Y = 4.10^{-5} \cdot 1.344^{x}$$

The greater the life expectancy at birth, the more incremental per capita national medical expenditure is required to generate a unit increase in life expectancy at birth. Therefore, "marginal cost," which is relative to the marginal increase in life expectancy at birth, is increasing continuously, as shown in Fig. 1. The above equation also indicates that the benefit of national medical expenditure in terms of life expectancy at birth does not increase linearly with amount of expenditure.

As previously discussed, the mortality rate has decreased remarkably because of medical advances and improved access to medical services, resulting in increased health, including improved life expectancy at birth. In spite of these objective improvements, the ratio of people who are ill and receiving medical treatment is increasing.

Figure 2 is a survival curve compiled from the 1979 Abridged Life Table and three different surveys conducted by Japan's Ministry of Health and Welfare the same year. Data used include the number of medical care recipients according to the Patient Survey; the morbidity prevalence rate according to the National Health Survey; and health consciousness according to the Basic Survey on Health Status. The combination is thought to represent the quality of life from the point of view of health.

This figure has some limitations due to inconsistencies in the timing of observations and surveys and differences among the sample groups of the

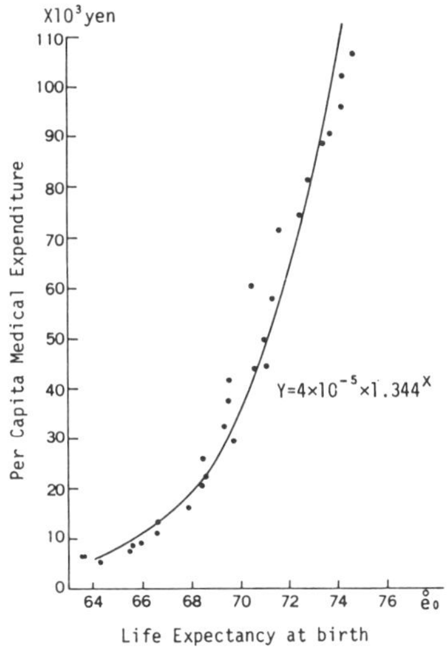

FIG. 1. Relationship between life expectancy at birth and per capita medical expenditure in Japan (Koizumi, 1985).
Note: Life expectancy is a weighted average of males and females.

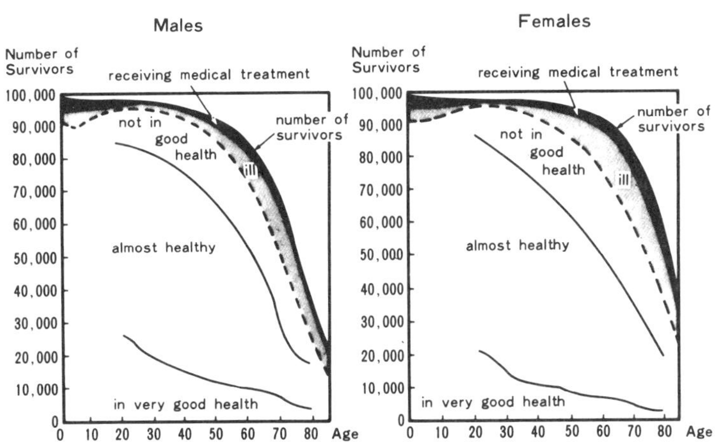

FIG. 2. Proportion of survivors by subjective feeling of health (Koizumi, 1985).

surveys of the original material. The death rate for the summarized life table is based on year-round data, while the medical care recipient data are confined to the third Wednesday in July, 1979, and the rate of disease data are limited to three days in the beginning of October. Material relating to health consciousness was obtained at the same time as the rate of disease material. With regard to the sample groups, the number living is based on annual death rates by sex and age calculated from national demographic statistics. The medical care recipient rate, morbidity prevalence rate and health consciousness measure data are based on sample plans for each survey and are equivalent in the sense that the total national population is the target, but the sampling error is not always the same.

Despite such shortcomings, Fig. 2 can serve as a sample for devising a new health indicator. The vertical axis represents the number living, and the horizontal axis represents the ages of males and females separately. The solid curve at the top represents the living population by age, the second solid curve represents the untreated population by age, and the dotted curve represents the nondiseased population by age. The "subjective" judgement of the condition of health is also shown in Fig. 2 and divided into "not in good health," a majority of "fairiy healthy," and "in very good health." This subjective consciousness is shown only among people over 20. Details of the survey data can be found in Tables 3 and 4.

Figure 3 shows the change in number living population 1965 to 1979

TABLE 3. Proportion of Sick People and People Who Visited Physicians (Koizumi, 1985)

	Year	Age group (%)		
		0–14	15–64	65–85
Sick People				
Male	1965	3.3	7.4	19.1
	1970	6.4	9.0	27.0
	1975	9.2	9.4	31.4
	1979	6.8	8.8	35.6
Female	1965	3.3	7.4	16.8
	1970	5.4	10.4	24.2
	1975	8.4	10.7	32.3
	1979	6.6	10.3	38.0
Medical Care Users				
Male	1965	5.1	6.5	8.6
	1970	6.4	7.0	12.0
	1975	5.5	6.2	16.8
	1979	6.5	6.0	17.2
Female	1965	4.5	6.3	7.0
	1970	5.9	7.5	10.8
	1975	5.7	7.1	18.3
	1979	5.8	6.0	19.1

TABLE 4. Subjective Feelings on Health (Koizumi, 1985)

Subjective feeling	Age group (%)			
	Male		Female	
	20–64	65–85	20–64	65–85
In very good health	17.4	10.7	11.8	5.9
Fairly healthy	62.6	43.8	62.3	38.2
Not in good health	20.0	45.5	26.0	55.9

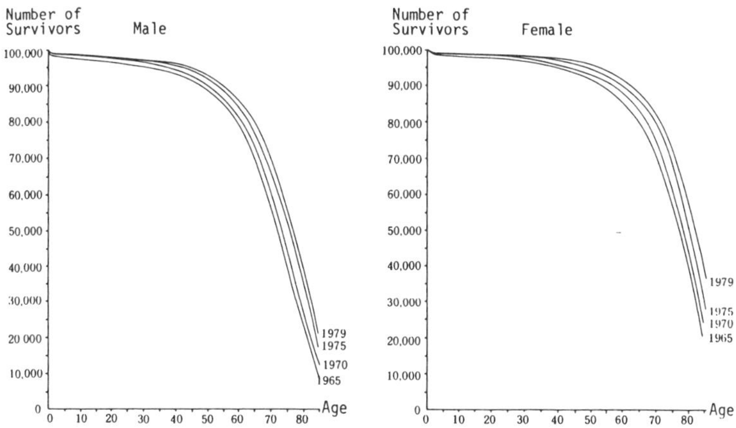

FIG. 3. Number of survivors (Koizumi, 1985).

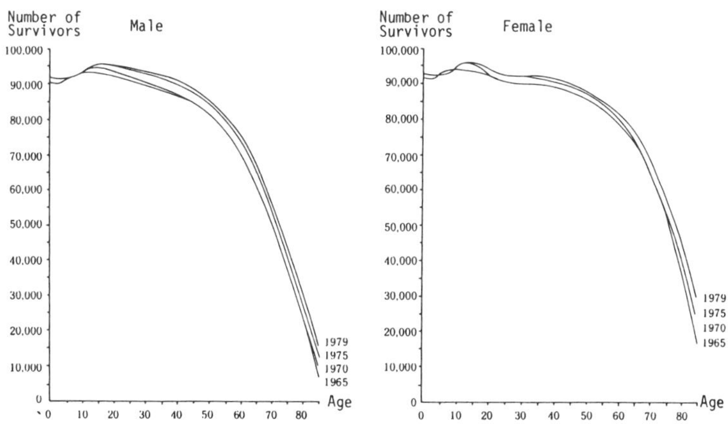

FIG. 4. Number of survivors who received no medical treatment (Koizumi, 1985).

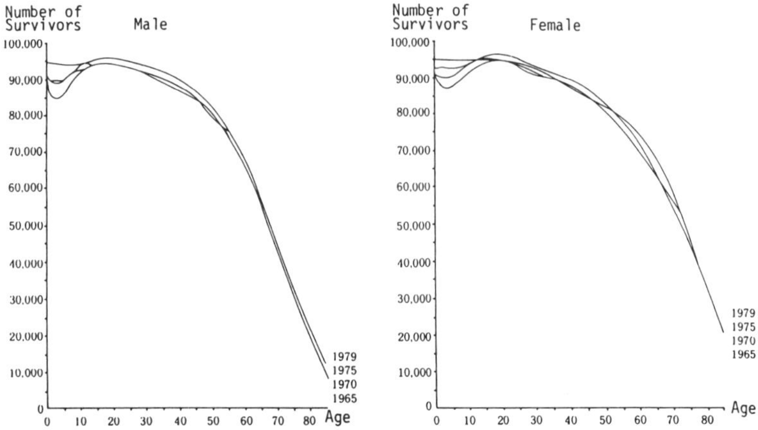

FIG. 5. Number of survivors with no disease (Koizumi, 1985).

for males and females separately. Figure 4 shows those who received no medical treatment, and Fig. 5 shows those with no disease. In Fig. 3, a constant and steady improvement is observed per year, but the same trend is not necessarily seen in Figs. 4 and 5. In Fig. 5, in particular, each year overlaps with the previous one except for the infancy period. This seems to have some significance.

The above are the results of part of the attempt to develop a new indicator of health levels based on data obtained in Japan. The development of this new indicator is still in its beginning stages and needs further improvement. It is presented here, however, as a possible indicator of the quality of life or the welfare environment.

BIBLIOGRAPHY

1. Koizumi, A. (1982). Ecology of human survival: A basic study of medico-economics. In Japan Medical Association (ed.) *Human Well-Being and Economic Welfare*. Tokyo, Japan Times. pp. 3–22.
2. Koizumi, A. (1985). Health problems of the year 2000 and beyond. *Health Policy* **4**: 307–319, 1985.

Problems of Health and Development Strategy in the Western Highlands, Papua New Guinea

Andrew STRATHERN

Institute of PNG Studies, Papua New Guinea

I. INTRODUCTION

Western Highlands Province (WHP), in the heart of Papua New Guinea, has experienced a relatively short but intensive history of contact with the outside world, beginning with its initial exploration in the early 1930s by gold miners and culminating today with its position as a major focus for the production of coffee and tea, as well as other cash crops. It contains one of the two major towns in the Highlands, Mount Hagen, which acts as a commercial centre for more outlying areas in the Southern Highlands (SHP) and Enga provinces, as well as Western Highlands itself. With all this economic development, not a great deal is known about the precise interaction of patterns of development with patterns of health. Obviously this represents an important area for investigation. In this paper I give a summary of information and ideas on the topic, in the hope that human ecologists and anthropologists may be thereby interested in carrying out further studies which could contribute to health planning in the province, and also to point out the main likely areas where government spending is needed to rectify deficiences in the existing health services.

II. TRADITIONAL AND INTRODUCED MEDICINE

I have discussed this topic at some length in three other publications (Strathern, 1984, 1985, in press), so a briefer statement will be given here. Traditionally a range of plant remedies was used to combat sickness. These might be used simply in themselves or more often in conjunction with the pronouncement of spells as well as sacrifices to putative spirit entities. Ritual experts (*mön wö*) held much of the knowledge to operate this medico-religious system. Their work included the task of combating lethal sorcery and the effects on men of female menstrual pollution. These complexes of activity have come under severe pressure since the coming of Europeans. On the one hand, the straightforward use of plant medicines has declined as a result of the availability of patent medicines such as aspirin, ointments, elastoplasts, bandages, disinfectants, cough mixtures, diarrhoea mixtures, and the like, all normally available at village level through the system of aid posts staffed by partly trained orderlies. On the other hand, the complex of ritual ideas has come under attack from the introduced Christian religion, which offers its own prayers and healing rituals instead of traditional ones. Nevertheless some activities do remain on both sides. One still sees the occasional use of leaves for the treatment of sores, especially boils. And indigenous rituals are performed to remove contaminating menstrual blood from male patients. (The treatment consists of sucking out blood from the patient through sugar cane peel and spitting this blood out onto a hot surface so that it burns. The pollution is then thought to be removed and the patient should recover.) Similarly rituals to prevent or to enhance the likelihood of pregnancy in women are still performed, sometimes by persons with some education. In these areas of experience where spirit forces or incalculable causes are held to be at work, recourse is had to anything which may possibly prove efficacious. There is definitely, then, a form of syncretism at work here.

In addition, the basic structure of ideas with respect to leading causes of sickness has hardly altered at all. Much sickness is held to result from anger (*popokl*) triggered by wrongdoing on the part of others, or else by one's own wrongdoing (e.g., breaking rules relating to sexual relationships). When the cause of sickness has been revealed by confession and appropriate expiation has been made, the way is open to healing; otherwise sickness may lead to death. Such ideas make a powerful contribution to social control. They also map easily onto Christian ideas of sin, confession, repentance, and redemption. Here again, we can see a fusion of traditional and introduced concepts.

Problems arising in this area are the following:

(1) The rather wholesale dropping of plant remedies should now be reviewed, with the thought of reviving the use of some of these traditional medicaments. For this purpose a thorough study is needed.

(2) The relationship between the use of ritual, whether indigenous or introduced, and the official health service agencies needs to be evaluated. Some data on this topic (not systematically gathered) suggest that on the whole the two systems do not greatly interfere with each other. However, these data relate one social group only. Sensitive survey work over a wider data base is needed.

III. THE IMPACT OF DEVELOPMENT ON DIET

No detailed studies of any kind have been done on this topic in the province. The traditional diet, like that of other parts of the Highlands, consists mainly of sweet-potato tubers and leafy greens, with seasonal supplementation by beans, corn, red fruit-pandanus, and regular consumption of sugar cane and bananas (both sweet and cooking types are eaten). These items remain a normal part of the diet nowadays. Pork was traditionally eaten only on ceremonial occasions, and pigs were saved for these. Often, too, pigs were not killed and eaten but passed on live between exchange partners several times before finally forming part of the diet. These circumstances still hold for the main part today.

The diet has changed with the addition of introduced foods, chiefly rice, meat, fish, sugar, salt, coffee, tea, bread, biscuits, and soft drinks (stimulants will be mentioned separately). The introduced foods are high in fats, carbohydrates, and protein. The introduction of regular protein supplies in the form of meat and fish (tinned) has probably been favourable, but the sharp increase in consumption of fats and sugar is less so. Problems of blood pressure and obesity may result. The people in general are extremely fond of fatty, sweet, and salty foods, partly because the traditional diet was relatively low in these ingredients, and it was perhaps adaptive in the past for people to seek them out. Ash salt was traded in from the Enga area, for example. Health education on these matters for villagers is almost nonexistent. In addition, to be "fat" is an admired condition rather than one to be deplored; again, when people regularly do physical labour and take exercise, a strong or firm body certainly indicates health and adequate food intake, but where they no longer do so obesity may take over, with associated problems of heart disease. (In the Hagen language the term *kopong* refers to "grease" or "fat," and a body in this condition is considered good.) Obesity may also lead over time to diabetes. Health tests comparing samples of urban with village dwellers would be enlightening in this regard.

Similarly, a comparison of patterns of tooth decay, controlling for age, sex, and lifestyle, could provide information on the likely effect of sugar consumption. Tooth brushing is rare in villages, but consumption of sugar cane may mitigate the effects of this situation.

These problems may be seen as likely to emerge over a slightly longer time-span, whereas in the short run the improved access to health services and to relatively cheap supplies of protein has reduced the level of malnutrition. Surveys in the Jimi Valley, in the north of the Province, in an area which is low in altitude and heavily forested, seem to indicate that the level of malnutrition is higher there than in other parts where a cash economy has penetrated more effectively. However, this should be interpreted with caution. It can too readily become an accepted dogma that economic development by itself alone will help to improve diet and therefore health. This is not so. Development brings with it a "basket" of results, some positive and some negative with respect to health. Further, traditional diets are not necessarily poor. The malnutrition which exists in the Jimi Valley may be influenced by factors such as parasitic infection, especially malaria, which reduces people's overall resistance to other infections, as well as, or more than, by the availability and intake of types of food.

Another problem lies with the methods of measuring malnutrition themselves. Figures supplied by the regional nutritionist for the Highlands in July 1985 are based on the percentage of children aged 0–5 years who are less than 80% of the standard weight for their age. The Highlands Provinces range from a 28% level in Simbu to 37% in SHP, with WHP at 29%, and within WHP the Jimi area is singled out as having a high rate. Two points should be noted:

(1) Malnutrition needs to be measured for other categories and ages of the population. Children depend on the breast for up to three years after birth. If their mothers are poorly nourished and/or carry a load of sickness, this will affect the children. The mother's nutritional status should therefore be independently assessed.

(2) In the Jimi area as a whole there are populations which tend to be smaller than those in the Wahgi Valley, for example.

Genetic as well as environmental factors may be at work here. The relevance of the statistics depends greatly on the standard being used as the 100% baseline for assessment purposes.

The same paper by the regional nutritionist acknowledges that "malnutrition is due to a combination of factors, not a single factor." She lists "land shortage, poor soils, lack of cash income, lack of education, diseases, dirty water supply, lack of nutritious food." Equally, however, forms of development themselves can lead to land shortage, decline of soil fertility, waste of cash income, pollution of water supplies, substitution of junk foods for nutritious ones, and an influx of new diseases. Ecosystemic effects of development patterns should also be taken into account. Coffee—and, to a greater extent, tea—plantations use up land which could otherwise be used for a variety of subsistence crops. The important thing to guard against in this process is reduction in the numbers of food plants available to the average family. Some new vegetables of course are available, e.g., cabbages, broccoli, cauliflower, tomatoes, lettuce, capsicums, onions, peppers, zucchini, aubergines, and potatoes, and these can add a pleasant touch to the diet although it is mostly Europeans who buy them. They are often grown in high-altitude areas otherwise short of cash income. Pigs are also sold in the Hagen market.

IV. THE IMPACT OF DEVELOPMENT ON DISEASE PATTERNS

It is well known that the arrival of colonial powers in remote parts of the world brings new epidemic diseases. In the Highlands the worst effects of these were mitigated by the fact that contact was relatively recent and administrative services were set up fairly quickly. Epidemics of diseases such as smallpox and tuberculosis seem not to have occurred, but others did. Perhaps the best known and remembered in oral history is the outbreak of severe dysentery which occurred in Hagen during the 1940s when the war with Japan was being fought. Groups placed ritual barriers at the edges of their territories in an attempt to keep outsiders from entering and bringing the disease with them. This early phase is now too easily forgotten. But periodic outbreaks of new strains of influenza, brought in by travellers from the outside world (especially at the time of the biennial Hagen show), occur to remind us. There is regularly an increased death toll as a result of these, particularly of adolescents and elderly persons, who have not been exposed to the virus before or who are in general less able to resist infections.

Historical evidence also suggests that malaria has increased since colonial contact, probably through the introduction of human and mosquito carriers. In places such as the Wahgi and Nebilyer valleys, this is now a major problem for the future. Extensive settlement in the Wahgi Valley allows for the proximate co-existence of populations of people and mosquitoes, with consequent infection of the humans. The increase in incidence of falciparum malaria is disturbing in this regard. The valley has been drained and opened to former traditional owners, plantations, and settlers on blocks. The land is exceptionally fertile, but water supplies are bad and there are many breeding grounds for mosquito larvae.

The Health Department at Mount Hagen Hospital has kindly supplied me with some figures on disease patterns in the province. The figures for blood slide examination, 1980–1984, are given in Table 1. If one compares the figures only for the two prevalent types of malaria, falciparum and vivax, the pattern is clear: falciparum is relatively on the increase. Table 2 summarizes this (comparing and totalling only plasmodium falciparum and plasmodium vivax). The trend was strengthened in the first eleven months of 1985, for which figures are supplied: plasmodium falciparum (PF) 78%, plasmodium vivax (PV) 22%. As PF is a dangerous type of malaria requiring treatment with Fansidar, a restricted drug with con-

TABLE 1. Blood Slide Examinations by Year, 1980–1984, Mount Hagen Hospital

Year	No. of slides examined	Total positive	PF	PV	PM	Mixed
1980	27,685	6485	3,241	3,135	75	98
1981	28,561	5227	2,757	2,371	40	50
1982	23,100	6630	3,501	3,030	37	62
1983	31,256	7014	4,203	2,724	38	50
1984	21,604	5066	3,171	1,793	40	62

Source: Health Department Statistics
PF, Plasmodium falciparum; PV, plasmodium vivax.

TABLE 2. Percentage Incidence of PF and PV from Table 1

Year	PF	PV
1980	51	49
1981–1982	53	47
1983–1984	62	38

Note: PM (Plasmodium malariae) and mixed types of malaria have been omitted here.

siderable side effects, these figures give cause for concern. At Kuk, in the Waghi Valley, where there is a Department of Primary Industry Research Station and a tea plantation, the mosquito population seems clearly on the increase and serious cases of malaria are common. The information given by the Health Department indicates that "current policy is to reduce the incidence rate by initiating several control measures such as spraying operations, introducing of gumbusa fish which eat up larvae of mosquito to swamps, lakes, pools, etc." The effectiveness of this has not, however, been measured. From the monthly figures for January–November 1985 it is interesting to note that the greatest number of cases is reported not in the wet season as such but from April–August when the weather is relatively dry. This suggests that mosquitoes which carry PF breed in stagnant areas. Possibly, they bite more energetically at certain times. Specific information on this pattern would be welcome.

Malaria currently runs second to respiratory diseases (principally pneumonia) as a cause of morbidity and mortality in the Western Highlands Province according to the hospital figures. Respiratory disease affects all age groups, as does malaria. It is probably related to two factors: (1) the pattern of hot days and cold nights, from which chills can develop; and (2) smoky houses and cigarette smoking.

Rural house design has not changed greatly. Fires are needed at night to keep warm, and while the smoke helps to keep mosquitoes away it also makes people cough. As the WHP health report says: "Remedial measures almost nil except to treat those affected and give health education." Both of course are helpful steps, but what is needed is a study of a house design which could be introduced rurally and would provide warmth without being smoky.

Respiratory disease has probably been in the Highlands for a long time, but is likely to have increased with the movements of people in and out as a result of development. It is generally agreed, however, that venereal diseases are a new introduction, specifically correlated with the arrival of Europeans. Concern has been shown about these for at least the last fifteen years in Hagen. Prostitutes ride up and down with trucks on the highway to Lae and back. Visits to social night dances, to cinemas, and to towns in general widen the likelihood of sexual contact and therefore the spread of such diseases. Cures are, of course, available for those who go to hospital and have their conditions diagnosed. The most common long-term effect of gonorrhea and/or chlamydia is sterility. Most often, women do not know that they have such diseases and are suprised or even indignant when one is diagnosed, and are reluctant even then to accept that sterility is the outcome. Given the desire of both men and women to have children, sterility is certainly a curse which they might have been more careful to avoid were they better acquainted with the dangers of untreated and undiagnosed disease. The concept of infection is itself not very strongly established. There is a term for things which are transmissible or "catching" (*oklmba etem*), but although colds for example fall into this category, diarrhoea is thought not to do so. Sufferers from venereal diseases are commented on behind their backs but this is not always accompanied by vigorous attempts to get them to hospital. Certainly further health education for the masses is important in this connection. Given the potential entry of the Acquired Immune Deficiency Syndrome (AIDS) into PNG, the point does need to be emphasized.

So far in this section I have emphasized the negative effects of development on the incidence of malaria, respiratory disease, and venereal diseases. Naturally, this is only part of the picture. The advent of modern medicine and surgery obviously has made it possible to treat and cure many diseases which could not be handled by traditional medicine. At any rate, since the first epidemics of introduced diseases were controlled, it is clear that new health care has allowed an overall growth in population; certain conditions, such as yaws and types of leprosy, have been almost entirely cleared up (the treatment of yaws, however, laid open the way for syphilis); and whole ranges of internal illnesses can be treated by antibiotics and surgery whereas they would have in the past led to death. One disease which is difficult to combat, though, is cancer. Only seven deaths from it appear to be listed in the hospital statistics for 1983, but reports of it regularly reach the rural areas. It would be interesting to reconstruct from more detailed records whether it is on the increase and to investigate why (changes in diet and social conditions would be involved). Table 3 lists the official statistics on leading causes of mortality derived from WHP hospital reports for 1983. The source is computer printouts from the Health Statistics Section, issued 26 November 1984. I have modified the designations slightly. More detailed breakdowns by age and sex indicate that peak periods for the major killer, pneumonia, are the first four years of life (175/242) and over 44 years (43/242). For malaria, however, deaths are evenly spread. These figures show the same pattern for both sexes, but the absolute number of deaths for males is higher (131 as against 111 for females in the case of pneumonia). A summary is given in Table 4.

Statistics are lacking on the possible effects in the WHP of the introduction of betel-nut chewing, alcohol consumption, and the smoking of introduced cigarettes; or of possible chemical pollution of rural water supplies, as well as the effects of allowing pigs to eat urban refuse and garbage, as is done near Mount Hagen. (The pigs may become infected

TABLE 3. Mortality in WHP 1983 (from Hospital Records)

Condition	No. of cases
Pneumonia	242
Malaria	75
Perinatal conditions	54
Ill-defined intestinal conditions	50
Meningitis	44
Anemia	32
Ill-defined conditions	22
Respiratory problems	16
Septicaemia	14
Heart disease	11
Pig bel	10
Malnutrition	10
Viruses	9
Traffic accidents	9
Childbirth	8
Malignant neoplasms	7
Other digestive disorders	7
Measles	5
Influenza	4
Chronic pulmonary diseases	4
Others	63
	696

Source: Health Department Statistics, based on records from the hospital and health centres. Note that such figures must be interpreted with caution. There is no real "total" against which to measure the incidence of these causes of mortality. I refer therefore only to the most obviously salient conditions, pneumonia and malaria.

TABLE 4. Mortality from Pneumonia and Malaria by Age and Sex, WHP, 1983

(1) Pneumonia

	Age			
Sex	1–4 years	5–14	15–44	44+
Female	78	3	8	22
Male	98	3	9	21

(b) Malaria

	Age			
Sex	1–4 years	5–14	15–44	44+
Female	9	6	17	5
Male	9	4	14	11

Source: Same as Table 3.

with worms which then pass into people when the pork is eaten.) All of these matters do, however, pose potentially serious problems. One may perhaps single out alcohol consumption, which is entirely of an introduced nature. Highlands males practise drinking to get drunk, and as often as not boast or fight with other males or beat their wives. Traffic accidents, rapes, murders, thefts, and strained inter-group relations can all partly be traced back to the fact that one of the parties involved was a drunk male. I have dealt with the cultural elaborations of this syndrome elsewhere (Strathern, 1982), so I merely note here that this is most certainly a deleterious result of development, and little can be done about it other than restricting the numbers of outlets for the sale of alcohol, something which the WHP provincial government is rather belatedly doing.

Betel-nut chewing may or may not have long-term health consequences. Lime in the chewed mixture can lead to mouth cancer. The habit has spread very rapidly and widely in the province among adults of both sexes and is now firmly established. Cigarette smoking has a traditional background. Whether introduced smoking is more or less dangerous than the traditional leaf is unknown, but the habit is entrenched. Only fundamentalist Christian churches forbid these activities. It is possible, then, to combat detrimental effects of development with ideas derived from another sphere of acculturation.

One final point may be mentioned in this section. Mental health is almost entirely uninvestigated in WHP (one young research worker from Auckland University is beginning a study in Tambul). Mount Hagen town has a number of well-known characters who dress, speak, and eat in an odd manner, and who advertise themselves in the town itself by walking about in rags, picking from the litter tins, orating in front of government offices, directing traffic while eyeing women, pushing at people in the street or market, or removing layers of clothing. It is plausible to suggest that these behaviour patterns may be a result of acculturative stress. The people themselves relate them all to specific curses, forms of wrong-doing, or intra-family conflict having repercussions on the supernatural plane. In this connection one should also mention another phenomenon which is rapidly increasing in the Western Highlands, that is, the consumption of marijuana. This plant is being grown in people's gardens and is now becoming a feature of "social night" dances, being particularly popular, of course, with younger people. It is reported to induce hilarity and mild hallucinations. Sometimes it is distributed for sale at traditional dances and ceremonies. It is said to be grown by settlers at Kindeng in the Wahgi Valley and by people from the Tambul and Chimbu areas. Europeans are sometimes approached and asked if they want it. Indications are that marijuana is on the way to becoming a new kind of cash crop in the province. Its cultivation and use are, however, illegal. Its likely effects on health should become a part of any government health education programme in the future.

V. THE INTRODUCED HEALTH CARE SYSTEM

Here information obtained from the Health Department on this topic is presented, followed by some personal observations and suggestions.

The health care system consists of three levels: hospitals, health care centres, and aid posts. There are about 115 aid posts, each staffed by a single orderly, who has had two years basic training in health care. Table 5 summarizes the distribution of facilities at the three levels. The figures indicate that while the hospital and aid posts are almost entirely government-run, at the intermediate level the churches play an important role. Indeed, to the people themselves church health centres are simply "hospitals" on a par with, or even preferred to, Hagen Hospital. The churches also run ante- and post-natal services for mothers and children, including immunization, and receive government subsidies.

The Health Department itself runs specialist services associated with the hospital, e.g., dental services, disease control, nutrition, malaria, and

TABLE 5. Health Facilities, WHP, 1985

Type of facility	Govt.	Church	Total	Pop. served
Hospital	1		1	77,169
Health centres	7	4	11	
Health sub-centres	2	5	7	217,338
Aid posts	112	3	115	
Totals	122	12	134	294,507

venereal diseases. The hospital authorities recognize that although the system is comprehensive and runs fairly well, there are still many operational difficulties and also areas where research is needed (some of the latter have already been indicated). They list staff development and training, family health services, malaria research, environmental health, communicable diseases, and health education as priority areas, *inter alia*. But the biggest general problems seem to exist at the top and bottom levels of the system. At the bottom there is insufficient surveillance of what aid post orderlies do. While some faithfully carry out their duties, others do not and they seem to get away with this. At the top level we may quote what the hospital authorities themselves say: "The Mount Hagen Hospital is one of the busiest hospitals in the country, therefore increase in workload and overcrowding is a problem now. Staff shortage is also a problem.* Upgrading of this hospital to a base hospital standard is a must in the near future."

My own observations certainly support this plea. Both hospital beds and the outpatient areas are greatly under pressure. People come to the hospital from the Enga and Southern Highlands provinces as well, while the doctors at Hagen must also visit other hospitals from time to time. Table 6 indicates the increase in pressure on the hospital's facilities since 1981. Some, but not much, of this pressure is relieved by the service offered by private doctors in Mount Hagen, but most people go to the hospital because its public facilities are much cheaper than visiting a private doctor; nevertheless, concerned kinsfolk do often pay the up to K20 (twenty kina) fee per visit to the doctor in order to gain the extra attention which can be obtained.

Upgrading of the hospital to base standard could cost up to K4 million, but it would be well worth it in order to create full confidence in the province's health system. Similarly, at the bottom level, retraining and good supervision of aid post orderlies would have a similar salutary effect.

VI. SUMMARY OF FINDINGS AND PRACTICAL SUGGESTIONS

This paper has been divided into four sections:
(1) traditional and introduced medicine;
(2) the impact of development on diet;
(3) the impact of development on disease patterns; and
(4) the introduced health care system.

Under (1) I suggested that there is a need to do research on the plant remedies used in traditional medicine and consider how these may be re-

* This may be related to Mount Hagen's unfavourable reputation with respect to crime, another effect of development; this situation has improved during 1985, however.

TABLE 6. Selected Statistics on Mount Hagen Hospital, 1984

(a) Admissions

Year	Total admissions	Total outpatients
1981	9,679	152,390
1982	9,561	140,895
1983	10,136	177,359
1984	10,665	179,300

(b) General Surgical Ward

	Adults and children (Public)	Intermediate
1981	1,806	449
1982	1,914	485
1983	1,893	438
1984	2,185	556

(c) Obstetric Figures

	Total figures
1981	1,522
1982	1,582
1983	1,713
1984	1,966

Simplified from Health Department Statistics.
Intermediate = paying ward. The vast majority of patients are cared for in the public wards.

cultivated or reintegrated with introduced medicines. The contribution of traditional rituals and Christian prayers to the overall healing process should not be ignored.

Under (2) I noted the need for much more research information on malnutrition patterns for all ages and on the effects of changes in diet. Although infant malnutrition is officially linked to lack of development, the overall picture is by no means so clear-cut. Development brings problems with it, particularly in the high consumption of fats and sugars by adults.

This is shown even more clearly in (3), where patterns of malaria, pneumonia, and venereal disease were linked at least partially to the effects of development. Health education and health extension work are badly needed to counteract these processes. More detailed research on the incidence of malaria would also be helpful. Healthy house designs for the Highlands need to be developed.

In (4) the major need pointed to is the urgent upgrading of the Mount Hagen Hospital.

To these points, all of which emerge based on hospital and government statistics, another viewpoint can be added, and that is that in future any plans for further development of the province should take into account and budget for the likely health implications, and the needs for new health facilities. For this to happen effectively there must be coordination between the relevant departments of the government itself. To give an example, alteration of terrain often gives new scope for insects to breed, as at Kuk when large drainage channels were dug to reclaim fertile land from swamp conditions. These channels form good breeding grounds for mosquitoes, and hence increase the likelihood of malaria in an area which now badly needs its own health centre to cope with the prbolem. The people themselves are well aware of this need and are busy collecting money as a contribution towards the costs involved. Although they feel that in general they are better off now than before contact with regard to health, they do also know that certain diseases, notably venereal disease, came with the white men, while others, like malaria, have become more prevalent.

VII. COMPARISON OF FINDINGS WITH OTHER STUDIES

A useful general article covering much of the same ground I have traversed here, but worldwide in focus, is by R. Wirsing (1985), entitled "The health of traditional societies and the effects of acculturation." Wirsing points out that in small-scale, traditional societies prior to Western contact people's health was protected by

(1) their isolation;
(2) their good knowledge of the environment and how to use its biota;
(3) subsistence practices that do not reduce ecological complexity; and
(4) practice of birth control.

It is obvious that development may decisively upset all of these factors. Some viruses, for example, such as that for measles, are less likely to survive in a small population, but when the virus can be re-introduced regularly from outside this advantage is lost and the small population becomes vulnerable. Other diseases, however, such as tuberculosis, syphilis, malaria, and pneumonia are all capable of persisting in small populations. While development may increase the incidence of these, it also brings with it some access to medicines which can cure them. After an initial period of susceptibility in which population may drop, the availability of modern medicine plus the arrival of pacification usually leads to a population upsurge. This has also probably occurred in the WHP.

It is in the field of diet that untoward long-term consequences of development must be carefully monitored. Wirsing notes that in the traditional societies diseases which are low in incidence are heart trouble, cancer, tooth decay, and diabetes mellitus. Their diets are good because of their low fat, high fibre, high mineral, and low sodium contents. Removal of this balance can lead to obesity, high blood pressure, and heart disease, as well as diabetes. This last is apparently because of a "thrifty genotype" by which the body is enabled to store food consumed in times of plenty against times when it is scarce (perhaps this is especially true for females)—the so-called "feast and famine" syndrome. When too much, and inappropriate, food is available, type 2 noninsulin-dependent diabetes mellitus can result. Another danger results from discontinuing the use of spring water containing iodine and replacing it with non-iodized salt as a condiment for food. This was done in the Jimi Valley of WHP and resulted in an increase in levels of endemic goitre. Wirsing also notes that the traditional diets in the New Guinea Highlands were almost entirely vegetarian, with only small regular intakes of protein, well below the daily allowance stipulated in health charts, yet Highlanders were strong and healthy on the whole. This shows that populations can develop their own metabolic methods of maintaining health. The finding underlines the point that metabolism and diet balance may be upset through acculturation. In WHP the positive result of improving protein consumption and health services seems to be increased patterns of overall individual growth (children taller and heavier than their parents and earlier sexual maturity, especially for girls), but this should not conceal the possible longer-term deleterious effects of diet change.

Wirsing summarizes the damaging effects of acculturation under the following headings:

(1) introduction of new diseases;

(2) population decline or per contra uncontrolled population increase;

(3) deterioration of lifestyle and hygiene conditions when more people live closely together; for example, fecal-oral transmission of infections and soil-transmitted helminths all spread more easily;

(4) paid work and consumption of junk foods (this is certainly true of Hagen, where such food is sold in great quantities);

(5) loss of cultivation of a range of plants when cash crops are introduced (this is not serious in WHP, where good vegetables are regularly grown for sale in the market);

(6) alterations in the environment, which allow diseases to proliferate; and

(7) disturbance of nutritional adjustment (as discussed already in relation to diabetes).

These factors could, and should, be used as a checklist against which to evaluate the effects of existing and future development on health patterns in the province and in Papua New Guinea as a whole.

Acknowledgments

For the preparation of these data and views I am greatly indebted to the WHP Minister for Health, Mr. Kar Kil; the Assistant Secretary for Health, Mr. Peter Eapaea; Mrs. Poisy Eapaea, Provincial Nutritionist; and especially to Mr. Kelly Kewa, Provincial Disease Control Officer; M.K. Gandi, Provincial Health Inspector; and Masakai Sikulaum, Provincial Malaria Supervisor. Mr. Kewa kindly compiled information from his colleagues and from departmental files and made them available to me in a consolidated form for perusal. Mrs. Susan Bonnel, Provincial Planner, Western Highlands Province, also gave kind assistance.

REFERENCES

Strathern, A.J. (1982). The scraping gift: Alcohol consumption in Mount Hagen. In M. Marshall (ed.), *Through a Glass Darkly*. Port Moresby: pp. 139–154.

Strathern, A.J. (1984). Health care and medical pluralism. *Bikmaus* 5 (1): 84–89.

Strathern, A.J. (1985). Digging out causes. Health care in Mount Hagen. In W.G. Jilek (ed.), *Traditional Medicine and Primary Health Care in PNG*. WHO, pp. 26–32.

Strathern, A.J. (1986). Health care and medical pluralism: Cases from Mount Hagen. In S. Frankel (ed.), D.Reidel (in press)

Wirsing, R. (1985). The health of traditional societies and the effects of acculturation. *Current Anthropol.*, **26** (3): 303–332.

Complex of Environment, Activity, and Health in Indonesian *Kampungs*

Shosuke SUZUKI

Department of Public Health, Gunma University School of Medicine, Maebashi, Japan

I. INTRODUCTION

The view that everything is connected with everything is a central tenet of ecology. Similarly, health, in an individual or a population, is an interconnected phenomenon, which has to be analyzed in the context of man's environment, activity, food consumption patterns, social organization, spiritual life, health services, and so on. This paper presents four examples of ill health in *kampung*s in rural Indonesia, and attempts to identify the set of cause and effect relationships contributing to these states of ill health.

Health, in this context, can be considered as occupying a "niche" in the human ecosystem of a specific time and place. In Indonesia, the ecosystem is essentially an agricultural one, in which village groups operate at a level of economic self-sufficiency, although many areas are moving toward a cash economy in an attempt to raise living standards. It is hoped that this kind of human ecological approach to health problems will also be useful in formulating programs for the primary health care movement being sponsored by the World Health Organization (WHO, 1978, 1983; Mahler, 1985).

The research in Indonesia was undertaken with the focus on the man-environmental system (Suzuki, 1985a), with man in this case being a population of several tens to a few hundred people constituting the rural community referred to as a *kampung*. *Kampung* society provides a social organization covering family and kinship ties, the institutions and actual practice of Islam, rituals and customs related to marriage, birth, and death, and other cultural aspects of human life.

The environment in which *kampung* residents live can be divided into two types: the natural and the manmade. The natural environment here is a tropical climate with its particular vegetation, soil, and water types. The manmade environment includes the rice fields, irrigation canals, fish ponds, *pekarangan* (home gardens), and others created and maintained through human labour.

As they go about their daily activities, the villagers both affect and are affected by their environment. Their health depends on the food they eat, their working and living conditions, and their social and cultural responses to the environment.

II. *KAMPUNG*s SURVEYED

Eight *kampung*s were surveyed for this report (Tables 1 and 4 and Fig. 1): Salamungkal, Pasirparahu, Brumbung, Sukoharjo, Desa Kintap, Pelaihari, and Bloks A and C. Bloks A and C, in South Kalimantan, is a transmigration area settled by peasants from Java. Sukoharjo is not actually a village *kampung*, but a town which serves as the capital of the Sukoharjo Regency, Central Java; the fathers of schoolchildren surveyed for our research tend to be government officials and merchants rather than agricultural workers (Hattori *et al.*, 1985).

III. METHODOLOGY

In order to identify the cause-and-effect relationships determining human ill health, the author stayed in a villager's home in each of the five *kampung*s surveyed. Household surveys provided information on demography, housing, land ownership, morbidity and mortality, and the kinds of health care resorted to in times of illness. The four health problems on which this paper focuses are acute conjunctivitis or eye inflammation (Suzuki, 1983a), ascaris and hookworm infestation (Suzuki, 1983b, 1985b), malaria (Suzuki *et al.*, 1985), and retarded child growth (Hattori *et al.*, 1985). Levels of ill-health were assessed by history-taking and eye examinations, parasite egg detection in faeces, blood smear tests and fluorescent antibody tests, and anthropometric measurements, respectively.

IV. RESULTS

1. Conjunctivitis

At *Kampung* Pasirparahu, the author was visited by many men suffering from acute conjunctivitis, contracted by mud splashing into their eyes as they hoed the wet rice fields. The incidence of conjunctivitis in three of

TABLE 1. Some Physiographic and Social Characteristics of the Area Surveyed

Kampung or Community *Desa* or Village *Kecamatan* or Subdistrict *Kabupaten* or Regency *Propinsi* or State	Pasirparahu Selajambe Ciranjang Cianjur West Java	Salamungkal Cigentur Paseh Bandung West Java	Brumbung Dukuh Sukoharjo Sukoharjo Central Java	Sukoharjo Sukoharjo (town) Sukoharjo Sukoharjo Central Java	Blok A & C Sebamban Lima Kintap Tanah Laut Kalimantan Selatan
Latitude	7°s	7°s	7°s	7°s	4°s
Altitude, m	260	900	90	90	40
Geological feature	Undifferentiated volcanic products		Alluvium, Holocene		Old alluvial region
Soil type	Grumsol from sedimentation of old cray	Latosol & Andosol from igneous rock in mountainous area	Alluvial flood plain of Solo River		Weathered siliceous shales and sandstones
Geography	Incline plain of Mt. Gede (2,962 m), Gradient less than 1°	Halfway up Mt. Salasih (1,944 m), Gradient 6° to 9°	Flood plain of Solo River, Practically no gradient		On a gentle hill near Java Sea, Practically no gradient
Major language of daily use	Sundanese	Sundanese	Javanese	Javanese	Javanese, Indonesian & Sundanese
Non-Islamic people, %	0	0	2 to 3	4 to 5	1 to 2
Primary school education, %	85	85	92	97	94
Population density, /km²	1,140	1,264	1,044	2,157	22
Fertility of the land	Very fertile	Very fertile	Very fertile	Very fertile	Very poor
Farmers and labourers, %	95	95	95	21	100

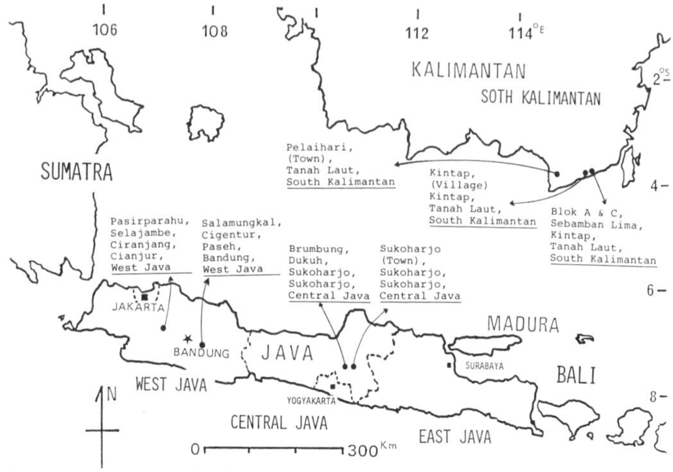

Fig. 1. Location where the health survey was carried out. From top to bottom, name of: *kampung* or community, *desa* or village, *kecamatan* or sub-district, *kabupaten* or regency, and *propinsi* or province.

TABLE 2. Incidence Rate of Conjunctivitis (Household Interview Survey)

Name of village	Brumbung, Dukuh	Salamungkal, Cigentur	Pasirparahu, Selajambe
Number of persons surveyed	475	427	330
Number having conjunctivitis in the last 15 days	0	5	14
Incidence rate of conjunctivitis for 15 days per 1,000 persons	0	11	42

Source: Suzuki, 1983.

the surveyed *kampung*s is shown in Table 2. Pasirparahu had the highest incidence, due to the fine, sticky soil in the region, which means that while working in the wet rice fields a full-strength swing of a hoe is needed to break up the soil. Conjunctivitis results when mud and soil particles enter and irritate the eyes during hoeing of the rice fields, and the Pasirparahu villagers see it as an occasionally unavoidable work hazard (Fig. 2). They were reluctant to accept recommendations that plastic glasses be worn while hoeing the wet rice fields. The other two *kampung*s surveyed have different soil types (Table 1), which seldom splash while being hoed, and thus the environment contributes less to the incidence of this disease.

A few days' rest at home is usually sufficient for recovery from acute conjunctivitis. However, one out of ten cases leads to varying degrees of permanent visual disability (Table 3).

CONJUNCTIVITIS

Soil type: fine clay

↓

Hoe the wet soil by hand

↓

Mud splashes into eye

↓ ←— Unwilling to wear glasses

Injured conjunctivae

↓ ←— Massage with hand
←— Wash with dirty water

Conjunctivitis or get into inflammation

↓

Recovery with nubecula and decreased visual acuity

FIG. 2. Cause-effect relationship of acute conjunctivitis observed among wet rice field cultivators at Kampung Pasirparahu, Cianjur, West Java.

TABLE 3. Visual Acuity of the Villagers Aged 10 Years Old or More, by Sex, *Kampung*, and the Three Classes of Visual Acuity; Number of the Examined Eyes and the Percentage in Parentheses

	Men				Women			
Visual acuity	1.0– 0.7	0.6– 0.3	0.2– 0	Total	1.0– 0.7	0.6– 0.3	0.2– 0	Total
Brumbung	47	10	7	64	173	30	5	208
	(73.4)	(15.6)	(10.9)	(100.0)	(83.2)	(14.4)	(2.4)	(100.0
Salamungkal	84	5	3	92	114	36	8	158
	(91.3)	(5.4)	(3.3)	(100.0)	(72.2)	(22.8)	(5.1)	(100.0)
Pasirparahu	115	23	10	148	74	6	0	80
	(77.7)	(15.5)	(6.8)	(100.0)	(92.5)	(7.5)	(0.0)	(100.0)
Total	246	38	20	304	361	72	13	446
	(80.9)	(12.5)	(6.6)	(100.0)	(80.9)	(16.1)	(2.9)	(100.0)

Source: Suzuki, 1983.

2. *Ascaris and Hookworm Infestations*

Ascariasis and hookworm infestations were surveyed in the *kampungs* of Pasirparahu, Salamungkal, and Brumbung. Faeces samples were examined for parasite egg contents under a light microcrope, although nearly half of the inhabitants were too shy to submit fecal samples to the author, who was a guest in the *kampung*.

In the two West Java *kampung*s of Pasirparahu and Salamungkal *Ascaris lumbricoides* was found in 61.8% and 52.6% of the faeces samples collected, respectively, while Brumbung in Central Java had a relatively low infestation rate of 15.5%. Hookworm infestation was highest (57.9%) in Salamungkal in the mountains of West Java; and that in the other *kampung*s was very low (Fig. 3) (Suzuki, 1983b, 1985b).

The reason for the high parasite rate in West Java is the use of fish ponds as lavatories. Fish ponds form an indispensable part of the Sundanese agricultural ecosystem, being used for human excreta and kitchen waste treatment, fertilizer, irrigation, as an occasional source of animal protein, and in rituals. A few wealthy individuals keep fish for sale. In *Kampung* Salamungkal the average household's fish pond occupies 41 square metres, while the average household dwelling space is 34 sq. m (Suzuki, 1984). Parasite eggs in faeces are partially digested by the fish in the ponds, although some of the eggs flow along with irrigation water down to paddy rice fields and this water is then later re-used by downstream inhabitants (Figs. 4 and 5).

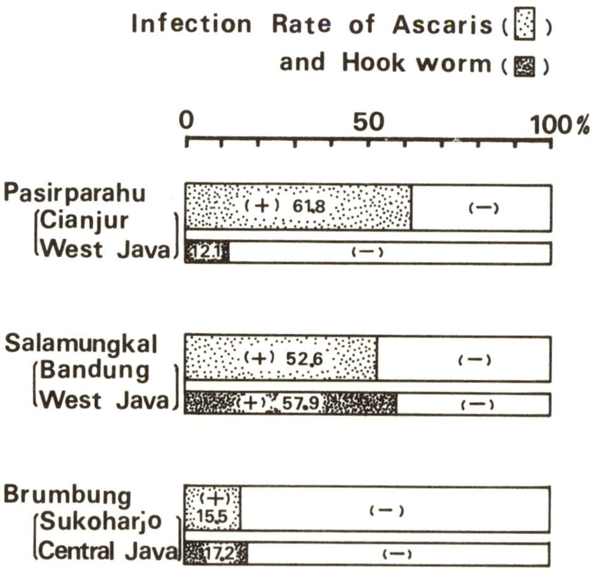

FIG. 3. Ascaris and hookworm infestation of villagers of the three *kampungs*, Pasirparahu, Salamungkal, and Brumbung. Location and characteristics of the *kampung*s are presented in Fig. 1 and Table 1 (Suzuki and Koyama, 1984; Suzuki, 1985b).

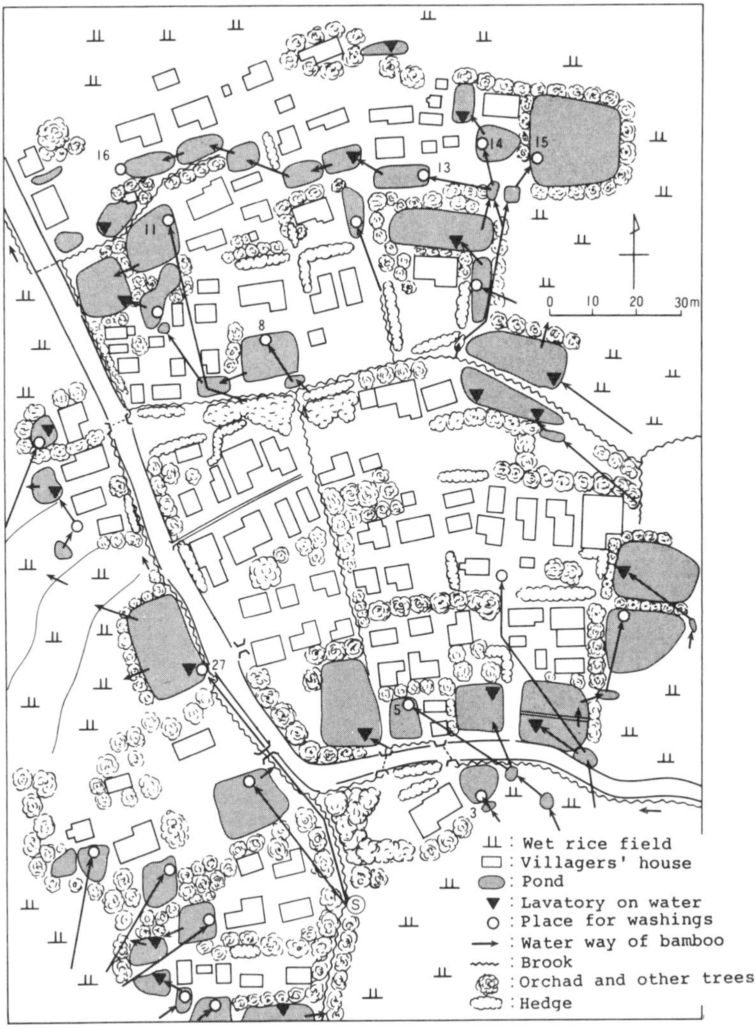

FIG. 4. Map of Kampung Salamungkal, Cigentur, Paseh, Bandung. Downslope from south to north with 6° to 9° gradient. Notice the water flow from rice fields to fish ponds, and the lavatory on the fishpond. Water is used repeatedly. Fishpond area is 41 m^2 per household on average. This map was made by T. Igarashi and revised by the author (1984).

In contrast, the ethnic Javanese inhabitants of Brumbung, Central Java, use concrete-sealed earthen latrines that do not pollute the surrounding soil or surface water. Latrine improvement programs as recommended

PARASITOSIS: ASCARIS AND HOOKWORM

WEST JAVA	CENTRAL JAVA
Traditional inland fishery	No tradition of inland fishery
↓	↓
Lavatory on fishpond	Green revolution and flood control
↓	↓
Digestion of human excreta by fishes and pond water	Increased income, higher education
↓	↓
Parasite eggs flow down to be used for home water and for irrigation	Village development program including separate and earthpit lavatory
↓	↓
High parasite infection	Decreased parasite infection

FIG. 5. Cause-effect relationship of parasitosis: ascaris and hookworm infection compared between *kampungs* of West and Central Java.

periodically by the municipal health authorities are easily accepted by *Kampung* Brumbung residents, who are better educated and freer of religious traditions than the West Java residents. This, coupled with the fact that the Javanese agricultural pattern places little importance on fish culture, has contributed to a low incidence of parasitosis here.

3. Malaria in Inmigration Districts

Malaria has been almost completely eradicated in Java. However, our malaria survey (Bakir Abisudjak *et al.*, 1985) in south Kalimantan showed that malaria is still a problem in areas with large numbers of inmigrants from Java.

The districts surveyed, Bloks A and C, Tanah Laut Regency, South Kalimantan, are inmigrated by Javanese (152/285 or 53.9%), Sundanese (29.8%), and Madurase (8.1%). The people of Bloks A and C inmigrated 3.4 and 1.8 months, respectively, before our survey team arrived early in 1984.

Malaria parasite rates in men aged 16 to 49 years old in Bloks A and C amounted to 28.1% and 13.9%, respectively, while those in women, children and old people were 0.0% (Table 4). This distribution is due to the fact that men aged 16 to 49 years often stay for two to three weeks in the forest some 70 km from Bloks A and C to collect perfume wood (*Aquillaria Malaccencis*) for sale, and those from Desa Kintap do the same traditionally to cut trees (*Eusideroxylon zwageri* T. & B.) used for roofing (Koyama and Suzuki, 1985; Suzuki *et al.*, 1985). During these extended stays in the forest they are infected by the malarial parasite *Plasmodium falciparum* via the *Anopheles balbacencis* mosquito.

The malaria fluorescent antibody-positive rate is higher among the inhabitants of Desa Kintap, Kintap Subdistrict, in which Bloks A and C are located, than among any of the other areas surveyed (Table 5) (Suzuki *et al.*, 1985). As the malaria antibody in serum lasts at least several months, a positive result is evidence of past infections. Diffuse distribution of the positive rate to all sex and age groups shows past prevalence of malaria in Desa Kintap. In Pelaihari, the capital of Tanah Laut Regency, malaria seems not currently endemic any more (Table 5).

Eradication of malaria in the transmigration district of South Kalimantan is rendered difficult by the fact that only one-third of adults in Bloks A and C are aware that the disease is transmitted by mosquitoes; as migrants from malaria-free Java, they are unfamiliar with the disease and the preventive measures against it (Fig. 6). Ideally, anti-malarial drugs should be taken before an extended stay in the forest, but as there is currently only one health officer of the transmigration service organization making weekly visits to each block of 500 persons, this is not possible.

One positive result of the malaria survey (Bakir Abisudjak *et al.*, 1985) was the finding that even without blood smear tests, health workers can

TABLE 4. Parasite Rate of Inhabitants, by Age, Sex, and Locality in South Kalimantan

Village	Age and Sex							
	0–15		16–49		50–		Total	
	M	F	M	F	M	F	M	F
Sebamban L.	0*/13**	0/14	18/64	0/46	0/9	0/3	18/86	0/63
Blok A	0***	0	28.1	0	0	0	20.9	0
Sebamban L.	0/13	0/6	5/36	0/55	0/6	0/2	5/55	0/63
Blok C	0	0	13.9	0	0	0	9.1	0
Desa Kintap	0/38	0/26	3/22	1/19	0/19	0/7	0/45	1/52
	0	0	13.6	5.3	0	0	0	1.9
Pelaihari	0/10	0/0	0/27	0/20	0/8	0/12	0/45	0/32
	0	–	0	0	0	0	0	0
Total	0/74	0/46	26/149	1/140	0/42	0/24	26/265	1/210
	0	0	17.4	0.7	0	0	9.8	0.5

* No. positive cases. ** No. examined cases. *** Parasite rate in %.
Source: Suzuki *et al.*, 1985.

TABLE 5. Fluorescent Antibody-Positive Rates of Inhabitants, according to Age, Sex and Locality in South Kalimantan

Village	Age and Sex							
	0–15		16–49		50–		Total	
	M	F	M	F	M	F	M	F
Sebamban L.	0*/14**	0/20	31/64	1/50	3/10	0/3	34/88	1/74
Blok A	0***	6	48.4	2.0	30.0	0	38.6	1.4
Sebamban L.	0/16	0/6	10/38	4/56	2/6	0/2	12/60	4/64
Blok C	0	0	26.3	7.1	33.3	0	20.0	6.3
Desa Kintap	4/38	1/31	14/22	3/20	11/19	3/7	29/79	7/58
	10.5	3.2	63.6	15.0	57.9	42.9	36.7	12.1
Pelaihari	0/19	0/3	5/31	2/27	1/9	3/13	6/59	5/43
	0	0	16.1	7.4	11.1	23.1	10.2	11.1
Total	4/87	1/60	60/155	10/153	21/44	6/25	85/286	16/238
	4.6	1.7	38.7	6.5	47.7	24.0	29.7	6.7

* No. positive cases. ** No. examined cases. *** Antibody positve rate in %.
Source: Suzuki *et al.*, 1985.

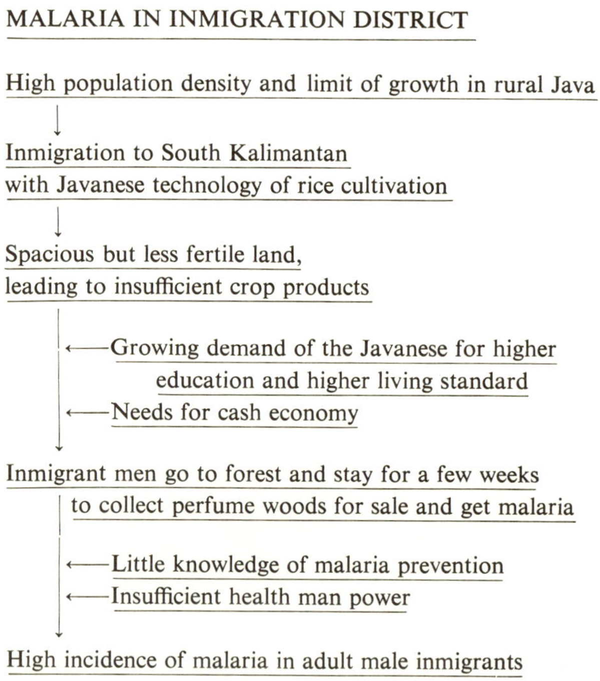

FIG. 6. Cause-effect relationship of malaria in a migration district Blok A & C, Kintap, Tanah Laut, South Kalimantan.

estimate with 75% sensitivity the incidence rate in a community simply by taking oral histories from the villagers.

4. *Retarded Growth of* Kampung *Children*

The average adult height of Sundanese and Javanese villagers is 5–10% less than the Japanese average adult height (Suzuki, 1983b, 1985b), although it is not known whether this difference is mainly of genetic or environmental in origin. Environmental factors, especially nutrition, certainly account for some of this difference (Tibault *et al.*, 1985), since the average Japanese height increased by approximately 10 centimetres between 1932 and 1982 during Japan's so-called modernization period (Figs. 7 and 8).

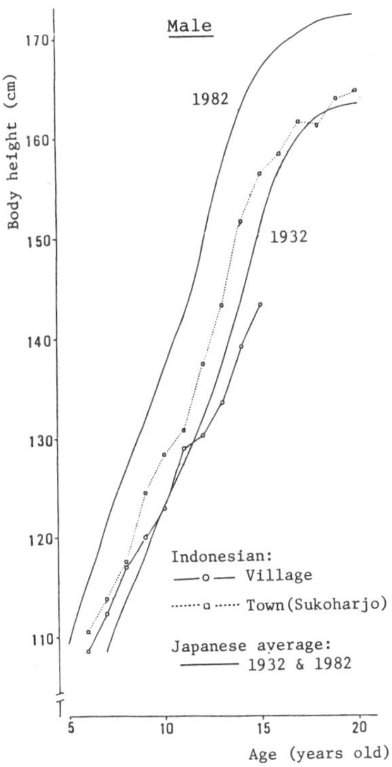

FIG. 7. Growth curve of body height of Indonesian villagers in the vicinity of Sukoharjo Town, Central Java, inhabitants of Sukoharjo Town, and Japanese average for the years 1932–1982 (males only). Differences in the growth curve between village and town inhabitant groups is distinct: growth of the former seems retarded (Hattori *et al.*, 1985).

The underlying factors causing retarded growth can perhaps be ascertained more clearly by comparing heights between rural and urban Indonesian populations. Hattori *et al.* (1985) compared the mean heights of school children in Dukuh Village, Sukoharjo Subdistrict, Central Java (the rural population) with those in the capital town of Sukoharjo, Sukoharjo Regency, Central Java (urban). The information used in the comparison came from primary, junior high, and high school records, which were checked to ensure that the measuring equipment used was accurate and that the day of measurement was recorded in order to calculate the exact ages of the children.

As can be seen from Figs. 7 and 8, the mean height of urban school children of both sexes is approximately equal to that of Japanese school children between 1932 and 1982, while rural Indonesian children are shorter, especially after the age of 8 or 9 years. The growth curve of rural Indonesian children up to age 9 nearly parallels that of Japanese children in 1932, while that after 9 years of age can be referred to as growth retardation.

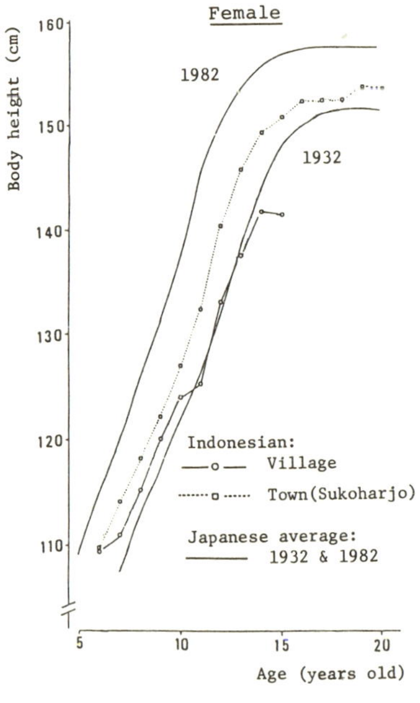

FIG. 8. Growth curve of body height of Indonesian villagers in the vicinity of Sukoharjo Town, Central Java, inhabitants of Sukoharjo Town, and Japanese average for the years 1932–1982 (females only). Difference is distinct in the growth curve between village and town inhabitants, and growth of the former seems retarded (Hattori *et al.*, 1985).

TABLE 6. Age of Adolescent Growth Spurt

		Village	Town (Sukoharjo)	Japan 1932	Japan 1982
Body Height	Male	15.6	12.6	15.0	12.4
	Female	11.8	11.5	13.1	10.8
Body Weight	Male	15.7	13.9	15.2	12.2
	Female	15.4	11.6	13.5	10.9

Source: Hattori *et al.*, 1985.

The adolescent growth spurt calculated by age is shown in Table 6, which shows that urban Javanese experience this spurt at nearly the same age as did Japanese children in 1982. These figures indicate that the maximum mean body height has nearly been attained in Sukoharjo town, Central Java. It seems that rural Javanese children have not yet experienced this growth spurt acceleration, although the sample size was too small for reliable estimates.

The results of a nutritional survey carried out in Central Java (Baily, 1961; Igarashi, 1984) have shown that the animal protein intake is estimated at between 4.6 and 3.9 grammes per day, corresponding to the Japanese level of between 7.3 and 6.8 g per day in 1931 to 1935 (Hattori *et al.*, 1985; Kouchi, 1983). Severe cases of malnutrition are rarely seen in Javanese and Sundanese villages (Igarashi, 1984), although a few cases of adult beri-beri do occur. Neither is parasite infection nor diarrhoea thought to be a major contributing factor to retarded growth among rural Javanese children, because they were never endemic to this area (Fig. 9) (Suzuki and Koyama, 1984), in sharp contrast to the situation in West Java (Suzuki and Koyama, 1984), Papua New Guinea (Suzuki *et al.*, 1984), and Bangladesh (Black, 1982). However, the prevalence of dermatitis in Javanese children may point to potential hyponutrition in some village populations (Suzuki and Koyama, 1984).

V. SUGGESTIONS FOR IMPROVEMENTS IN HEALTH STATUS

The four types of ill health focused on in this paper, conjunctivitis, parasitosis, malaria, and retarded child growth, are caused by environmental and human activity factors. They could be reduced in incidence, if not eradicated completely, by a series of rather simple measures.

Social education on the causes of conjunctivitis could lead to the wearing of protective glasses while at work in wet rice fields. As fish ponds are extremely important in agriculture in West Java, and as villagers are uninformed about separate sewage and latrine systems, it is suggested that small water reservoirs be constructed to receive water discharged from the

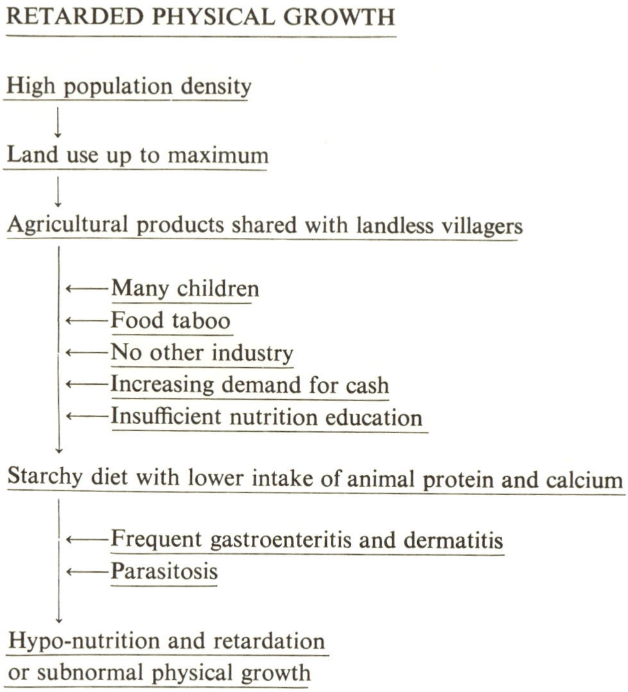

FIG. 9. Cause-effect relationship of insufficient physical growth of village children.

ponds. After the water has been stored in these reservoirs for a certain period, the parasite eggs will die and the water can then be re-used safely for other purposes, such as irrigation. Malaria can be prevented by taking anti-malarial drugs before men go into the forests to collect wood, provided people are educated about the causes of the disease and the health service system becomes established. Least serious medically is the retarded child growth seen in rural areas of Indonesia. The recommendation here is to concentrate on improving nutrition so as to cure and prevent skin lesions. Better nutrition will lead to gradual improvement of growth rates.

As Edmundson (1986) noted, "There is no single set of solutions to the problems of development." The health status of a rural community is specific to that community, and thus the set of actions taken to improve health should be specific to that community. The most important single action regarding health improvement in rural Indonesia is to consciously extend the chance for education to all villagers.

Acknowledgements

The article is based on two research projects collaborated with Professor Otto Soemarwoto, Director of Institute of Ecology, Padjadjaran University, Bandung, Indonesia, carried out in 1978 to 1974, under financial supports by Nissan Science Foundation (#781009), and the Ministry of Education, Science and Culture, Japan (#58041014 & #5904301). The author is grateful to the two organizations; Indonesian Institute of Sciences (LIPI); Ministry of Education of Indonesia; Associate Professor Tadataka Igarashi at the Centre for South East Asian Studies, Kyoto University, Japan: the other team members of the research project; and finally Indonesian villagers.

REFERENCES

Baily, K.V. (1961). Rural nutrition studies in Indonesia, I: Background to nutritional problems in the cassava areas. *Tropical and Geographical Medicine*, **13**: 216–233.

Bakir Abisudjak, H. Koyama, R. Kosugi, and S. Suzuki (1985). Field survey of malaria at South Kalimantan, Indonesia; Applicability and validity of inhabitants' malaria history to primary health care. In: S. Suzuki and Otto Soemarwoto (eds.), *Health Ecological Survey in Indonesia in 1983/1984, Part 1*. Shibukawa, Japan: Tanaka Pub. Print. Co., pp. 125–133.

Black, R.E., K.H. Brown, S. Becker, A.R.M. Abduk Alim and Imdadul Huq (1982). Longitudinal studies of infectious diseases and physical growth of children in rural Bangladesh. *American J. Epidemiology*, **115**: 315–324.

Edmundson, W.C. (1986). Diet, disease and development in India and Indonesia: Some general comments on planning priorities. A position paper presented at a Symposium on *The Comparative Human Ecology of Health and Survival Strategy in Asia and South Pacific*, this volume.

Hattori, T., S. Suzuki, H. Koyama, M. Ogawa, S. Aoki, and T. Igarashi (1985). Differential growth of body height of rural and urban Indonesian with special emphasis on modernization. In: S. Suzuki and Otto Soemarwoto (eds.), *Health Ecological Survey in Indonesia in 1983/84, Part 1*. Shibukawa, Japan: Tanaka Pub. Print. Co., pp. 12–26.

Igarashi, T. (1984). Food intake pattern at two rural Sundanese villages. In: *Human Ecological Survey in Indonesia: A Compilation in Japanese*. Tokyo: Nissan Science Foundation, pp. 54–65 (in Japanese).

Kouchi, M. (1983). Historical changes of and the environmental factors concerned with Japanese physical characteristics. In: R. Ohtsuka (ed.), *Ecological Anthropology* (*L'esprit d'Aujourd'hui*). Tokyo: Shibundo, 96–109 (in Japancsc).

Koyama, H. and S. Suzuki (1985). Comparative study on the way of life of the three communities in South Kalimantan, Indonesia. In: S. Suzuki and Otto Soemarwoto (eds.), *Health Ecological Survey in Indonesia in 1983/84, Part 1*. Shibukawa, Japan: Tanaka Pub. Print. Co., pp. 104–116.

Mahler, H. (1985). Targetting on health for all. *WHO Chronicle*, **39**: 219–222.

Suzuki, M., H. Koyama, Bakir Abisudjak, and S. Suzuki (1985). An immunological malaria survey in a hypoendemic transmigration community in South Kalimantan in Indonesia. In: S. Suzuki and Otto Soemarwoto (eds.), *Health Ecological Survey in Indonesia in 1983/84, Part 1*. Shibukawa, Japan: Tanaka Pub. Print. Co., pp. 117–124.

Suzuki, S. (1983). Conjunctivitis due to cultivation work observed among Indonesian peasants. *J. Human Ergology*, **12**: 55–63.

Suzuki, S. (1983b). Human life and health: A case study in rural communities in Java Islands. *Kitakanto Igaku* (The Kitakanto Medical Jounal), **33**: 1–10 (in Japanese).

Suzuki, S. (1984). Use and quality of water of Sundanese and Javanese villagers. In: *Human Ecological Survey in Indonesia: A Compilation in Japanese*. Tokyo: Nissan Science Foundation, pp. 31–37 (in Japanese).

Suzuki, S. (1985a). Procedure of research. In: S. Suzuki, O. Soemarwoto, and T. Igarashi (eds.), *Human Ecological Survey in Rural West Java in 1978 to 1982, A Project Report*. Tokyo: Nissan Science Foundation, pp. 4–8.

Suzuki, S., (1985b). Morbidity rate, blood pressure, stature, parasite infestation, and the living environment. A comparative study of the three *kampungs*: Pasirparahu, Salamungkal, and Brumbung, West and Central Java. In: S. Suzuki, O. Soemarwoto, and T. Igarashi (eds.), *Human Ecological Survey in Rural West Java in 1978 to 1982, A Project Report*. Tokyo: Nissan Science Foundation, pp. 145–154.

Suzuki, S. and H. Koyama (1984). Health status of three peasant communities in Java Island with special emphasis in stature, skinfold thickness, parasite infestation, morbidity rate, disability days, and the method of therapies. In: *Human Ecological Survey in Indonesia: A Compilation in Japanese*. Tokyo: Nissan Science Foundation, pp. 66–83 (in Japanese).

Suzuki, T., T. Akimichi, T. Kawabe, T. Inaoka, and R. Ohtsuka (1984). Growth of the Gidra in lowland Papua New Guinea. In: N. Kobayashi and T.B. Brazelton (eds.), *The Growing Child in Family and Society*. Tokyo: Univ. of Tokyo Press, pp. 77–93.

Tibault, H.W., L. LaPalme, R. Tanguay, and A. Demirjian (1985). Anthropometric differences between rural and urban French-Canadian schoolchildren. *Human Biology*, **57**: 113–129.

WHO (1978) Alma-Ata 1978. Primary Health Care. *Report of the International Conference on Primary Health Care*. Alma-Ata, USSR, 6–12 September 1978. Geneva, World Health Organization (Health for All Series, No. 3).

WHO (1983) New Approaches to Health Education in Primary Health Care, Report of a WHO Expert Committee. *Technical Report Series 690*. Geneva, World Health Organization.

Invariable Daily Energy Expenditure of Sundanese Villagers with Recent Changes in Their Time Allocation

Kazuhiko MOJI

Department of Human Ecology, School of Health Sciences, Faculty of Medicine, University of Tokyo, Tokyo, Japan

I. INTRODUCTION

Recent detailed time allocation studies have revealed inter- and intra-group diversities of work hours in many human societies. It is necessary to discuss why these variations exist and how they affect the health and survival of the people. Two considerations help to identify the determining factors and the resultant influences of work hours.

First, it is important to explain changes or persistence of time allocation. Anthropologists, economists, and human ecologists have paid considerable attention to seasonal variations in work hours (Hart, 1979; Montgomery and Johnson, 1977; Ohtsuka, 1983). However, there does not seem to be any diachronic study of time allocation spanning a number of years. Because of this lack, cross-cultural comparisons instead of longitudinal data were utilized to assess changes in work hours (Boserup, 1965; Minge-Klevana, 1980; Munroe *et al.*, 1984). Cross-cultural comparison may clarify long-term cultural evolution, but more precise data will be obtained by ascertaining changes in work hours within a group in accordance with changes in its natural and socio-cultural environments as well as with population increase. In other words, work hours should be traced by repeated time allocation studies, and be connected with changes in man-environment relations.

Secondly, it is important that time allocation data be converted into energy expenditure, from which the energy balance can be studied. Conversion of time allocation data into energy must be contrasted with individual or group energy intake, thus yielding the individual or group energy balance. The advantage of energy balance study is twofold. First, we can assess the nutritional status of individuals or of a group. Secondly, it enables us to check the plausibility of sets of data on energy intake and expenditure. Such energy-balance studies in the field as the work of Norgan, Ferro-Luzzi, and Durnin (1974) in Papua New Guinea and the work of Edmundson (1976) in Java have rarely been conducted in spite of the great number of studies dealing individually with energy intake or energy expenditure. There have been several input-output studies, but none has assessed the energy balance. Many input-output studies started off on the false premise that energy intake and expenditure were always in balance. Energy balance analysis seems to have been avoided for fear of difficulties if the intake and expenditure data were not in balance. Thus, most input-output studies have little practical value to health scientists.

The aim of this paper is to show the results of field work in a Sundanese village. To begin with, an energy balance study carried out in 1979 is described. Next, changes in work hours from 1979 to 1981–1984 are shown, and finally those work hours are converted into energy expenditure. Daily energy expenditure of the Sundanese villagers did not vary with recent changes in their time allocation. This means that work hours can change without a change in energy expenditure, or that energy expenditure can remain constant even if work hours change in response to changing conditions.

II. THE VILLAGE STUDIED

These studies were done in Tanu, a small *kampung* situated on a ridge in a southern mountainous area of the Priangan highlands. Its elevation is 900 metres above sea level, and it is part of Desa Dukuh of Kabupaten Bandung in West Java. In West Java, the major ethnic group is the Sundanese, in a population of 20 million. According to the 1980 Desa Dukuh census, there were 1,503 households containing 6,352 people living in the 32 *kampungs* of Desa Dukuh, all of which covers an area of only 1,440 hectares (ha). Tanu, with 200 villagers, covers 26 ha and

TABLE 1. Population Dynamics in Tanu

	N	Annual rate ‰
Live births	43	46.9
Deaths	13	14.2
Infant deaths	6	139.5
Out-migrants	50	54.6
In-migrants	24	26.2

The duration of observation was 51.5 months from 1979 to 1983, and the mid-period population was 213.5.

thus its population density is approximately 800 people per square kilometer. The city of Majalaya, the economic center of the area, is between 8 and 10 km from Tanu, and is well known for its textile industry.

Between February and May 1979, the daily maximum temperature in Tanu ranges between 24.5–29.0°C and the daily minimum temperature between 18.5–20.5°C. The rainy season, during which the area receives

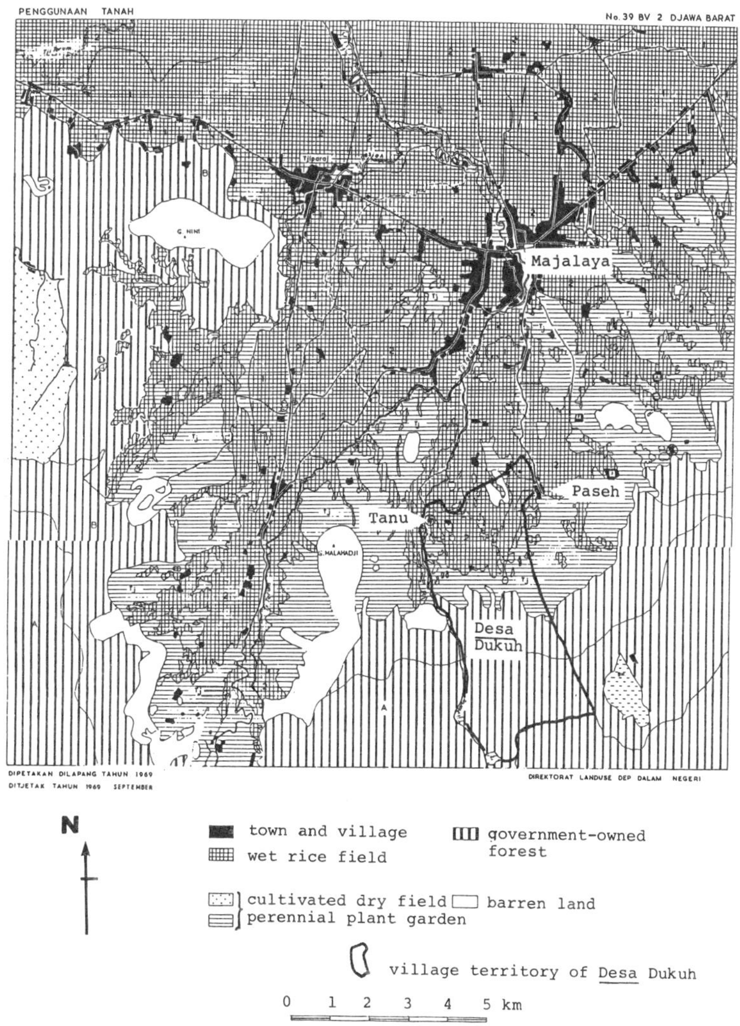

FIG. 1. Land utilization around Tanu.

80% of its annual precipitation of 2,440 mm, lasts for approximately seven months from mid-October to mid-May.

The number of births, deaths, infant deaths, and out- and in-migrations during 51.5 months from 1979 to 1983 are listed in Table 1. There were 48 households with 214 people in 1979 and 45 households with 218 people in 1983. The high out-migration rate keeps the population size stable despite a high fertility rate (total fertility rate during this period was 7.9).

The land utilization map is shown in Fig. 1. In total, 48 households owned 6.9 ha of year-round wet rice fields, 3.6 ha of seasonal wet rice fields, 2.0 ha of dry fields, and 2.9 ha of perennial plant gardens. The distributions of households by areas of land owned, land cultivated, and land controlled are listed in Table 2. In Tanu, the average household can be sustained by 0.3 ha of year-round wet rice fields. According to the villagers, economic value is similar between year-round wet rice fields, the seasonal wet rice fields, and the dry fields. A household can thus earn its livelihood exclusively by agriculture if it controls more than 0.3 ha of land. However, as shown in Table 2, only one-third of the house-

TABLE 2. Distribution of Households by Area of Land Owned, Land Cultivated, and Land Controlled (ha)

	0	<0.1	<0.2	<0.3	<0.4	<0.5	<1.0	<1.6	Total
Land owned	9	9	6	3	7	4	7	3	48
Land cultivated	5	6	9	9	9	2	8	0	48
Land controlled	3	7	17	5	5	3	7	1	48

Figures indicate the sum of year-round wet rice fields, seasonal wet rice fields, and dry fields.

The area of land controlled is adjusted to the area from which the net harvest is available to a household.

TABLE 3. Agricultural Production of Tanu

Crops	Area harvested ha/yr	Yield /ha* ton/ha	Yield /yr ton/yr	Energy supply 10^6 kcal	Protein supply 10^5 g	Income /ha 10^4 Rp	Gross income 10^4 Rp
Rice (polished)	17.5	1.40	23.5	85	160	21.5	376
Tobacco	4.3	–	–	–	–	43.0	185
Corn	0.6	1.52	0.9	3	7	8.3	5
Cassava	0.6	9.40	5.6	6	5	13.3	8
Sweet potato	2.4	2.86	6.9	7	1	5.7	14
Beans	2.1	1.40	2.9	9	6	33.3	70
Shallot	4.3	1.43	6.1	2	1	28.1	120

Figures indicate the production by 48 households in 1979

* yield/ha/harvest, including refuse; rice 0%, corn 10%, cassava 25%, sweet potato 14%, beans 5%, shallots 10%.

holds control more than 0.3 ha of land.

Agricultural production in Tanu is shown in Table 3. Rice harvested by Tanu villagers provides only 80% of the total consumed. Despite this, rice still supplies the bulk of energy and protein. The sum of the gross income from dry field crops is the same as the possible amount of income from rice, though rice is usually not sold.

III. METHODOLOGY

The first field work in Tanu was conducted from November 1978 to September 1979. After two months of general excursions in the Priangan highlands, Tanu was selected as the site of study because of its suitability for direct observation. Tanu, situated 200 metres from the main Desa road, has few passersby. It is a densely built-up village within an area of 3 ha. Follow-up surveys in Tanu were conducted in October 1981 and July-August 1983 by myself, and in the rainy season of 1984 by my colleague, Dr. Koyama.

Time Allocation

Time allocation studies were conducted five times between 1979 and 1984 (Moji, 1980; Moji and Koyama, 1985). In the first three studies, i.e., a 60-day study between February and April 1979 and two seven-day studies in October 1981 and in July 1983, data were collected by the 24-hour recall method. The subjects were eight married couples, although this paper deals exclusively with the male subjects. The eight men ranged from 25 to 56 years in age and weighed from 47 to 55 kg. In the last two studies, for four days each in August 1983 and in February 1984, the spot-check method was applied. The subjects were 36 married men in 1983 and 35 married men in 1984. The work hours in this paper include directly productive activities and exclude household maintenance and non-work activities. The directly productive activities consist of wet rice cultivation, dry field cultivation, tobacco processing after harvest, firewood collection, stock animal care, work in factories, weaving and spinning in the village, handicraft making, non-agricultural wage labour, garden work, trading, and lumbering.

Energy Expenditure

Energy expenditure of the subjects in this study was calculated from time allocation data. Energy expenditure rates of activities studied in East Java by Edmundson (1978) were used for converting the time allocation data into energy expenditure. The mean age, mean body weight and mean energy intake of the subjects were almost the same as those in

Edmundson's study. The energy expenditure rates proposed by Edmundson are lower than Japanese standards, especially in heavier work (Fig. 2). I recorded activities in 91 different categories and assigned them to Edmundson's 13 categories, based on my observation and the villagers' classification of activities into light, medium, or heavy work.

Food and energy intake

In the 1979 survey period, food consumption by all the eight households was recorded for 28 days using the 24-hour recall method. During this period, I visited each household every evening to ask what food had been consumed since the previous evening meal. Energy intakes were calculated using the Indonesian Food Composition Table (1972).

IV. RESULTS

Energy Balance Study

Energy expenditure

In 1979, the average daily work hours of the eight subjects were 6.45 hours (Fig. 3), ranging from 4.7 to 9.1 hours. The coefficient of variation was calculated as 21.5%. On average, 30%, 23%, and 47% of work

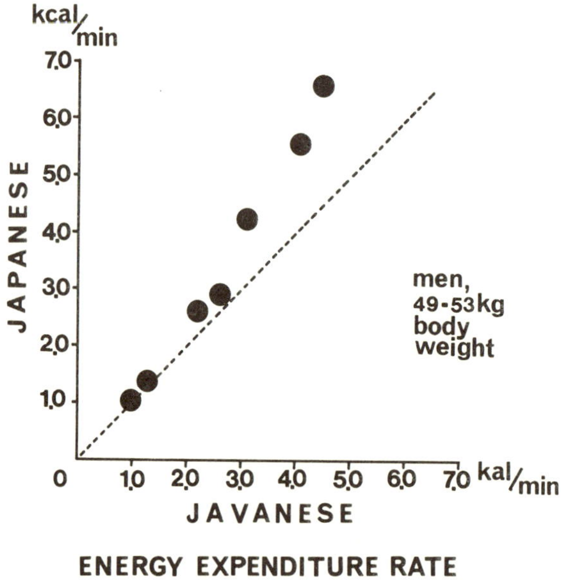

FIG. 2. Comparison of energy expenditure rate between Japanese and Javanese males.

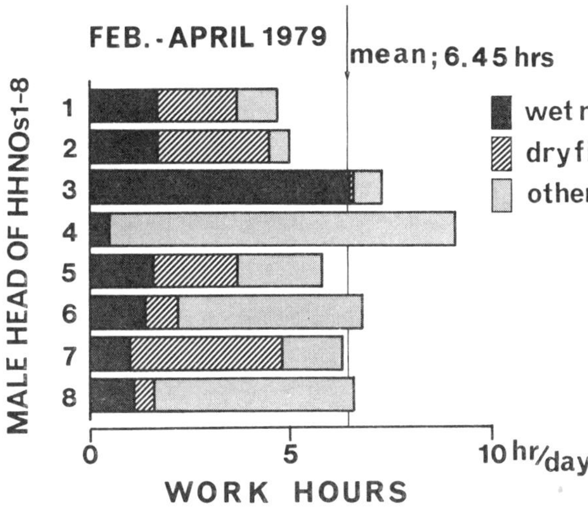

FIG. 3. Work hours of the eight Sundanese villagers in 1979 (60 days, by 24–hour recall method, directly productive activities alone).

hours were allocated to wet rice cultivation, dry field cultivation, and other productive activities, respectively.

Figure 4 shows the daily energy expenditure of the eight subjects. The mean and standard deviations (S.D.) are 2,450 ± 170 kcal; the mean

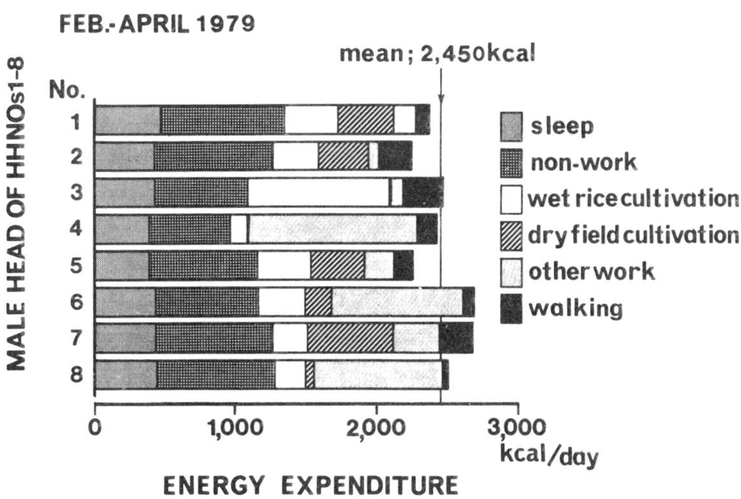

FIG. 4. Energy expenditure of eight Sundanese villagers in 1979.

energy expenditure was the same as that of the Javanese farmers studied by Edmundson. The coefficient of variation of energy expenditures is 6.9%, which is much smaller than that of work hours. Spearman's rank correlation coefficient (r_s) between the work hours and the energy expenditure of the eight subjects is 0.524 ($p = 0.09$). That is, the work hours account for only 27% of the variation in energy expenditure. The correlation between body weight and energy expenditure is even smaller ($r_s = 0.393$).

Wet rice cultivation, dry field cultivation, other productive activities, and walking associated with productive activities represent 15%, 10%, 20%, and 6% of energy expenditure, respectively.

Table 4 compares the mean energy expenditure rate (per-kg body weight per minute) of each category of productive activities. The energy expenditure rate is the highest in wet rice cultivation followed by that in

TABLE 4. Energy Expenditure Rate of Productive Activities

Activities	1979 rainy season	1981–1983 dry season
Wet rice cultivation	0.081	0.074 kcal/min/kg
Dry field cultivation	0.069	0.069
Tobacco processing	0.043	0.050
Firewood collection	0.062	0.060
Stock animal care	0.061	0.060
Working in factories	–	0.043
Weaving and spinning	–	0.043
Handicraft making	0.055	0.043
Non-agricultural wage labour	0.074	0.085
Garden work	0.038	–
Trading	0.079	0.036
Lumbering	0.060	0.060

TABLE 5. Food Consumption

Food group	No. of foods in group	Frequency per day	Weight per day
Rice	1	1.00	585.8 grammes
Sambel sauce	1	0.98	15.8
Vegetables and fruits	16	0.96	44.1
Salt	1	0.74	no data
Other starchy foods	8	0.68	77.3
Dried and salted fish	1	0.53	12.5
Sweets and sugar	3	0.34	20.2
Legumes and legume products	7	0.24	12.2
Other fish	5	0.13	5.3
Oil	2	0.08	1.4
Meat and eggs	4	0.07	1.9

APPENDIX A. Food Consumption of Eight Adult Males of Tanu (February—March 1979)

Food and foodstuffs: English name	Food and foodstuffs: Indonesian name	Food group	Frequencies per day	Weight per day (gm.)
rice	beras	I	1.00	585.8
sambel sauce	sambel	X	0.98	15.8
salt	garam	IX	0.74	(no data)
dried and salted fish	ikan asin	V	0.53	12.5
Chinese radish	daun lobak	VI	0.30	10.7
fried chips of casava flour	kerupuk	II	0.29	6.5
black nightshade (leaf)	daun leunca	VI	0.20	7.6
cassava	singkong	II	0.19	46.5
glutinous rice	beras ketan	I	0.15	14.3
sweets made of sugar/ coconut	puyur	VII	0.10	3.7
sugarpalm sugar	gula aren	VIII	0.09	2.2
Limnocharis Flava	genjer	VI	0.08	2.2
carp	ikan mas	V	0.07	2.8
soybean curd	tahu	III	0.06	3.1
cassava leaf	daun singkong	VI	0.06	2.6
eggplant	terong	VI	0.06	3.5
coconut oil	minyak kelapa	IX	0.06	0.8
red kidney bean	kacang merah	III	0.05	2.6
goat meat	daging kambing	IV	0.05	1.2
cucumber	ketimun	VI	0.04	4.3
cabbage	kool	VI	0.04	1.7
hyacinth bean	roay	III	0.03	1.7
fermented peanut cake	oncom	III	0.03	1.4
gnemon tree leaf	daun melinjo	VI	0.03	1.4
watercress	salada air	VI	0.03	1.0
pumpkin	waluh	VI	0.03	2.8
Leucaona Clauca (leaf)	pete cina	VI	0.03	0.9
banana	pisang	VI	0.03	3.7
corn	jagung	II	0.02	2.4
taro	talus	II	0.02	5.1
mixed rice with dishes	nasi rames	I	0.02	3.0
bean curd refuse	dage	III	0.02	2.0
mold-treated soya	tempe	III	0.02	0.5
congealed shrimp paste	petis udang	V	0.02	1.0
fish paste	trasi	V	0.02	0.5
shallot	bawang	VI	0.02	0.7
ketchup	kecap	IX	0.02	0.6
duck egg	telor bebek	IV	0.01	0.2
boggy earth eel	belud	V	0.01	0.3
shallot caulis (leek)	prei	VI	0.01	0.5
Chinese cabbage	pecay	VI	0.01	0.4
mushroom	jamur kuping	VI	0.01	0.7
jack fruit	nangka	VI	0.01	0.3

chicken	ayam	IV	0.01	0.4
potato	kentang	II	0.01	0.04
pond snail	tatut	V	0.01	0.7
bread	roti	II	0.004	0.05
seed of sugar palm	candil	II	0.004	0.9
water buffalo meat	dagin kerbau	IV	0.004	0.1

Using 24-hour recall method, eight households for four weeks.
food group: I rice; II other starchy foods; III legumes and legume products; IV meat and eggs; V fish; VI vegetables and fruits; VII sweets; VIII sugar; IX condiments; X *sambel* sauce

trading and non-agricultural wage labour. The high energy expenditure rate for trading in the 1979 records is mostly attributable to carrying 50–100 kg of shallots to the market.

Food Consumption and Energy Intake

The daily consumption frequencies of 49 foods/foodstuffs and the weight consumed by the subjects are listed in Appendix A. Table 5 allocates these foods/foodstuffs into 11 categories. On average, an adult male consumed 600 grammes (g) of rice (1,280 g after steaming) with 16 g of *sambel*, a sauce made of fish paste, red pepper, shallots, tomatoes, salt, sugarpalm sugar, and chemical seasoning. Dried and salted fish was the usual side dish, although only available once every two days.

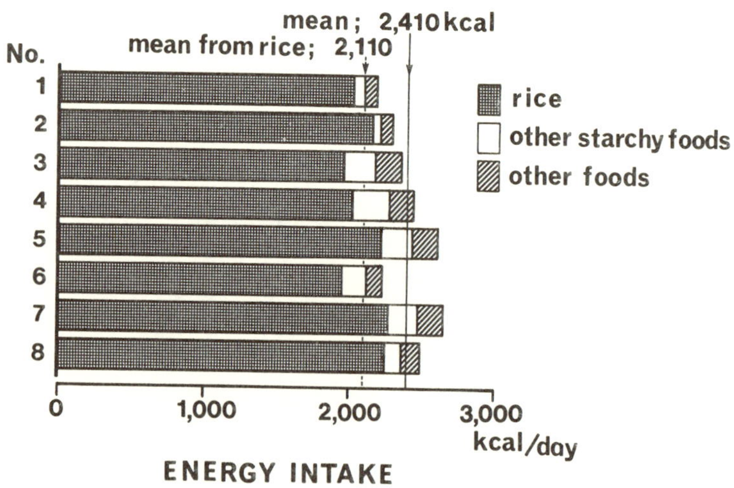

FIG. 5. Energy intake of eight Sundanese in 1979 (28 days, by 24-hour recall method).

When no fish was available, villagers sprinkle salt on rice. *Lalabs*, raw or boiled vegetables such as cassava leaves and radish leaves, were usually eaten once a day. The amount of other foods consumed weighed less than 120 g per day.

The daily energy intake of the eight subjects (Fig. 5) ranged from 2,190 to 2,650 kcal (mean and S.D.: 2410 ± 170 kcal). Rice provided 87% of the total energy intake. The coefficient of variation, 7.0%, was almost the same as that of energy expenditure.

Energy Balance

The mean energy expenditure was almost equal to the mean energy intake, with the former exceeding the latter by only 2%. However, there was no significant correlation between individual energy intake and expenditure (Fig. 6). Ratios of energy expenditure to energy intake ranged from 0.87 to 1.21. The subjects' body weight changes up to 1983 are shown in Fig. 7. The expenditure/intake ratios in 1979 did not coincide with the weight changes for four years.

Comparison of Energy and Nutrient Intake with RDA

Figure 8 compares energy and nutrients intake with the Indonesian Recommended Dietary Allowance (RDA) of 1968. After adjusting body weight differences, mean energy intake equals RDA. Protein, thiamine, and iron, more than a half of which is derived from rice, reached nearly

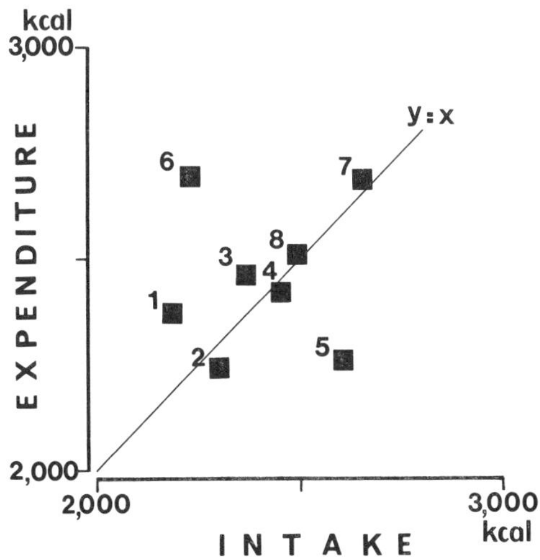

FIG. 6. Individual energy expenditure and intake in 1979.

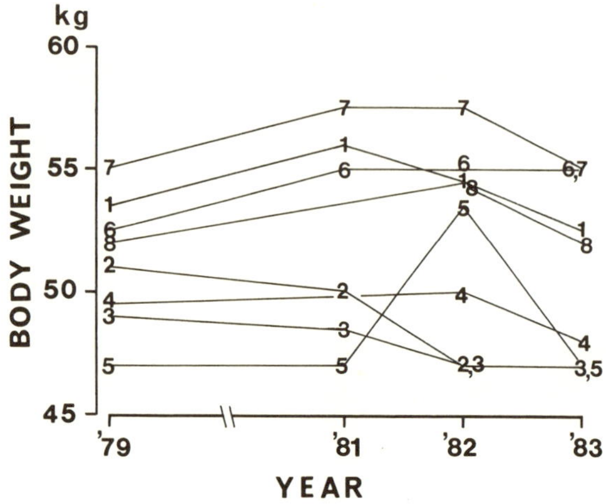

FIG. 7. Body weight change between 1979 and 1983.

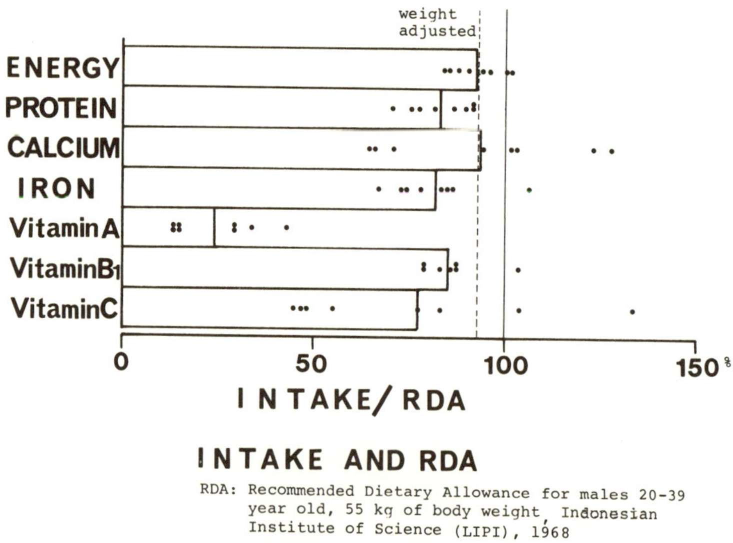

FIG. 8. Proportion of intake to RDA.

90% of the adjusted RDA. Other nutrients, mainly from foods other than rice, tended to vary in fulfillment of RDA. Among them, vitamin A showed the lowest percentage of RDA, although no villagers seemed to suffer from severe vitamin A deficiency.

Changes in Work Hours from 1979 to 1981–1984

Work hours from 1979 to 1983

The mean work hours (6.45 hrs) of the eight men in 1979 were shorter than those (7.93 hrs) in October 1981 (paired t-test, $t = 2.47$, $p < 0.05$), and those (7.95 hrs) in July 1983 ($t = 1.71$, $p = 0.13$). Individual work hours in 1979 and those in 1981 were significantly correlated ($r_s = 0.905$, $p = 0.001$), and those of 1981 and 1983 were marginally correlated ($r_s = 0.571$, $p = 0.069$). The mean hours allocated to different activities between 5: 00 a,m, and 6: 30 p.m. in 1979, 1981, and 1983 are listed in Table 6, with the total work hours each year being 6.3, 7.4, and 7.5 hours, respectively. The longer work hours in 1981 and in 1983 were

TABLE 6. Male Activity: 5:00–18:30, 1979, 1981, and 1983

		1979	1981	1983
Activity	No. of subjects	8	8	8
	mean age	36.0	38.0	40.0
	age range	25–56	27–58	29–60
1) Idleness		No data	4.5	3.3
2) Eating		No data	1.1	0.9
3) Hygiene		No data	0.1	0.4
4) Illness		No data	0	0.0
5) Visiting		0.1	0.1	0.2
6) Wet rice cultivation		1.9	2.6	1.5
7) Dry field cultivation		1.6	0.4	1.6
8) Tobacco processing		0	0	1.7
9) Firewood collection		0.6	0.2	0.3
10) Stock animal care		0.1	0.2	0.2
11) Work in factories		0	0.7	0
12) Weaving and spinning		0	0.5	0.8
13) Handicraft making		1.0	1.4	0.8
14) Non-agricultural wage labour		0.4	0.5	0.5
15) Garden work		0.1	0	0
16) Trading		0.2	0.7	0.2
17) Lumbering		0.2	0.3	0
18) Childcare		No data	0	0.1
19) Food preparation		No data	0.1	0.1
20) Other HMA		No data	0.1	0
6)–17) DPA		6.3	7.4	7.5
18)–20) HMA		No data	0.2	0.2
6)–20) TAW		No data	7.6	7.7

DPA: directly productive activities;
HMA: household maintenance activities;
TAW: total of all work.
Work time indicates DPA alone in this paper.
The results were recorded using the 24-hour recall survey method.

related to increases in tobacco processing, to the commencement of work in factories, and to more weaving and spinning in the village. Both seasonal and diachronic changes influenced time allocation in 1981 and 1983. Tobacco processing is exclusively carried out in the first half of the dry season, whereas factory work and weaving and spinning show scarcely any seasonal variation.

Work Hours as Determined by the Spot-Check Method in 1983 and 1984

Time allocation as determined by the spot-check method of the married male subjects in August 1983 and February 1984 are shown in Table 7.

TABLE 7. Male Activity: 5:00–18:30, 1983 and 1984

Activity		August 1983		February 1984
	Sample size	36		35
	Mean age	39.9		40.3
	Age range	20–65		20–65
1) Idleness		3.3		3.7
2) Eating		0.8		0.5
3) Hygiene		0.3		0.3
4) Illness		0.4		0.2
5) Visiting		0.1	≪	0.7
6) Wet rice cultivation		1.3	>	0.6
7) Dry field cultivation		0.2	≪	3.0
8) Tobacco processing		0.9	≫	0.1
9) Firewood collection		1.1		1.3
10) Stock animal care		0.9		0.6
11) Work in factories		0.5		0.7
12) Weaving and spinning		0.3		0.3
13) Handicraft making		0.9		0.4
14) Non-agricultural wage labour		0.9	≫	0.1
15) Garden work		0.2		0.2
16) Trading		0.6		0.2
17) Lumbering		0.1		0.0
18) Childcare		0.2		0.2
19) Food preparation		0.1		0.2
20) Other HMA		0.3		0.2
6)–17) DPA		7.9		7.5
18)–20) HMA		0.6		0.6
6)–20) TAW		8.5		8.1

DPA: directly productive activities;
HMA: household maintenance activities;
TAW: total all work.
≪, ≫ : significantly different at $p < 0.01$ by χ-square test.
> : significantly different at $p < 0.05$ by χ-square test.
Work time indicates DPA alone in this paper.
The results were recorded using the spot-check survey method.

There is no marked difference in work hours between the two years (7.9 hours in August 1983 and 7.5 hours in February 1984). These work hours are very close to those recorded in 1981 and 1983 using the 24-hour recall method. Work activities to which significantly longer times were devoted in the dry season (August 1983) than in the rainy season (February 1984) were tobacco processing, non-agricultural wage labour (for both, χ-square test, $p < 0.01$), and wet rice cultivation ($p < 0.05$). Only dry field cultivation showed a reverse trend; time spent on this activity was longer in the rainy season than in the dry season ($p < 0.01$).

Comparison of Rainy Season Work Hours between 1979 and 1984

Comparing the time allocation in 1979 with that in 1984, agricultural activities required almost the same amount of time: 3.5 hours in 1979 and 3.7 hours in 1984. In other words, prolongation of work hours was attributable to non-agricultural work, especially to work in factories, weaving and spinning, and firewood collection. However, among agricultural activities, dry field cultivation took more hours in 1984 than in 1979.

Although a few questions remain regarding the seasonality of activities and the reliability of data collected, an overall comparison of the five records proved that the work hours of Tanu villagers increased from 1979 to 1981–1984.

Causes of Changes in Work Hours

The prolongation of work hours was due to an increase in the importance of cash crops, the prosperity of the textile industry in the nearby city of Majalaya, and a rise in the price of firewood.

In the second half of the 1970s, the national economic growth rate of Indonesia slowed down. The Indonesian government then devalued the rupia (Rp) in November 1978 from Rp415 to 625 to one U.S. dollar. Although this devaluation caused stagflation in following years, it effectively stimulated domestic industrial production in the first half of the 1980s. The revival of the textile industry in Majalaya in the 1980s produced many employment opportunities, and some villagers began to devote their time to weaving and spinning in the village or commuting to factories near Majalaya.

The devaluation also stimulated agricultural production for export, and cash crops such as tobacco benefitted. On the other hand, in the 1980s the price of oil has increased sharply. Many town-dwellers began to substitute firewood for oil, and the price of firewood rose. Consequently, the villagers spent much more time collecting firewood in 1983–1984 than before.

Thus, changes in the Tanu villagers' work hours were impelled by changes in national and international economics and policies.

Invariable Energy Expenditure through the Observation Period

Energy expenditure in 1981 and 1983

The energy expenditure of the subjects in the 1981 survey was 2,500 ± 340 kcal (mean ± S.D.), ranging from 2,130 to 2,960 kcal (Fig. 9). In 1983 it was 2,450 + 340, ranging from 1,950 to 3,000 kcal (Fig. 10). These two average values, being approximately identical, did not differ from the mean energy expenditure in 1979 (2,450 kcal). Thus, the mean energy expenditure remained constant, in contrast with the increase in work hours (Fig. 11). Coefficients of variation in individual energy expenditure (13.5% in 1981 and 14.0% in 1983) were larger than that in 1979 (6.9%). Presumably, this was due to the shorter survey periods in 1981 and 1983 (seven days each) in comparison to the 60-day survey in 1979. However, the coefficients of variation of individual energy expenditure were still smaller than those of individual work hours both in 1981 (34.2%) and in 1983 (33.1%).

Energy expenditures of each individual in 1979 and 1981 and in 1981 and 1983 were compared. The correlation coefficient between 1979 and 1981 for the eight subjects is 0.810 (r_s, $p < 0.01$) and that between 1981 and 1983 is 0.714 ($p < 0.05$). High correlations indicate the lack of variation in individual energy expenditures. The intra-individual variation among the three records, as calculated by (maximum − minimum energy expenditure) × 100 divided by minimum energy expenditure

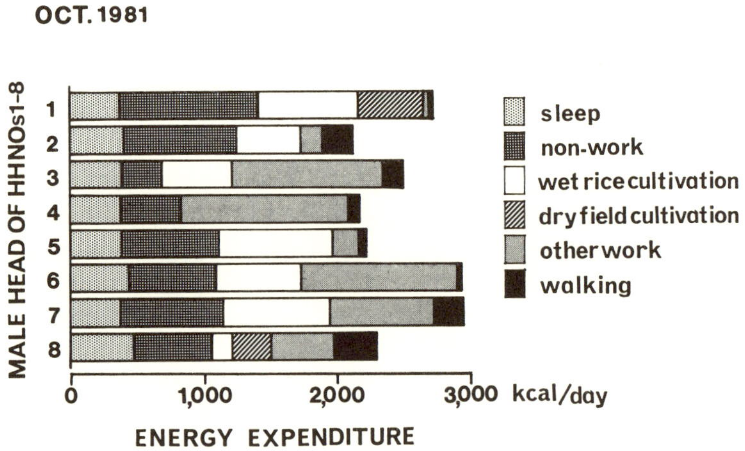

FIG. 9. Energy expenditure of eight Sundanese villagers in 1981 (seven days).

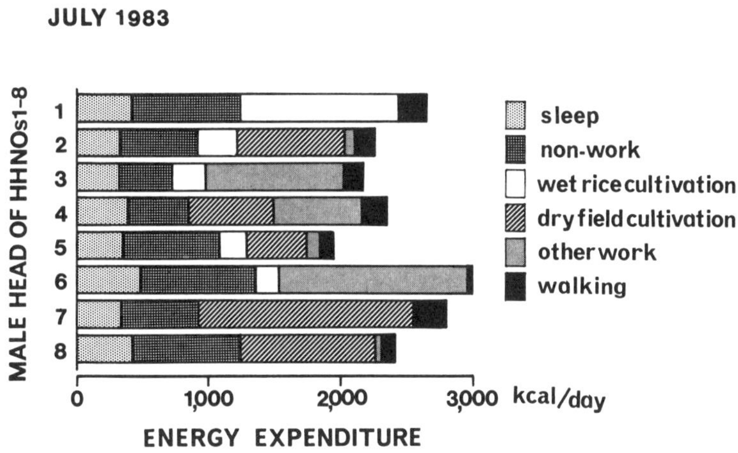

FIG. 10. Energy expenditure of eight Sundanese villagers in 1983 (seven days).

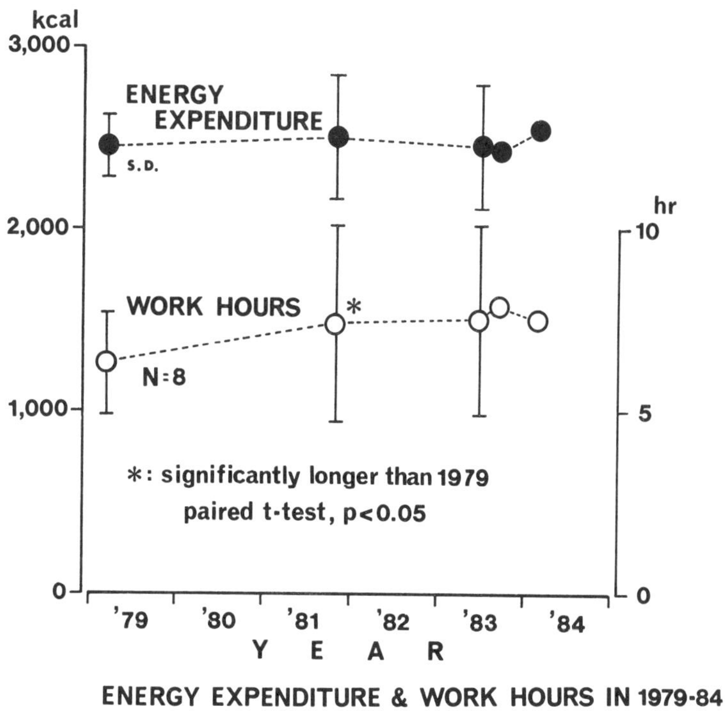

FIG. 11. Work hours and energy expenditure between 1979 and 1984.

of the individual among the three records, ranges from 6.1 to 15.6 (mean 11.7).

In both surveys, 57% of daily energy expenditure was on work activities, but the proportions of energy expended on each activity differed between the surveys: in 1981 21% was for wet rice cultivation, 4% for dry field cultivation, 26% for other productive activities, and 6% for walking associated with work, while in 1983 the percentages were 11%, 23%, 17%, and 6%, respectively.

Energy Expenditure in 1983 and 1984

The mean daily energy expenditure of the 35 men surveyed in 1983 and the 36 men in 1984 was calculated from the spot-check data by applying energy expenditure rates of activities listed in Table 4. The mean daily energy expenditure in 1983 was 2,430 kcal and that in 1984 was 2,550 kcal; both were very similar to the results of the previous three studies. Of the total daily energy expenditure in 1983, 57% was expended on work activities (12% for wet rice cultivation, 7% for dry field cultivation, and 38% for other productive activities, all including walking associated with those activities), and in 1984, 56% was expended on work activities (6% for wet rice cultivation, 25% for dry field cultivation, and 25% for other productive activities).

V. DISCUSSION

The repeated time allocation studies reported here revealed the Tanu villagers' changing time allocations and their unvarying energy expenditure during our survey period from 1979 to 1984. Discussion begins with the changing time allocation; the dynamic nature of time allocation which must be common in various societies has been neglected in many studies. Instead, as has been pointed out by Vayda *et al.* (1980), special attention should be paid to the people's continuing responsiveness to changing circumstances at the behavioural level. Though living in a non-urban locality, the villagers of Tanu have quickly responded to changing circumstances. In this case, national and international economic trends and policies have profoundly influenced their time allocation. This fact implies that the examination of a small group of people contributes to regional studies. At the same time, it implies that time allocation is very sensitively influenced by circumstantial changes, suggesting the importance of an analysis of circumstances themselves simultaneously with time allocation studies.

The next concern is whether this time allocation change of Tanu villagers is progressive or recessive. There are two possibilities: the change may be progressive in that it responds to the recent progressive industrialization of Indonesia, but it may be recessive when it responds merely to a boom-or-bust type of fluctuation. Variable time allocation and persistent energy expenditure may be advantageous if they revert to the previous time allocation pattern to cope with recessive changes in conditions. The Sundanese farmers may have experienced such recessive changes in the past, although they may be disadvantageous in the sense that they suppress or delay evolutional changes in life style.

The unvarying energy expenditure level may be related to the almost unchanging energy supply in the village, and sustained by unchanged dietary habits. Thus time allocation patterns may be constrained by the available supply of energy. The balance between the mean energy expenditure and the mean energy intake is maintained at a relatively low level, presumably through high energy efficiency and elaborate use of land and labour. Nevertheless, the villagers in general do not suffer from severe underweight or nutritional deficiency, and can allocate their time to various activities to ensure their health and survival.

However, if outside forces disrupt this traditional balance, radical changes will occur in the structure of energy expenditure and intake and in the variations in time allocation.

Acknowledgments

This research has been supported by a generous grant from the Nissan Science Foundation, the Tokyo Medical Association, and the Ministry of Education, Science and Culture, Japan, and conducted as a part of the project research directed by Shosuke Suzuki and Otto Soemarwoto. This paper has benefitted from critical reading by Ryutaro Ohtsuka and Tsuguyoshi Suzuki.

REFERENCES

Edmundson, W.C. (1976). *Land, Food, and Work in East Java*. New England Monographs in Geography, Monograph Series No. 4. The University of New England.

Gross, D.R. (1984). Time allocation: A tool for the study of cultural behavior. *Ann. Rev. Anthropol.*, **13**: 519–558.

Hart, G. (1980). Pattern of household labour allocation in a Javanese village. In H.P. Binswanger, R.E. Evenson, C.A. Florencio, and B.N.F. White (eds.), *Rural Household Studies in Asia*. Singapore: Singapore University Press, pp. 188–217.

Minge-Klevana, W. (1980). Does labor time decrease with industrialization: A survey of time allocation studies. *Curr. Anthropol.*, **21**: 279–287.

Moji, K. (1980). Labor allocation of Sundanese peasants, West Java. *J. Human Ergology*, **9**: 159–173.

Moji, K. (1982). Labor, household budget, and health of Sundanese peasants, West Java. *Proc. 10th Asian Conference on Occupational Health*, Singapore.

Moji, K. and H. Koyama (1985). A time-saving spot-check method applied to a Sundanese peasant community in West Java. *Man and Culture in Oceania*, **1**: 121–127.

Montgomery, E. and A. Johnson (1977). Machiguenga energy expenditure. *Ecology of Food and Nutrition*, **6**: 97–105.

Munroe, R.H., A. Koel, R.L. Munroe, R. Bolton, C. Michelson, and C. Bolton, (1983). Time allocation in four societies. *Ethnology*, **22**: 355–370.

Norgan, N.G., A. Ferro-Luzzi, and J.V.G.A. Durnin (1974). The energy and nutrient intake and the energy expenditure of 204 New Guinean adults. *Phil. Trans. R. Soc. Lond. B.*, **268**: 309–348.

Ohtsuka, R. (1983). *Oriomo Papuans, Ecology of Sago-Eaters in Lowland Papua*. Tokyo: University of Tokyo Press.

Vayda, A.P., C.J.P. Colfer, and M. Brotokusumo (1980). Interactions between people and forests in East Kalimantan. *Impact of Science on Society*, **30**: 179–190.

Diet, Disease, and Development in India and Indonesia: Some General Comments on Planning Priorities

Wade C. EDMUNDSON

Department of Geography, University of New England, Armidale, N.S.W., Australia

I. DIET, DISEASE, AND DEVELOPMENT

Development and health are intimately related to numerous factors influencing the individual within the totality of the surrounding environment. Given this complexity, where does one begin studying the interrelationships between diet, disease, and development? It seems that the central issue is always the individual changing over time and existing at different levels in a health continuum during the cycle of life. There are only two states which can be clearly defined as possessing health or not possessing health. These are the states of birth or the quickening of the embryo, at which time the human organism begins to have some homeostatic level of health, and the state of death, at which time health no longer exists. In the intervening period it is only the quality of health that will vary over time and space within the confines of an environment which may encourage or retard development.

The specific purpose here is to examine the biologic environment. The size, strength, and longevity of the individual is the key to health. The first question that arises is, how does one define and quantify health? Working at the highest level of generalization, to obtain a quantitative definition of health one must consider longevity and its mirror image, mortality. If data are accurately and reliably collected, life expectancy at birth (LE0) measures the general quality of the biologic environment. Nations, regions, and races with longer life expectancies may be "healthier" than those with low expectations of life. Likewise, an increase in longevity will represent development in the health sphere. Thus India with an estimated LE0 of 55 years in 1982 and Indonesia with an estimated LE0 of 54 years in 1982 may both be considered to be less healthy than

Australia with an estimated LE0 of 76 years in 1982 and the United States with an estimated LE0 of 75 years in 1983 (World Bank, 1985).

Diet and disease are clearly important components of health. A very basic question that occurs when considering the practicalities and priorities involved in changing or developing the biologic endowment of man is: are these two factors indeed, the basic components of health and if so, are they equally important?

The answer most commonly given is that diet and disease are equally important. However, little research has been devoted to this basic question. The reason is that very little data exist concerning national levels of nutritional sufficiency and much that does is of questionable reliability. Some national nutrition survey data do exist for India and some estimates of gross nutritional intake do exist for Indonesia, but these data are not reliable. Some post-1980 survey data for India may now be of acceptable quality, but the time span covered by reliable data is short and the relative change in life expectancy during this most recent period has been small. As for the international data sets published by the United Nations, nutritional data are insufficient and based on unreliable estimates of food production, not actual intake. To be accurate nutritional data must be based on actual household surveys and ideally must be based on actual weighed food intake, not simply on recall. Even in the United States it is only in the last decade that 10-state weighed survey data have been available. In the developing agricultural nations the quality of mortality statistics, which are often gathered by the village chief or other low-level government officials with little or no health training, is also very poor. With mortality data poor and nutritional survey data often non-existent, it is not surprising that little large-scale quantative statistical analysis has been undertaken to determine the relative significance of diet and disease in development.

Only two countries have accurate long-term national nutritional surveys: Switzerland and Japan. The data for Switzerland are not suitable for our purposes simply because Switzerland has been highly developed during the entire period of reporting. However, the data for Japan are highly suitable because they can be related to a period of extremely rapid development during which time Japan moved from a health status in terms of life expectancy very similar to that of the poor nations today to a high level of health status equal to that of most of the developed nations. The post-World War II situation in Japan was appalling. In the immediate post-war period Japan was a highly urbanized society in which the majority of the population were essentially living in hutments or makeshift squatter settlements. Industry was almost non-existent and agriculture was devastated not only by internal distruption but also by the withdrawal of food imports which were, and still are, an important part of Japan's economy.

However, by 1949, the Japanese government had re-instituted a national nutritional stratified sample survey based on the actual weighing of three days of food intake for 10,000 families. The Japanese nation is noted for its high level of organization, and thus there are reasons to assume that both nutrition survey data and disease mortality data for Japan are unusually accurate.

For this reason I performed an analysis of both nutritional sufficiency and disease mortality as surrogate measures for diet and disease in relation to change in life expectancy for Japan during the period 1949 to 1964. An index of nutritional sufficiency was developed based on the average percentage fulfillment of nutrient requirements for eight food groups equally weighted. An index of change of disease status was based on the total mortality rates for the five most common causes of death in 1949. Figure 1 illustrates the interrelationship between the dietary sufficiency index, the disease mortality index, and life expectancy at birth for Japan during this 15-year period. Figure 2, a visual illustration of the high degree of correlation between these three data sets based on fitted curves for length of life, disease mortality rates, and nutritional sufficiency ratios. The correlation between change in nutritional status change in disease status ($r = -.89$), illustrates the very high degree of relationship, or synergistic covariance, between diet and disease. Diet and disease are highly synergistic under most circumstances. For example, if someone is suffering from acute diarrhoea not only will he have an

Fitted curves for length of life, communicable disease rates and nutritional sufficiency ratios in Japan from 1949 – 1963

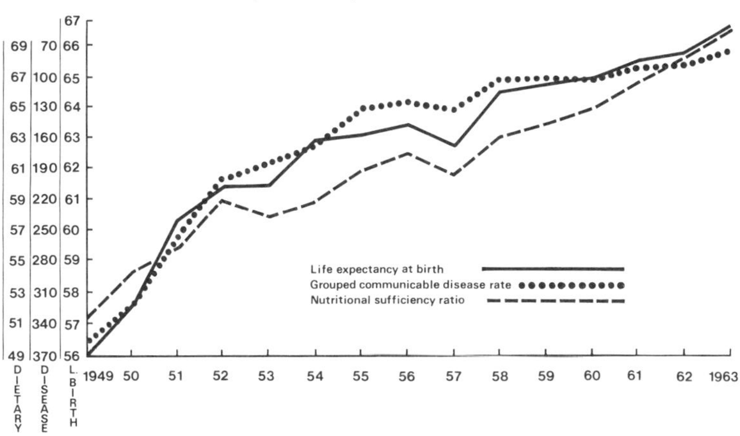

FIG. 1

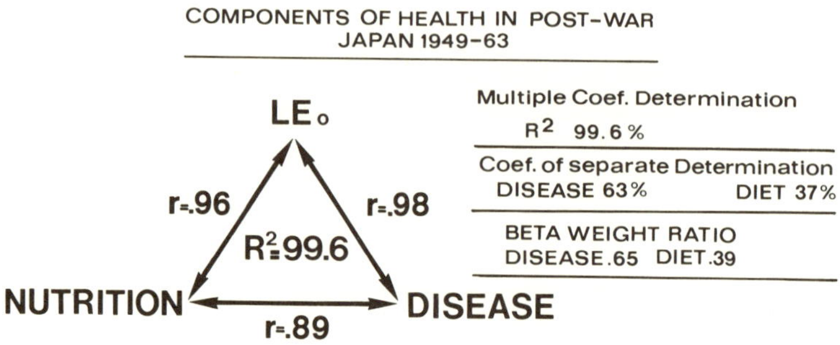

FIG. 2

extremely low intake of food but he will also be unable to effectively assimilate what little they are able to eat because of the rapid food transit time and disturbances in absorptive mechanisms. This is a clear example of disease synergizing malnutrition. A good example of malnutrition synergizing disease is the well-known effect of low protein intake on the development and course of tuberculosis. When protein intake is low the human organism will be far more susceptible to tuberculosis. Even a small inoculation of the tubercule bacillus is likely to result in the development of clinical symptoms in a malnourished individual, and infection in a severely protein-deficient child may result in a rapid and fulminating case of tuberculosis which can lead to death in as short a period as three months. In general, malnutrition strongly synergizes almost all common bacterial and protozoal illnesses. Viral illness may be either synergized or antagonized by malnutrition (Scrimshaw, 1966). Likewise the majority of illnesses will tend to synergize malnutrition by demanding higher energy intakes to meet the rise in basal metabolic rate which will accompany fever and by requiring higher intakes of protein and other nutrients to form antibodies to fight the illness and to replace damaged tissue. Most illness also tends to be accompanied by anorexia or loss of appetite. And finally, a severely ill individual can produce neither food nor income and may further reduce productivity by demanding the care of someone who is not actually ill. Both these figures illustrate the extremely close relationship between our surrogate measures of diet and disease and health as measured by LE0. The correlation between nutrition and health status is extremely strong and highly significant ($r = .96$). In other words, as nutritional sufficiency increased and the intakes of the eight food groups approached or exceeded recommendations, life expectancy also increased. The correlation between the fall in mortality from the five most significant diseases and life expectancy was even higher ($r = -.98$). Of course all three factors under examination were without doubt affected by changes in the cultural, economic, and physical environment, and it is difficult to say that whether the most important underlying factors influencing change in life expectancy were diet or disease. However, there is no doubt that the diet and disease indices do fully explain the change in life expectancy. Explanation is not causation, but in this instance, since we know the mechanism of the interrelationship, we can state that there is a clear deterministic and causal relationship among diet, disease, and life expectancy. This is nothing new, but the quantification is interesting, and in post-war Japan, change in the diet and disease indices accurately predicted 99.6% of all changes in life expectancy.

From a statistical point of view, the important factor here is that, given almost perfect determination of the health index by the two independent variables, it is possible to use statistical analyses to separate out the relative inputs of each of the independent variables. Using both beta weights and coefficients of separate determination, it became clear that in this case the disease input was more important than the nutritional input. Using both techniques the indications were that the fall in disease mortality accounted for more than 60% of the increase in life expectancy whereas the increase in nutritional sufficiency accounted for less than 40% of the improvement in health. Even though this is a regionally specific survey over a short period of time, this result is both interesting and statistically significant.

II. THE SIGNIFICANCE OF NUTRITIONAL MORBIDITY IN INDIA AND INDONESIA

Although the above result need not necessarily apply in India or Indonesia, it has been the author's empirical experience in the combined course of several decades of village research that a far greater proportion of deaths within the study villages must be attributed primarily to a specific disease insult which may or may not be synergized by an underlying complex of nutritional deficiency. A very significant proportion of the nutritional deficiency deseases found occurring in my four study villages have as their underlying cause a communicable disease insult. This is especially true in the case of protein calorie malnutrition in infants and children, where the underlying factor precipitating fully developed clinical symptoms of PEM is usually prolonged diarrhoea, a simple attack of German measles (*rubella*), or both.

Published data are limited and highly variable in terms of method of presentation, but they do support the conclusion that disease control is more important than dietary improvement in improving human health. It would be ideal for planning purposes if detailed morbidity data were available before setting developmental priorities. Clear economic priorities for health programmes cannot be set until we can define the areal incidence of diet and disease morbidity. The highest benefit per unit cost could then be determined by comparing the empirical significance of morbid conditions with the estimated cost of cure. However, collecting and collating these data in detail is a task far beyond the scope of this paper, and is rendered even more difficult by the fact that morbidity as opposed to mortality data are available only on the basis of individual case studies or in unpublished hospital or clinic attendance records. Nevertheless, some data will be cited here which suggest the relative importance of clinically significant as opposed to theoretical or subclinical dietary and disease morbidity in India and Indonesia.

III. ENERGY AND PROTEIN MALNUTRITION

In 1976, after eighteen months in the field, the present author "went to Java believing that calories, proteins, vitamins, and minerals should be stressed in that order, but he left thinking that the order should be reversed." In regard to their incidence and their influence on development, both energy and protein malnutrition are not as significant as many think them to be. Certainly protein-energy malnutrition (PEM) is no longer a major problem in Indonesia (see Edmundson, 1976 and 1980). In 1978, working in the outer islands of Indonesia, Hofler and Peach also concluded that PEM was not a major problem, stating that "hospital records of sick children showed no manifest Protein-Energy Malnutrition." Sukhatme and Margen (1982) and Edmundson (1980) have pointed out that the human organism can adapt to a wide range of energy intakes without any significant deterioration in health status or work output. Edmundson, (1976) in reference to 324 subject-days of data from East Java, stated: "Severe deficiency syndromes were found to exist for only vitamin A and iodine. Caloric intakes varied greatly from subject to subject, and in some cases caloric intakes were low enough that one would expect a lowered energetic output. However, the study subjects were, regardless of caloric intake, hard working and industrious."

Working in India, the author has observed a small but significant incidence of clinically significant marasmatic kwashiorkor. However, even in poor villages in isolated regions, the incidence of PEM is not high, even in India. In 1983 Chitre, Deshpande, and Nimbalkar working with an impoverished tribal population in Maharashtra found the incidence of protein-energy malnutrition to be only 0.6%. In their extensive review of the health status in Kerala, Panikar and Soman (1984) also found that the incidence of nutritional deficiency disease was low relative to the incidence of other diseases and said that "the proportion of patients suffering from nutritional deficiency diseases is quite small throughout the period under review, suggesting that despite considerably low intakes, florid clinical signs of deficiency do not exist among the people."

The problem with the overstatement of the incidence of malnutrition, PEM, and especially undernutrition has been a gross disregard of the empirical evidence and the failure to consider human variability and adaptation. We cannot assume that all Indians and Indonesians with energy intakes lower than Western recommendations are clinically undernourished. Those populations with low intakes have been labeled "undernourished" and those with high intakes have been called "overnourished." These naïve classifications have relatively little economic or clinical significance.

Minimum as opposed to optimum human energy requirements are significantly lower than recommendations, and field observations show many populations living healthful and productive lives on energy intakes about 30 to 40% lower than some Western standards, often based on obsolete data uncorrected for weight differentials. Until these empirical truths are recognized we will continue to be exposed to common misinterpretations of the incidence of clinically significant undernutrition.

Many recommendations for human energy intake have been set too high because of failures to consider human variation and adaptation. The recommendations have been misinterpreted by international agencies and developmentalists who have viewed failure to meet these recommended levels as indications of "permanent states of hunger" or even "starvation."

The key to understanding the economic impact of any health problem is to separate out the clinically significant, serious forms of illness from the mild forms and the theoretical estimates of potential illness or sub-optimal conditions. Thus, although according to the United Nations 15% of the world's population may be sporadically "hungry" and 500 million may be in the category of "mildly malnourished or stunted," the significant figure in relation to energy and protein malnutrition is that the "prevalence of clinical cases of kwashiorkor and marasmus" is estimated at only one million (Latham, 1984). Then, if this figure of one million is compared to the same UN prevalence estimates of six million for blindness resulting from vitamin A deficiency and six million for cretinism resulting from iodine deficiency goitre, the planning priorities begin to come into perspective. In the future more emphasis needs to be placed on the quality of the diet and less on the quantity of food intake (see Edmundson, 1980).

A statement that many people in the Third World are underfed and therefore physically underactive has no more significance than its illogical corollary, that many Westerners are overfed and therefore hyperactive. Many people are periodically "hungry" and would eat more and better food if it were available, but a very small proportion are actually "starving." They are suffering from "psychic hunger" and malnutrition, but not from widespread physiologic hunger and starvation. Data are unreliable and incomplete, but after thorough examination of news reports for the decade of the 1970s (*Facts On File*) and famine research (Curry and Hugo, 1984) it appears that about 400,000 people starve to death throughout the world on average each year at present, with deaths rising to about 800,000 during "famine years." This represents a mortality incidence of 0.01 to 0.02%, which is unacceptably high but somewhat lower than the figures in UN press releases, which state that "15% of the world's population is starving."

IV. VITAMIN A DEFICIENCY

In both India and Indonesia vitamin A deficiency appears to be one of the most important nutritional problems cxhibiting clearly defined clinical symptoms. In their sample of school boys in six villages near Udaipur, Bhandari and others (1975) found active xerophthalmia to be the most clearly defined nutritional disease, with an incidence of 9%. However, the incidence and severity of vitamin A deficiency varies considerably from region to region, and Panikar and Soman (1984) reported an incidence of only 0.7% for Bitot's spots in Kerala in 1976. Although this was the most common nutritional deficiency sign noted in their study, Bitot's spots alone are not indicative of a clinically significant morbid condition. Nevertheless Bitot's spots are often associated with fully developed clinical cases of kertomalacia at a ratio of about 10 to 1, and Banik (1977) in a survey of 2,000 children in urban Delhi observed some visible sign of a vitamin A deficiency, mainly Bitot's spots, in 8.5% of the higher caste children and 24% of the lower caste children. In the author's survey of a poor Indian village there was no active kertomalacia in a population whose staple was sorghum, but Shelia Pereira (1966), in a study of 175 patients with kwashiorkor, observed that 14.3% of these were also suffering from severe kertomalacia, usually leading to total blindness. This indicates an incidence of binocular blindness of about 0.1% in *Harijan* villages near Velore in South India (personal communication).

In the poorest of my three study villages in Indonesia, one person in five was suffering from either active kertomalacia or partial blindness due to prior bouts with this vitamin A deficiency disease. Vitamin A deficiency is the largest cause of blindness in Indonesia. Various pre-war studies by Oomen, van Veen, Maas, van Manen, and others reported incidence rates for xerophthalmia ranging from as low as 3% in Java to 20% in Sumatra. More recent studies in Indonesian journals have focussed on pre-school children, with Saroso reporting a 13.9% incidence in Jakarta, Daarwin Karyadi reporting 11.1% incidence in Bogor, and Tarwotjo reporting 4.3 and 5.2% incidence in Salatiga. Data available in international journals indicate a 7% incidence of xeropthalmia in Javanese village children and a 17% incidence in Sumatran children (see Oey *et al.*, 1967; Gyorgy, 1967; and Kusin, Sinaga, and Marpaung, 1977). Among 4,595 children surveyed by Sommer and others in Java (1981), the yearly incidence of active corneal keratomalacia was 0.5%. Sommer extrapolates his findings to estimate about 500,000 new cases of xerophthalmia, half of which result in blindness, occur each year in India, Bangladesh, the Philippines, and Indonesia combined; however, this may be an overestimate in the case of India because on the basis of these limited data and my own experience, it is probable that vitamin A deficiency is only about half as common in India as it is in Indonesia.

The relatively high intake of milk products in India as opposed to the extremely low intake in Indonesia might account for these differences. On the basis of these data, I would estimate the Indian incidence of xerophthalmia at about 2.5%, with about 0.5% suffering visual impairment and about 0.05% permanently blinded. It would appear that the Indonesian incidence for xerophthalmia is about 5%, with about 1% of all Indonesians suffering some degree of permanent visual impairment and perhaps 0.1% permanently blinded because of inadequate vitamin A intake.

V. IODINE DEFICIENCY

The next most important nutritional problem in India and Indonesia is goitre. In mapping world goitre there is a narrow belt of extremely high incidence which extends from the Hindu Kush mountains through India and Indochina to Indonesia and New Guinea. The Himalayan region is noted for the prevalence of endemic goitre. According to Ramalingaswami (1973), 98% of the population living just south of Mt. Everest have goitre and 5.7% are cretins. Mathur in his study "Endemic Goitre in India" estimates there may be 25 million or about 3.3% of all Indians with some form of goitre; however, they include small palpable goitre, and the vast majority with these would suffer no significant or debilitating effects from this adaptation to low iodine availability. Stanbury and Hetzel (1980) estimate the number of Indians afflicted with goitre to be only 10 million or about 1.3%, but they are talking about visible goitre which may or may not be clinically significant. Again the problem is one of defining the level of clinical significance. Nevertheless, simple diffuse goitre is the main abnormality of the thyroid encountered in India, and it is most common in females, the majority of whom are euthyroid and lead perfectly normal lives. Goitre is extremely common in the northern states, significant in the central states, and less common in the coastal states. Panikar and Soman in their study of health in the coastal state of Kerala, where fish is the most important source of animal protein, make absolutely no mention of goitre.

In Indonesia goitre is clearly associated with andesitic and rhyolitic *lahar* from the numerous volcanoes. Hardly any part of Indonesia is free from endemic goitre. Prevalence rates are about 90 % in parts of West Sumatra and East Java and 60 % in North Sumatra and Central Java, as noted in various studies by Abu Nain, Maspaitella, and Djokomuljanto (1973). Village studies show ranges of incidence of palpable goitre from 25 % to 97 % (Soewondo *et al.*, 1966). However, it should be stressed that overt hypothryoidism and cretinism have only been found in areas of severe endemic goitre (80–90 % incidence), with the incidence of moderate neurologic change measured at 8 % or about one-tenth the goitre rate and this change being found mainly in non-goitrous individuals whose thyroid glands have been unable to adapt to environmental iodine deficiency (see Goslings et al., 1977). Therefore, iodine deficiency causes economically significant long-term debilitation only at the extremes, in those who are unable to adapt or those whose goitres have grown extremely large.

Personal records taken during an east-west transcept of Java show the incidence of larger visible goitre to range from 1 to 40 %, averaging about 5 %, with perhaps 0.5 % of the Indonesian population suffering a significant degree of physiological debilitation leading to about 0.05 % frank cretinism. Detailed data for India are even more difficult to obtain than data for Indonesia, and goiterous terrains are more localized than in Indonesia. However, given the fact that in the more densely populated parts of India, rainfall is only 40 to 60 inches per year compared to 60 to 80 inches per year in Indonesia, and thus leaching of iodine from the soil is less, one might estimate an overall incidence of visible goitre of about 2 % or less, with about 0.2 % of the population suffering a significant degree of debilitation leading to about 0.02 % frank cretinism.

VI. SIGNIFICANCE OF DISEASE MORBIDITY IN INDIA AND INDONESIA

The purpose of this paper is not to go into diet and disease morbidity in detail but rather to present data to support a general estimate of the relative significance of diet and disease and to suggest what are the most significant morbid conditions in terms of incidence and severity. Even a limited analysis of available data makes it very clear that disease morbidity is far more common than dietary illness. Nutritional illness is common in India and Indonesia and of major significance, but infectious and communicable respiratory and enteric diseases are far more common occurrences of incredible magnitude. Also heavy infestation of intestinal and skin parasites are the norm for the majority of the population, and even though these parasitisms seldom result in death, they cause acute suffering over time. The synergistic interactions of disease and diet are also clear, and Tandon (1984) has pointed out that diarrhoea, short fever, and respiratory illness were the associated diseases which contributed to 42.6% of the deaths in his Indian study of 4,292 children with severe PEM. His was a study of disease following malnutrition; however, it is also clear that a significant proportion of the most common nutritional insults, especially PEM and anaemia, are strongly synergized by acute diarrhoeas in the case of PEM and exceptionally high rates of intestinal parasitism in the case of anaemia. Specific field studies and hospital outpatient records as well as personal observation strongly support these conclusions, and McLaren (1983) correctly suggests that we should not talk of malnutrition but rather of the "diarrhoea-malnutrition complex."

P.V. Sukhatme's study of infant and child morbidity in eight villages near Poona has now been under way for four years, and preliminary data indicate that the most common cause of childhood morbidity is diarrhoea, followed by helminthic infection, respiratory distress, and skin infection. There are seasonal variations in the incidence of diarrhoea, with this condition affecting between 15 and 22% of the children at any given time. In the dry season respiratory illness is more common than diarrhoea, affecting about 18% of the children throughout the year. Another 10 to 15% of the more than 800 children observed in this survey of villages in Maharashtra have skin disorders. Sukhatme's survey has not yet been published but is quoted because actual observations of morbid conditions in the villages on the basis of home visitation every other day for five years are very rare. Sukhatme did not measure helminthic infestation; however, in 1982 when Sukhatme's associates Drs. Edmundson and Rao examined 122 stool samples of children and adults from an adjacent study village after the administration of an antihelminthic to all individuals, they found 98% to be infested with *Ascaris lumbricoides*. The average worm load per stool sample was 14 and the average weight of the worm load was 21 gramme. Multiple stool samples were collected from those villagers with heavy worm loads. At least 5% of the villagers were carrying over 100 worms, and at least 1% were carrying over 500 worms. Furthermore, after deworming children with heavy worm loads showed rapid weight gain.

This pattern of disease morbidity and nutritional synergy seems to be quite common throughout India. The mobidity patterns seen in outpatients attending clinics in Kerala also showed diarrhoeal disorders, helminthic infections, respiratory infections, and skin infections to be the most common complaints, in that order. Panikar and Soman (1984) listed major classes of disease as diagnosed in the outpatient clinics of three rural hospitals. Their data indicate that diarrhoeal disorders account for 20.4% of the diagnoses of all illness, helminthiasis accounts for 20.5%, respiratory infections for 19.9%, skin infections for 8.6%, fevers for 5.5%, and injuries for 2.5% of the diagnoses. It should be noted that these observations were made during the dry season when one expects the prevalence of diarrhoeas and dysenteries to be at their lowest, and 80% of this disease group were bacterial dysenteries, the rest being of amoebic origin. Faecal contamination of drinking water and food were chiefly responsible, and one can readily see that proper disposal of excreta and the provision of safe drinking water would control this major cause of morbidity which is the biggest killer of children and the most important contributory factor in protein energy malnutrition. Roundworm infestation was more common than hookworm infestation which ranked second, but massive intestinal parasitism appeared to be common throughout India, and the synergistic interaction between diet and disease is once again clear. Anaemia, malabsorption, malnutrition, and eosinophilia associated with acute respiratory illness have all been found to be correlated with helminthiasis.

VII. STOOL SAMPLES OF INTESTINAL PARASITISM IN INDIA

Intestinal parasitism is responsible for a significant proportion of the total morbidity in India. Data on the point incidence of helminthic infection and its absolute significance are extremely difficult to obtain. Data on the incidence of diarrhoea are a bit better. Chakraborty and others (1978) reported that 3.3% of their study population of 12,214 individuals in West Bengal were actively suffering from "diarrhoea-dysentry" at any given time; this accounted for a proportion equal to 14.2% of the total morbidity, with 23.5% of their sample ill at any given time.

Chaudhri (1983) examined 1,452 stools of individuals in the state of Haryani. He found *Entamoeba histolytica* in 4.41% of the stools. This does not necessarily indicate active cases of ameobic dysentery. Nevertheless, most of these individuals would suffer sporadically. It should also be noted that his sample included mostly upper-class "individuals associated with the university."

Poirriez and others (1984) found *Entamoeba histolytica* in 7% of their sample of 82 children and *E. coli* in 38% of the faecal specimens. *Necator americanus* were found in 86% and *Ascaris lumbricoides* in 30%.

Amin and others (1979) examined 50,000 faecal samples in Bombay. Motile *E. coli* protozoa were found in 26.62% of the samples and *E. histolytica* were found in 16.05%. In this urban sample, helminthic infestation was on the order of only about 2%. However, in another urban study of 1,003 faecal samples from Bareilly, Garg and Pande (1980) found 20% *A. lumbrocoides* and 11% *N. americanus.*

VIII. STOOL SAMPLES OF INTESTINAL PARASITISM IN INDONESIA

Diarrhoea, dysentery, and human parasitism also appear to be among the most common causes of sickness, with infant diarrhoeas being the most common cause of child mortality in Indonesia. According to Lo and Walker (1983) diarrhoea is the most common cause of morbidity in infancy and often becomes protracted, leading to malabsorption and malnutrition. Specific morbidity data are once again incredibly difficult to obtain, but data on parasites in faeces have been collected from many regions of Indonesia.

Hiagins and others (1984) examined stools from 1,387 individuals in Flores, Sumatra, and Java. They found that parasitism was lowest in Flores where population densities were also low; intermediate levels were found in Sumatra; and the highest levels were found in Java where the population densities were highest. Protozoa were found in about half the population sampled, with *Entamoeba coli* and *Entamoeba histolytica* being the common diarrhoeal agents. However, it is probable that only about one in ten of the infected individuals was actively ill at any given time. *Ascaris lumbricoides*, *Trichuris trichiura*, and *Necator americanus* were the most common parasites but egg counts were low, suggesting that much of the infection was subclinical.

Purnomo and others (1980) examined 198 stool samples from Flores and recovered *Entamoeba histolytica* from 21% and *Entamoeba coli* from 19% of their samples. *Ascaris lumbricoides* were found in 43% and *Necator americanus* in 18% of their samples.

Stafford and others (1980) examined 270 stool specimens from the inhabitants of three villages in Bali. The most common protozoan was *Entamoeba coli*, found in 22% of the samples, but *Entamoeba histolytica* was found in only 5% of the samples. The most common helminths were *Ascaris lumbricoides* (91%), *Trichuris trichiura* (90%), and *Necator americanus* (59%).

Joesoef and Dennis (1980) examined 311 faecal samples on Alor Island. *Entamoeba coli* were found in 31.8% of their samples and *Entamoeba histolytica* in 31.2%. Evidence of *Ascaris lumbricoides* was found in 55.3% of the samples, *Necator americanus* in 28.6%, and *Trichuris trichiura* in 96.8%.

Joseph and others (1978) studied human parasitoses in South Sulawesi. Examining 765 stool samples, they found *Entamoeba coli* in 24% and *Entamoeba histolytica* in 6% of their samples. They discovered evidence of *Ascaris lumbricoides* in 74% of the stools, *Trichuris trichiura* in 65%, and *Necator americanus* in 62%.

IX. ESTIMATING THE INCIDENCE AND SIGNIFICANCE OF GUT INFESTATION

Although data concerning specific diarrhoeal parasites found in stool samples are more complete for Indonesia than India, available evidence indicates that in both countries levels of gut infestation are similar, with an average of about 25% of all individuals carrying *Entamoeba coli* and 15% carrying *Entamoeba histolytica.* If we assume that all carriers are ill at least once a year, this would represent an annual incidence of clinical diarrhoea of about 40%. If we compare incidence of diarrhoeal illness at the same level of clinical severity with the incidence of the most significant nutritional deficiencies, it appears that disease morbidity is exponentially higher than nutritional morbidity, and the same is true for mortality at all levels.

Worm infestations are often perceived as little more than a "fact of life" in the relatively crowded rural regions of India and Indonesia. Because these helminthic infestations are seldom the direct cause of death, they tend to be regarded as relatively insignificant. However, with reports indicating that 20% of all rural outpatient morbidity is attributed to helminths and given that some infestation is almost universal, this problem is of major significance. The problem of worm load is stressed here because it is so closely correlated with sanitation, and we are dealing with a synergistic syndrome of poor sanitation, gut infestation, and malnutrition. Available data indicate that in rural India and Indonesia about 50 to 60% of all individuals are carriers of *Ascaris lumbricoides* and 40 to 50% are carriers of *Necator americanus.* Probably about 10% of these have heavy worm loads with mild but measurable clinical symptoms, and about 1% are severely affected.

X. CONCLUSIONS AND RECOMMENDATIONS

Planning is a matter of priorities. Before beginning action programmes to improve health conditions, it is necessary to do three things:

1. try to delineate the relative importance of the specific health problems in terms of incidence;
2. try to determine the significance of these problems in terms of their severity and duration; and
3. by examining these data in relation to ease of cure, try to set practical priorities for developmental programmes in terms of estimated benefit per unit cost.

This means knowing what problems are clinically significant and knowing what solutions are economically feasible. In India and Indonesia during the 1970s, the entire national health budget never amounted to more than US $1 per person per year. Most of this money is already budgeted. Any planner who is not aware of this economic restriction will probably choose an inappropriate response to programme planning.

Although the data presented in this paper are incomplete, they do clearly point out the significance of certain problems which can be solved by the people themselves at low cost. In the course of twenty years of village research in India and Indonesia, specific vitamin and mineral deficiencies appeared to be of greater clinical significance than undernutrition or protein malnutrition. Problems of intestinal parasitism are far more significant.

Appropriate nutritional technologies were sought to cure xerophthalmia and goitre, and it was found that the villagers could cure themselves of the former by eating a mixture of cassava and papaya leaves and of the latter by rubbing their necks with tincture of iodine (see Edmundson, 1980). The problems of intestinal parasitism not only are more significant than specific vitamin and mineral deficiencies but also synergize undernutrition and malnutrition. One may cure these diseases when they occur or one may remove the underlying causes. During the course of four years of action research in eight villages, P.V. Sukhatme has halved child mortality by capping the wells, supplying reliable pump sets, chlorinating the water, and providing cement, shovels, picks, and plans for sanitary latrines. All these measures are of course preceded and accompained by education on the importance of sanitation.

These data support a general philosophical approach to rural health priorities, which suggests that on a cost-benefit basis, curative clinical programmes and direct food supplementation may have less practical potential than educational programmes which motivate the individual villager to improve his or her own health environment. In relation to present morbid conditions in Indonesia and India, I would suggest that a primary school health education programme with an applied sanitation component might be integrated with clinical elements to stress the following priorities in order of importance:

a. provision of clean water;
b. building of latrines;
c. extension of child inoculation programmes;
d. better provision of protective foods;
e. continuation of projects to increase food quantity; and
f. continuation of family planning programmes.

A human being is an extremely complex biologic organism. Diet and disease are intimately related to each other and to the surrounding environment. Malnutrition is one fact of life in the less developed world and disease is another. The mechanisms of human nutrition and human disease are extremely complicated: no single health insult can occur without facilitating others. Most nutritional disease states normally occur as complex malnutritional syndromes covering a wide spectrum of deficiencies interrelating in a complex manner. Disease insults are equally complex, and few villagers can be found suffering from clear textbook cases relating to only one specific illness. Careful examination will generally reveal a co-incidence of poor sanitation, intestinal parasitism, and chronic subclinical diarrhoea coupled with a history of recurring respiratory illness synergizing failure to thrive and various clinical or subclinical dietary deficiencies. These dietary and disease insults interact with each other and with the surrounding economic, physical, and cultural environment.

Health development and the development of human resources will always be evolutional and seldom revolutional. Important long-term improvement begins with attitudinal change in the minds of the individual villagers. Economic development begins the change from traditional to innovative ways of thinking. Social development begins with change from elitist to communal thought patterns. Biologic development begins with awareness of the communal importance of public health as the key to private health. Health is a bio-social complex. There is a wide range of acceptable health standards for any measurable aspect of diet or disease. There is a wide range of inter-individual and intra-individual biologic variability which makes it impossible to set a single standard requirement or index below which all are unhealthy or malnourished and above which all are healthy and well nourished. Accurate measurement of health standards depends on the acceptance of the reality of human variability and adaptation and the complex interaction of humankind and nature over a wide range of inputs and conditions. Not all disease conditions are equally significant. Not all instances of the same disease in different individuals are of equal significance. Health is not a constant, but a continuum. Homeostatic autoregulation comes into play whenever there is any disturbing influence and helps to bring the system back into balance with the general biologic needs dictated by the ontological demands of growth, development, differentiation, and decay.

Because of the complexity and variability of these intense interactions it is necessary to try to maintain a highly flexible and holistic approach if we are to satisfactorily even attempt to answer questions like what is the relationship between diet and disease and which elements of the health equation are most economically and socially significant.

In this study specific problems were selected to receive special emphasis while an attempt was made to maintain an awareness of human biologic and social variability. I tried to examine economic priorities in terms of the incidence or number of people suffering from the health insult, in terms of the severity of the specific problem being examined, and in terms of the resources available to solve the problem and most especially the cost of the solution relative to an estimation of the potential benefit to be obtained. Although certain extremely common nutritional deficiencies can be cured at very low cost, disease is more important than diet, and it is clear that at present in India and Indonesia simple improvements in public sanitation would yield the greatest health benefits at the lowest cost.

REFERENCES

Abu Nain, *et al.* (1973). The prevalence of endemic goitre among school children in some parts of Sumatra, Java, and Bali. *Bull. Health Studies in Indonesia*, **1**: 2–12.

Amin, A.B., *et al.* (1979). Incidence of helminthiasis and protozoal infections in Bombay. *J. Indian Med. Assn.*, **72** (10): 225–227.

Banik, N.D.D. (1977). Some observations on feeding programmes, nutrition and growth of pre-school children in an urban community. *Indian J. Pediatrics*, **44**: 139–149.

Bhandari, B., *et al.* (1975). Nutrition and health status of rural school boys of Udaipur District. *Indian J. Pediatrics*, **42**: 330, 186–193.

Chakraborty, A.K., *et al.* (1978). Health status of rural population of Singur as revealed in repeat general health survey 1975. *Indian J. Med. Research*, **68**: 6, 1018–1028.

Chitre, R.D., S. Deshpande, and S.N. Nimbalkar (1983). The process of human adaptation in a malnourished population with special reference to tribals. *Indian J. Nutrition and Dietetics*, **20** (2): 46–55.

Demeester, N. and A.M. Ermans, (1967). Euthyroid 'hot' nodules: A physiologic approach. In W.J. Irvine (ed.), *Thyrotoxicosis*. London: Livingstone.

Djokomoeljanto, R. and R. Harijono (1974). Endemic goitre prevalence in school children of the Merapi area, Java. *Tropical and Geographical Med.*,

26 (4): 363–367.
Edmundson, W.C. (1976). *Land, Food, and Work in East Java.* New England Monographs in Geography, University of New England, Armidale, Australia.
Edmundson, W.C. (1977). Individual variation in work output per unit energy intake in East Java. *Ecology of Food and Nutrition*, **6** (3): 147–151.
Edmundson, W.C. (1980). Adaptation to undernutrition: How much food does man need? *Social Sci. and Med.*, **14** D: 119–126.
Edmundson, W.C. (1980). Applied nutritional geography; priorities and praxis. *Social Sci. and Med.*, **14** D: 133–137.
Garg, R.K. and A.K. Pande (1980). Studies on the incidence of human parasites in Bareilly. *Indian Vet. Med. J.*, **4** (1): 33–36.
Gillei, B. (1971). Endemic goitre. *Scientific American*, **224**: 6–12.
Goslings, B.M., R. Djokomoeljanto, and C. van Hardeveld (1977). Hypothyroidism in an area of endemic goiter and cretinism in Central Java, Indonesia. *J. Clinical Endrocrinol. and Metabol.*, **44** (3): 481–490.
Gyorgy, P. (1967). Red palm oil in the prevention of vitamin A deficiency. *Am. J. Clinical Nutrition*, **20**: 1267–1275.
Hiagins, D.A., *et al.* (1984). Human intestinal parasitism in three areas of Indonesia, a survey. *Ann. Tropical Med. and Parasitol.*, **78** (6): 637–648.
Hofler, W. and H. Pech (1978). Nutrition and health of children less than five years old on the Mentawi Island of Sipora, Indonesia. *Tropen Medizin und Parasitologie*, **29** (4): 497–508.
Joesoef, A. and D.T. Dennis (1980). Intestinal and blood parasites of man on Alor Island, Southeast Indonesia. *SE Asian J. Tropical Med. and Pub. Health*, **11** (1): 43–47.
Joseph, S.W., *et al.* (1978). Human parasitoses of the Malili area, South Sulawesi (Celebes) Province, Indonesia. *SE Asian J. Tropical Med. and Pub. Health*, **9** (2): 264–271.
Karyadi, D. (1976). *Hubuganan Ketahanan Fisik dengan Keadaan Gizi dan Anemi Gizi Besi.* Bogor: Archipel.
Kusin, J.A., H.S.R.P. Sinaga, and A.M. Marpaung (1977). Xerophthalamia in North Sumatra. *Tropical and Geographical Med.*, **29** (1): 41–46.
Lala, V.R. and V. Reddy (1970). Absorption of beta carotine from green leafy vegetables in undernourished children. *Am. J. Clinical Nutrition*, **20**: 110–118.
Latham, M.C. (1984). Strategies for the control of malnutrition and the influence of the nutritional sciences. *Food and Nutrition*, **10** (1): 5–31.
Lo, C.W. and W.A. Walker (1983). Chronic protracted diarrhea of infancy; a nutritional disease. *Pediatrics*, **72** (6): 786–800.
Mathur, C.B.L. (1975). Endemic goitre in India. *Baroda J. Nutrition*, **2** (2): 157–165.
McLaren, D.S. (ed.) (1983). *Nutrition in the Community: A Critical Look at Nutrition Policy, Planning and Programmes.* Chichester: Wiley and Sons.
Oey, K.L., *et al.* (1967). Red palm oil in the prevention of vitamin A deficiency. *Am. J. Clinical Nutrition*, **20**: 1267–1276.
Oomen, H.A.P.C. (1961). An outline of xerophthalmia. *Int'l. Rev. Tropical Med.*,

1: 271–279.

Panikar, P.G.K. and C.R. Soman (1984). *Health Status of Kerala*. Trivandrum: Centre for Development Studies.

Poirriez, J., *et al.* (1984). Human trichostrongyliasis in India. *Trans. Royal Soc. Tropical Med. and Hygiene*, **78** (3): 425–426.

Purnomo; F. Partono, and A. Soewarta, (1980). Human intestinal parasites in Karakuak, West Flores, Indonesia, and the effect of treatment with mebendazole and pyrantel pamoate. *SE Asian J. Tropical Med. and Pub. Health*, **11** (3): 324–327.

Ramalingaswami, V. (1973). Endemic goiter in Southeast Asia: new clothes on an old body. *Ann. Inter. Med.*, **78**.

Rohde, J.E. (1979). What we can do about weanling diarrhoea, how to do it. *Indian J. Nutrition and Dietetics* **16** (4): 127–144.

Scrimshaw, N.S. (1966). Synergistic and antagonistic interactions of nutrition and infection. *Fed. Proc.*, **25**: 1679–1681.

Soewondo, H. (1966). Endemic goitre in East Java. *Am. J. Tropical Med. and Hygiene*, **15**: 116–125.

Sommer, A., *et al.* (1981). Incidence, prevalence, and scale of blinding malnutrition. *Lancet*, **1** (1): 8235; 1407–1408.

Stanbury, J.B. and B.S. Hetzel (1980). *Endemic Goiter and Endemic Cretinism.* New York: Wiley and Sons.

Stafford, E.E., *et al.* (1980). Human parasitoses in Bali, Indonesia. *SE Asian J. Tropical Med. and Pub. Health*, **11** (3): 319–323.

Sukhatme, P.V. and S. Margen (1982). Autoregulatory homeostatic nature of energy balance. *Am. J. Clin. Nutrition*, **35** (2): 355–365.

Tamboli, B.L. and R. Sharma (1980). Prevalence of helminthic infection and associated anaemia in Sindhi Colony, Jaipur. *J. Commun. Dis.*, **11** (2): 51–58.

Tandon, B.N., *et al.* (1984). Management of severely malnourished children by village health workers in integrated child development services in India. *J. Tropical Pediatr.*, **30** (5): 274–279.

World Bank, U.N. (1985). *World Development Report* 1985, New York: Oxford.

Pejaten, a Village Developing into Advanced and Self-Sustaining Growth

Adnyana MANUABA

Department of Physiology, Udayana University, Bali, Indonesia

I. INTRODUCTION

According to its stage of development, a *desa*, or village, in Indonesia belongs to one of three types: *desa swadaya* (traditional and less-developed village), *desa swakarya* (village in transition) or *desa swasembada* (village developing into advanced and self-sustaining growth).

Pejaten is a *swasembada* village in Bali, covering 150 hectares (ha), with 3,347 inhabitants in 624 households. It is located 3 kilometres (km) from the coast, 8 km from the district capital of Tabanan, and 21 km from Denpasar, the provincial capital of Bali. The village has a head (*bendesa*), and is divided into eight community institutions (*banjar*), each of which has its own head (*kelian*). The *bendesa* is assisted in village management by an office administrator of his own choosing and also by a village social committee (*lembaga sosial desa*, or LSD) before 1980, or a village reliance council (*lembag ketahanan masyarakat desa*, or LKMD), following Presidential Decision No. 28 promulgated on 31 March 1980. The LSD or the LKMD is composed of people's representatives with the special tasks of planning, coordinating, and inspecting village development, and is a vehicle for community participation in development projects. Since the *bendesa* is also the chairman of the LSD or the LKMD, village management proceeds smoothly.

Although Pejaten is surrounded by the Dati River on the south and east and the Panan River on the north and west, most of its area is dry land (68.0 ha, 45.3%) on which residents farm and from which they take the raw materials for the "soil industry." House yards comprise 52.2 ha (34.8%); public utilities in the form of roads, schools, temples, graveyards, sports fields, etc., 5.8 ha (3.8%); and areas owned by outsiders,

22.5 ha (15.0%). Pejaten inhabitants also own 148.2 ha of wet rice fields outside the village proper, meaning that an average rice field holding is only 4.4 acres per person, too small to eke out a living.

Given these conditions, development efforts based on the traditional agricultural pattern are doomed to failure and other avenues must be sought. The current focuses of development are on "soil handicraft industry," encouragement of transmigration, active participation in family planning programmes, creating new employment opportunities, and intensifying the use of existing agricultural land. Recently, Pejaten has become well known as a roof tile-producing village with an extensive market (1,500,000–2,000,000 tiles per month), and was designated one of the *swasembada* villages in Bali (Table 1).

This paper attempts to illustrate the efforts made by the people of Pejaten to achieve their present status, with special reference to the holistic approach to development, including survival strategy and health issues.

Information was collected through secondary data, local observation, and interviews. The present author's personal experiences as director of the Regional Institute of Occupational Health, Industrial Hygiene, and Safety of Bali Province (1969–1983) and as Deputy Dean of Student Affairs of the Faculty of Medicine, University of Udayana, Bali (1962–1965), have also been drawn upon.

II. HISTORY OF DEVELOPMENT IN PEJATEN

Before 1969 Pejaten was considered a very poor and underdeveloped village whose inhabitants had to depend on not only rice but also banana

TABLE 1. Distribution of Main Occupations in Pejaten (1982)

Occupation	Male	Female	Total
1. Roof-tile manufacturer	700	845	1,545
2. Farmer	249	—	249
3. Teacher	31	16	47
4. Labour farmer	42	—	42
5. Carpenter	35	—	35
6. Civil servant	26	—	26
7. Merchant	—	23	23
8. Driver	22	—	22
9. Cattle breeder	11	10	21
10. Member of armed forces	20	—	20
11. Private	4	3	7
12. Nurse	—	2	2
13. Physician	1	—	1
14. Midwife	—	1	1

trunk and sweet potatoes as staple foods. Some of the reasons for this lack of development were problems between *banjars* which had continued since the days of Dutch colonial rule; distracting quarrels between various political parties; a lack of mutual understanding between leaders and the common people; and disruption by outsiders. It can be said that development was non-existent. Education was limited to one primary school in the village and health care suffered as a result of ignorance and poverty. Crime was on the increase and chaos reigned. Several projects to improve conditions, including construction of a bridge between Pejaten and Bongan, and building a clinic with the help of Udayana Medical School students and local youths, were begun but were abandoned before being completed.

Indonesia's first five-year plan began in 1969 and brought changes to the village of Pejaten. The youth of the village and the students, organized into the Pejaten High School Students Association (Ikatan Pelajar Sekolah Lanjutan Pejaten, or IPSLP), and the village social committee (LSD) in concert took the initiative in the changes by motivating villagers to assume responsibility for their own development, and a new village head was elected. The motto for this new era was: "Develop better welfare in the village through self-reliance."

The newly elected village head quickly took steps to consolidate his own staff and that of the LSD. Regular monthly meetings were held to plan for and evaluate elements of the village development programme proposed by the people and aimed at the "bottom-up." Funds for this were collected from villagers as well as from government sources.

In June 1970 a Civil Defence Force (*pertahanan sipil*, or HANSIP) was organized to maintain peace and order, with a resultant decrease in crime and gambling. Civil legal cases were reduced by solving problems under the supervision of village authorities before resorting to the courts. But perhaps the most significant contribution to the establishment of a foundation for development lay in the mutual cooperation between institutional leaders and between the leaders and the citizens of the village.

III. THE ROOF TILE CO-OPERATIVE

In order to begin one meaningful economic development project to benefit Pejaten as a whole, certain problems faced by the roof tile industry with its small-scale and/or cottage nature had to be identified and solutions found. The main problems were a lack of capital and a lack of knowledge of fund raising; limited materials of poor quality; outdated technology; poor organization and production management; lack of skills; and limited marketing abilities.

After thorough discussion and analysis of the problems faced by the roof tile industry, the following decisions were taken to improve the situation: (1) Roof tiles were manufactured to size specifications under the trademark "Pejaten" to aid in marketing efforts. (2) Technical courses were organized with government assistance to improve quality and introduce new technology. (3) Kerosene stoves were used from 1973 in the firing process for economic and ecological reasons. (4) Ergonomics principles were applied to the production process, thus increasing productivity and improving working conditions for those involved, especially women and children. (5) A marketing co-operative was established for advertising campaigns and for participation in trade exhibitions. (6) A new ceramic tile project was begun, which has recently received technical assistance from a private Dutch foundation for the transfer of new technology.

The roof tile co-operative was founded originally by several volunteers to strengthen the economic position of the manufactures. At that time, tile prices were largely set by the buyers, and the so-called "pre-paid" system (*ijon*) was in wide use. After an initial success, the community at large responded favourably to the idea of the co-operative, and on 1 September 1978 the Pejaten Roof-Tile Co-operative was formally established. Monthly profits from the co-operative are used as follows: payment of 3% interest to members; staff salaries (12.5%); working funds (10%); salaries for the LSD members (5%); and development projects to benefit the whole village (69.5%). Members are entitled to interest-free loans and various other benefits, including increased income and employment opportunities, direct sales to the co-operative without waiting for buyers' orders, and the general upgrading of the standard of living in Pejaten village.

The statistical data, though fragmentary, demonstrate that the number of workers in roof-tile manufactures increased from 120 in 1969 to 1,280 in 1980 and then to 1,545 in 1984; and the gross profit increased from Rp 260,040 to Rp 915,040 during just the year and a half from September 1978 to February 1980.

The establishment of the co-operative system in the roof tile industry has had a major impact on the Pejaten community at large, economically as well as socially. The success of this co-operative system has been followed by similar co-operatives in building construction, in a consumers' group, in credit, and in a health insurance and medical system.

As a result of this success, villagers' patterns of expenditures have changed; besides being used for daily economic and social needs, income is used for other purposes, but priority is still given to rice fields over luxuries. Materials related to building local industries are the second most important expenditure after agricultural materials.

IV. MEDICAL CO-OPERATIVE

Although a clinic had been open in Pejaten since 1963, this facility was not used to the full by village residents. But since the establishment of the Health Fund/Insurance System in 1976 monthly visits to the clinic have increased, with beneficial results for all. The initial members of this system numbered 430 in 76 households, but all of the villagers had joined it by August 1978.

At the clinic's inception, funds for medical supplies and operation were raised in a variety of ways, including film and drama shows and donations of roof tiles by members. However, in January 1983 the Health Insurance Co-operative was set up with contributions of Rp 12,500 per household as capital, with any subsequent profits to be divided among the members.

Improvements in health have occurred at a personal and village-wide level. More wells and latrines have been dug; the proportion of households using a well and latrine in 1984 was respectively 91.8% and 62.5%. Due to better sanitary conditions and campaigns to promote the wearing of shoes, hookworm-related illnesses have drastically decreased (Tables 2 and 3). Productivity gains of "soil handicraft industry" have also been recorded as fewer work days have been lost to illness and injury.

Transmigration and family planning have been encouraged in Pejaten. Since 1973, more than 400 persons have migrated to other places in Indonesia. The most recent data show that 86.8% of eligible families participate in family planning and that during the period 1969–1979 the rate of population increase has been only 1.18% annually; this changing pattern is illustrated in the age composition of the Pejaten population (Table 4).

V. OTHER RESULTS

In addition to steady economic and health care improvements in the

TABLE 2. Qualitative Survey on Soil-Transmitted Helminths

Year	Number of house-holds	Positive			Prevalence (%)			Hb
		AL	TT	An	AL	TT	An	(gr%)
1981	318	294	234	256	92.5	73.6	80.5	11.0
1983	282	116	142	92	41.1	50.5	32.6	12.6
1984	325	54	155	16	16.6	47.7	4.9	13.8

AL = *Ascaris lumbricoides*
TT = *Trichuris trichiura*
An = *Ancylostoma* (Duodenale)
Hb = Hemoglobin concentration

1982: Pyrantel 3 times a year.
1984: Pyrantel 3 times a year.

TABLE 3. Quantitative Survey on Soil-Transmitted Helminths

Year	Number of house-holds	Positive			Prevalence (%)			Hb
		AL	TT	An	AL	TT	An	(gr%)
1981	29	27	21	24	93.1	72.4	82.8	11.0
1983	36	10	17	10	27.8	47.2	27.8	12.3
1984	36	6	25	5	16.7	69.4	13.9	13.8

AL *Ascaris lumbricoides*
TT *Trichuris trichiura*
An *Ancylostoma* (Duodenale)
Hb Hemoglobin concentration

1982: Pyrantel 3 times a year.
1983: Pyrantel 3 times a year.

TABLE 4. Population Distribution in 1983 and in 1986

	No. of people	
	1983	1986
55–	381	523
50–54	126	132
45–49	150	136
40–44	146	203
35–39	99	237
30–34	161	271
25–29	230	297
20–24	314	376
15–19	293	459
10–14	504	367
5–9	474	314
0–4	322	220

village, a number of other development projects have been undertaken, with varying degrees of success. For example, education has been given priority by the local authorities and the people. Three primary schools have been built, a kindergarten has been opened, and national educational regulations have been more strictly enforced, resulting in a lower school drop-out rate and higher literacy rate among the people. Adult education classes in such subjects as agriculture, animal husbandry, cooking, and the arts have also been conducted.

In executing development projects, villages were subsidized by the central government (with grants ranging from Rp 100,000 to 1,250,000 in recent years); however, such grants are considered to trigger fundraising in the community. It is evident that many development projects are finally funded mostly by the communities themselves.

Cultural and entertainment activities have not been neglected. Music and dance programmes and classes are held regularly for all interested participants and television sets have been installed in each of the eight *banjars*. Sports facilities financed by village funds have been constructed and are widely used. Because most of the villagers are Hindu, religious activities have focused on the construction of a new temple for the entire community and rehabilitation of older temples.

Public transportation infrastructure has also been improved, with footpaths being widened, existing roads extended, and water pipelines for irrigation being laid under roads and footpaths.

VI. CONCLUSION

After an analysis of how the people of Pejaten have managed to improve their living conditions, it was found that the following were the most important: (1) better local administration fostered the spirit of leadership and mutual trust necessary for the success of co-operative systems, and (2) the co-operative system first applied to the roof tile industry was adapted to suit health, educational, and social institutions.

Coping with Industrialization: Experiences in Small Enterprises of Asia

Kazutaka KOGI

ILO Regional Office for Asia and the Pacific, Bangkok, Thailand

I. INTRODUCTION

Work, life, and health conditions of workers in many developing countries have been greatly affected by local industrialization. In particular, workers in small enterprises labour in difficult conditions. Though the industrialization process differs from country to country, its effects on working conditions, particularly those in small enterprises, have many common aspects (Phoon, 1975). As available reports show, these common aspects include generally poor working and living conditions, uncontrolled use of imported machinery, exposure to specific hazards often unknown to employers and workers, poor welfare facilities, and lack of enterprise-level services and training (Kogi, 1985). It should be noted that these small enterprises fall outside the scope of conventional regulatory measures and organized services (Dy, 1984; ILO, 1984). It is difficult for an inspectorate or service institutions to deal with all the problems of the many widely dispersed small enterprises.

It is important, on the other hand, that small enterprises and their workers make voluntary efforts to cope with these difficulties. These efforts should extend not only to areas covered by regulatory standards but also to various aspects of production and the working life (Kogi, 1985). These efforts must be incorporated into the long survival process of the enterprise and the occupational life of individual workers and thus need frequent adjustment. It is therefore necessary to go beyond the conventional protective measures and look at the support required to facilitate voluntary efforts (Dy, 1984; Kogi, 1985; Wisner, 1985).

Our recent experiences in developing countries in Asia show that when self-help is facilitated by training, small enterprises take serial actions for improvement (ILO, 1985). This paper discusses what kinds of self-help action can be taken by small enterprises and what kinds of support are effective for them. This will help us to find more ways to encourage self-reliance using existing scarce resources.

II. TRAINING APPROACH TO WORKING CONDITIONS IMPROVEMENT

A training approach focussing on voluntary action of employers and workers in small enterprises has been developed within the framework of the International Programme for the Improvement of Working Conditions and Environment (PIACT) launched by the International Labour Organisation (ILO) in 1976. The approach is based on the awareness that active participation of employers and workers can lead to concrete improvements, and that emphasizing voluntary action is complementary to regulatory measures.

Small enterprises do not always have the time and resources to carry out necessary improvements of working conditions in a consistent manner. These enterprises are preoccupied with the need to acquire appropriate materials, to obtain financing, to market their products, to overcome inadequacy in infrastructure, to ensure the smooth operation of the enterprise, and to deal with labour and personnel matters. They need to be backed by well-organized support that provides technical and management training and advice (Bromley, 1985). Therefore, it was deemed necessary to design a voluntary programme for very busy people that would show practical results.

The principles of the training approach which has led to good results include: building on local practice; focus on achievements; linking working conditions and management goals; learning-by-doing; exchange of experience; and worker involvement. Especially important is to begin with gathering positive examples found in the participating enterprises (Louzine, 1982). The participants are then guided to carry out similar, specific improvements through self-help.

These improvements carried out through self-help are of particular interest, as they represent improvements that can be accomplished in a practical, low-cost way consistent with the enterprise goals.

III. AREAS FOR SELF-HELP ACTIONS

The improvement of working conditions and environment covers a broad scope. PIACT encourages a comprehensive approach looking at occupational safety and health, length and arrangement of working time, organization of work and job content, and welfare facilities and services.

An ILO pilot study in eight developing countries in Asia has shown that improvement actions actually taken by respondents to a postal survey were reasonably balanced in terms of success rates in different topic areas (Table 1). Actions by small enterprises had generally lower success ratios than those by large enterprises. Nevertheless, small enterprises experienced some success in virtually all topic areas. The success rate, including partial

TABLE 1. Number of Successful and Unsuccessful Interventions Reported in a Postal Survey of Experts in Eight Developing Countries in Asia

Area of intervention	Successful	Partially successful	Unsuccessful
Relocating machines	6	3	7
Changing work postures or machine designs	6	4	7
Reducing workload	8	6	4
Working time and rests	2	1	4
Heat and ventilation	11	7	12
Noise and lighting	7	9	12
Hazardous chemicals	12	14	11
Accidental injuries	5	5	10
Welfare facilities	5	3	5
Cultural adaptation and others	8	4	3
Total	70	56	75

TABLE 2. Three-month Follow-up Results of Improvements Suggested at the End of a Small Enterprise Training Programme (Madras, 1985) (Results for 27 enterprises)

Types of action	Number of improvements suggested	Three months later		
		Done or in progress	To be done soon	Not done
Good housekeeping	19	14	3	2
Better materials handling	8	4	3	1
Changing work height or machine designs	5	4	1	—
Improved lighting	11	9	2	—
Screening hazard sources or providing exhausts	11	11	—	—
Providing guards or protective equipment	6	4	2	—
Reducing fire hazards	2	2	—	—
Sanitary facilities or lunchroom	8	8	—	—
Total	70	56	11	3

success, for small enterprises was 62% for areas related to machines and work methods, 57% for areas related to working environment, and 47% for areas concerning working time, welfare facilities, and others. The corresponding rates for large enterprises were 77%, 65%, and 79%, respectively.

Improvements carried out by small enterprises in our recent training programmes in the Philippines and India included a range of simple measures. The majority of these measures were not only proposed but also implemented by the participants themselves. The rate of implementing the proposed measures was quite high (Table 2). An enterprise usually took multiple measures, meaning that each tried to make a comprehensive evaluation of its problems.

Examples of improvements carried out in the course of the training programme and during its follow-up period are listed in Table 3. Typically, these improvements concerned: layout, storage, and materials handling; work station design; production-related physical environment; work organization and scheduling; and welfare facilities.

These improvements accomplished through self-help have some common characteristics. First, almost all of them are practical, low-cost improvements. Second, strong linkages can be identified between these improvements. Improved materials handling, for instance, is related to better work postures, good housekeeping, and work organization. Third, most of these improvements were associated with major workload factors of the jobs involved. The improvements made were thus relevant to management priorities which were perceivable on the shop floor. Finally,

TABLE 3. Low-cost Examples of Improvement Carried Out in Small Enterprises through a Training Programme Encouraging Self-help

Area	Low-cost examples
Layout, storage, and materials handling	– Marking and clearing passageways – Storage racks/pushcarts – Improved feeding of materials
Work station design	– Adjusting work height – Easy-to-reach materials/controls – Non-confusing displays/instructions
Physical environment	– Lighting and ventilation – Screening noise/hazard sources – Providing guards/safety device
Work organization and scheduling	– Increased communication – Providing buffer stock – Group work by rotation – Inserting short breaks
Welfare facilities	– Sanitary facilities well maintained – Providing or improving a lunchroom

both short-term and long-term effects seemed to have been taken into consideration.

IV. EFFECTIVE SUPPORT

In conclusion, a mechanism to match the self-help efforts of small enterprises is necessary, because the ill effects of industrialization appear when there is a serious gap between rapid changes in production methods and working life and the self-help efforts to cope with them. The support therefore should go beyond conventional approaches and take into account the nature and areas of potential self-help actions by these enterprises.

Self-help is successful when it starts from locally available achievements, selects priorities, and focusses on low-cost measures simple to conceive and usable on the shop floor as suggested by our previous results (Kogi, 1985). It is interesting that immediate, effective self-help actions concern major workload factors. Direct support should be developed to facilitate self-help through the exchange of experience in the local context in these multiple areas.

REFERENCES

Bromley, P. (1985). *Planning for Small Enterprises in Third World Cities*. Oxford: Pergamon Press.

Dy, F.J. (1984). Improving working conditions and environment: Problems and approaches in the Asian context. In *Humanizing Work*. Manila: Institute of Labor and Manpower Studies, pp. 74–83.

International Labour Conference, 70th Session (1984). *Report VII: Evaluation of the International Programme for the Improvement of Working Conditions and Environment (PIACT)*. Geneva: ILO.

International Labour Office (1985). *Improvement of Working Conditions and Productivity in Small and Medium-sized Enterprises: Intensive Training Course and Short Training Course* (Madras), *Proceedings*. Geneva: ILO.

Kogi, K. (1985). *Improving Working Conditions in Small Enterprises in Developing Asia*. Geneva: ILO.

Louzine, A.E. (1982). Improving working conditions in small enterprises in developing countries. *Intl. Labour Rev.*, **121**: 443–454.

Phoon, W.O. (1975). The impact of industrial growth in South-east Asia. In *Ciba Foundation Symposium 32: Health and Industrial Growth*. Amsterdam: Elsevier, pp. 107–126.

Wisner, A. (1985). Ergonomics in industrially developing countries. *Ergonomics*, **28**: 1213–1224.

Epilogue

The present book is a collection of 14 papers read at the symposium, "The Comparative Human Ecology of Health and Survival Strategy in Asia and the South Pacific," which was held at the University of Tokyo's Hongo Campus in March 1986. The symposium was organized to look at the current condition of human ecology research in the target area, and simultaneously to contribute to future research design. The symposium papers and the associated discussion tapped out a number of theoretical and practical suggestions, which were quite diversified because people's survival varies from country to country and even within each country, and because this symposium dealt with human survival and health from a wide angle.

To my mind, the most constructive achievement of this symposium was the proposing of several ideas to further research in human ecology; they are here classified into four categories. First, as has been pointed out by T. Suzuki in his introductory essay, "production," "consumption," and "reproduction" are recognized as a set of key concepts in understanding human survival. This set seems prevalent in animal ecology, but in the field of human ecology primary attention has been paid to production and consumption and less to reproduction, as typically seen in so-called cultural ecology. The stress on reproduction here parallels, in some sense, that on fertility in Kobayashi's methodological discussion of micro-level demography. My own paper, whose subjects are a non-literate population in lowland Papua, is an attempt to examine reproduction or inter-generational replacement in a human population.

Second, "time depth" is emphasized in the analysis of human survival and health. The structure and function of the man-environment relationship are basic concepts in human ecology, although it is important to recognize that the state of a man-environment system at any moment reflects both its history and a moment in the ever-changing course of time. With different time spans and with different topics, several papers touch on the ecological significance of time depth in local ecosystems. Production is treated by Kano in his analysis of agricultural history in Java; energy consumption and expenditure are discussed by Moji for Sundanese peasants; and reproduction is related to production and consumption in my own paper on a Papuan population. Ellen provides an extensive analysis of long-term human survival in the Banda Arc in the light of natural and man-made environmental perspectives, and Manuaba presents the developmental history of a Balinese community, focusing on social and economic organization and health status.

Third, attention is directed to the importance of emic analysis in human ecology study, as emphasized by Funabiki in his paper on a population in Vanuatu and by several other authors, for instance Strathern. Human ecology has been principally concerned with the etic dimension; consequently the emic dimension which backs it up tends to be neglected. In my understanding, however, it is fair to say that etic analysis should pay more attention to emic aspects, and emic analysis, to etic aspects.

Fourth, our approach to health is characterized by special notice to its relation with living and working conditions. Human groups treated along this line include indigenous peoples in the New Guinea Highlands (Strathern), rural populations in Java (S. Suzuki), Javanese, Sundanese and Balinese transmigrants into Kalimantan (Abdoellah), local populations in India and Indonesia (Edmundson), and workers in small enterprises in several Southeast Asian countries (Kogi). Based on their own findings, these authors not only relate the people's health conditions to their living and working conditions but also propose solutions to the current problems of each group. In this connection, the drastic change in the survival curve of the Japanese, and associated problems over the last century, which are presented by Koizumi, may be suggestive to the researchers and policy-makers who work in developing countries.

Since shortly after this symposium took place, I and my collaborators have been in a remote area of Papua New Guinea conducting research on the comparative human ecology of populations in lowlands, foothills, and highlands. In the course of this ongoing field research I have been impressed with the diversified living systems in these different habitats and even within each group of several hundred to a few thousand people. This experience, together with the stimuli given to me in this symposium, again persuades me of the importance of the comparative approach to human survival and health.

Finally, with hearty thanks to the contributors, other participants in the symposium, the President of the University of Tokyo, and the Japanese Ministry of Education, Science and Culture (financial sponsor of the symposium), it is my sincere hope that this book will make a contribution to the advancement of human ecology studies.

September 1986

Ryutaro Ohtsuka
at Fly River Headwater,
Papua New Guinea

Index